UNDERSTANDING FINANCIAL STATEMENTS

TENTH EDITION

Lyn M. Fraser

Aileen Ormiston

International Edition contributions by

Abhik Kumar Mukherjee

St. Xavier's College, Kolkata

Boston Columb ... er Saddle River
Amsterdam Cape Tow ... ris Montréal Toronto
Delhi Mexico City S ... pore Taipei Tokyo

Editorial Director: Sally Yagan
Editor in Chief: Donna Battista
Director Editorial Services: Ashley Santora
Editorial Project Manager: Karen Kirincich
Editorial Assistant: Jane Avery
Editorial Assistant: Lauren Zanedis
VP Director of Marketing: Patrice Jones
Marketing Assistant: Ian Gold
Senior Managing Editor: Nancy Fenton
Publisher, International Edition: Angshuman Chakraborty
Acquisitions Editor, International Edition: Somnath Basu
Publishing Assistant, International Edition: Shokhi Shah
Print and Media Editor, International Edition: Ashwitha Jayakumar
Project Editor, International Edition: Jayashree Arunachalam
Senior Manufacturing Buyer: Carol Melville
Creative Director: Jayne Conte
Cover Designer: Jodi Notowitz
Media Project Manager: Sarah Peterson
Full-Service Project Management and Composition: Integra
Printer/Binder: Courier/Westford
Cover Printer: Courier/Westford

Pearson Education Limited
Edinburgh Gate
Harlow
Essex CM20 2JE
England

and Associated Companies throughout the world

Visit us on the World Wide Web at:
www.pearsoninternationaleditions.com

Authorized adaptation from the United States edition, entitled Understanding Financial Statements, 10th edition, *ISBN 978-0-13-2655064 by Lyn M. Fraser and Aileen Ormiston published by Pearson Education © 2013.*

ISBN 10: 0-273-76903-0
ISBN 13: 978-0-273-76903-3

British Library Cataloguing-in-Publication Data
A catalogue record for this book is available from the British Library

10 9 8 7 6 5 4 3 2 1
14 13 12

Typeset in Times Ten Roman 10/12 by Integra
Printed and bound by Courier/Westford in The United States of America

The publisher's policy is to use paper manufactured from sustainable forests.

For Eleanor
—Lyn M. Fraser

For my father, Mike, Josh, and Jacqui
—Aileen Ormiston

Contents

Preface to the Tenth Edition

In this new edition of *Understanding Financial Statements*, Aileen and I continue with our objective of taking readers behind the numbers, dazzling presentations, and slick brand marketing of corporate annual reports to assess the reality of a firm's financial condition and performance. Based on the dramatic events that have unfolded in financial markets and the accounting environment as well as extensive feedback from our readers—faculty, students, practitioners, and many others who use the book to develop a better understanding of financial statement analysis—we have introduced some significant new elements in this tenth edition.

- Chapter 1 has been updated to include examples relating to ongoing financial turmoil, the evidence of corporate fraud, the rash of major corporate failures, and the staggering collapse of financial markets. The first chapter also introduces a new company, Sage Inc., which is used throughout the book to illustrate how to read and interpret financial statements.
- Material has been added and reorganized to emphasize the importance of *financial reporting quality* and to provide relevant examples from current corporate reporting.
- In every edition, we have focused on *cash flow from operations* as a measure of financial performance, but Chapter 4 in this tenth edition offers new material to underline its importance as an analytical tool and to enhance the discussion of the usefulness of the *statement of cash flows*, especially in light of the magnitude and quantity of recent business failures.
- Four new cases based on real-world companies have been added at the end of each chapter, along with new study questions and problems and an updated template for financial statement analysis.
- The text addresses current issues in financial reporting, including financial reporting reforms, the process for developing accounting standards, and the potential for requiring the adoption of international accounting standards.
- To lighten the load, we have introduced in this tenth edition a variety of "illustrations" that we hope will appeal to our readers. Let us know!

As always, our intent is to present the material in this book in a manner that is accessible, readable, and relevant in order to help readers make practical sense of complex financial information.

Lyn M. Fraser

Organization of the Tenth Edition

Chapter 1 provides an overview of financial statements and presents approaches to overcoming some of the challenges, obstacles, and blind alleys that may confront the user of financial statements: (1) the volume of information, with examples of specific problems encountered in such areas as the auditor's report and the management discussion and analysis section as well as material that is sometimes provided by management but is not useful for the analyst; (2) the complexity of the accounting rules that underlie the preparation and presentation of financial statements; (3) the variations in quality of financial reporting, including management discretion in some important areas that affect analysis; and (4) the importance of financial information that is omitted or difficult to find in conventional financial statement presentations.

Chapters 2, 3, 4, and 5 describe and analyze financial statements for a mythical but potentially real company, Sage Inc., which sells recreational products through retail outlets in the southwestern United States. The specifics of this particular firm should be helpful in illustrating how financial statement analysis can provide insight into a firm's strengths and weaknesses. But the principles and concepts covered throughout the book apply to any set of published financial statements (other than for specialized industries, such as financial institutions and public utilities).

Because one company cannot provide every account and problem the user will encounter in financial statements, additional company examples are introduced throughout the text where needed to illustrate important accounting and analytical issues.

Chapters 2 through 4 discuss in detail a basic set of financial statements: the balance sheet in Chapter 2, the income (earnings) statement and statement of stockholders' equity in Chapter 3, and the statement of cash flows in Chapter 4. The emphasis in each of these chapters is on what the financial statements convey about the condition and performance of a business firm as well as how the numbers have been derived. Appendix 3A discusses and illustrates issues that relate to the quality of earnings—and thus the usefulness—of financial reporting. The chapter contains a step-by-step checklist of key items to help the analyst assess the quality of reporting, and real-company examples of each step are provided.

With this material as background, Chapter 5 covers the interpretation and analysis of the financial statements discussed in Chapters 2 through 4. This process involves the calculation and interpretation of financial ratios, an examination of trends over time, a comparison of the firm's condition and performance with its competitors, and an assessment of the future potential of the company based on its historical record. Chapter 5 also reviews additional sources of information that can enhance the analytical process. Appendix 5A shows how to evaluate the segmental accounting data reported by diversified companies that operate in several unrelated lines of business.

Self-tests at the ends of Chapters 1 through 5 provide an opportunity for the reader to assess comprehension (or its absence) of major topics; solutions to the self-tests are given in Appendix B. For more extensive student assignments, study questions and problems are placed at the end of the chapters. Cases drawn from actual company annual reports are used to highlight in a case-problem format many of the key issues discussed in the chapters.

Appendix A covers the computation and definition of the key financial ratios that are used in Chapter 5 to evaluate financial statements.

Appendix B contains solutions to self-tests for Chapters 1 through 5.

Appendix C presents a glossary of the key terms used throughout the book.

The ultimate goal of this book is to improve the reader's ability to translate financial statement numbers into a meaningful map for business decisions. It is hoped that the material covered in the chapters and the appendixes will enable each reader to approach financial statements with enhanced confidence and understanding of a firm's historical, current, and prospective financial condition and performance.

Uses for the Tenth Edition

Understanding Financial Statements is designed to serve a wide range of readers and purposes, which include:

1. Text or supplementary text for financial statement analysis courses.
2. Supplementary text for accounting, finance, and business management classes, which cover financial statement analysis.
3. Study material for short courses on financial statements in continuing education and executive development programs.
4. Self-study guide or course material for bank credit analysis training programs.
5. Reference book for investors and others who make decisions based on the analysis of financial statements.

Features of the Tenth Edition

In revising the text, we have paid close attention to the responses received from faculty who teach from the book, from students who take courses using the book as a primary or supplementary text, and from other readers of the book. Our primary objective remains to convey to readers the conceptual background and analytical tools necessary to understand and interpret business financial statements. Readers and reviewers of earlier editions have commented that the strengths of this book are its readability, concise coverage, and accessibility. We have attempted to retain these elements in the tenth edition.

The tenth edition incorporates new requirements and changes in accounting reporting and standards, as well as the following items:

- New examples are provided in all chapters to illustrate accounting concepts and the current accounting environment.
- Chapter 1 has been updated to include examples of accounting fraud that have occurred in recent years.
- Chapter 1 introduces Sage Inc., the company used throughout the book to illustrate how to read and interpret financial statements.
- Appendix 1A is new to this edition and includes excerpts from the Form 10-K of Sage Inc., including the financial statements and notes for the company, the auditor's report, and the management's discussion and analysis.
- The content found on the balance sheet has been updated in Chapter 2 to better reflect the current format of balance sheets.
- The section on the quality of financial reporting on the balance sheet (in Chapter 5 of the ninth edition) has been moved to Chapter 2.
- The interpretation of the income statement, using Sage Inc., in Chapter 3 now illustrates how the management's discussion and analysis can be used when completing an analysis of a company.
- Appendix 3A (formerly Chapter 5) has been updated with new examples and includes a discussion of the quality of earnings.
- A new introduction has been written for Chapter 4 to explain the importance of the cash flow statement and enhance the discussion of the preparation of the statement of cash flows.

- The section on the quality of financial reporting on the statement of cash flows (in Chapter 5 of the ninth edition) has been moved to Chapter 4.
- Chapter 5 was Chapter 6 in prior editions and has been updated to be consistent with the reorganization of the entire text.
- Study questions and problems have been updated in each of the five chapters.
- The writing skills problems, research problems, and Internet problems have been retained in this edition.
- The Intel cases offer the student the opportunity to analyze a real company throughout the text, and in this edition the highlighted company is Intel, a high-technology firm. Information for the Intel cases is available on the Pearson Web site: *www.pearsoninternationaleditions.com/fraser*.
- The comprehensive analysis case has been retained in the textbook to illustrate how to complete a financial statement analysis using the template available on the Pearson Web site: *www.pearsoninternationaleditions.com/fraser*. The company used is Avnet, and each chapter contains a case to help students apply the content of the chapter as well as learn to use the financial statement analysis template.
- Four new cases (including the Intel and Avnet cases) have been added at the end of all chapters based on real-world companies.
- Appendix 5A illustrates how to analyze segmental data using Sage Inc., the firm used throughout the textbook.
- The footnotes provided throughout the text contain resources that may be used by instructors to form the basis of a reading list for students.
- The tenth edition includes other features of earlier editions that readers have found useful: self-tests at the end of each chapter, with solutions provided; end-of-chapter study questions and problems; and a glossary of key terms used in the text.
- The Solutions and Instructor's Manual and Test Item File, available at *www.pearsoninternationaleditions.com/fraser*, contain solutions to study questions, problems, and cases; a sample course project with assignment outline and a test bank for Chapters 1 through 5 are also provided. Both objective and short-answer test questions are included.
- The Web site for the text has been updated and includes templates to use for financial calculations, PowerPoint slides that can be downloaded for use in class, and an online version of the self-tests.

We hope that readers will continue to find material in *Understanding Financial Statements* accessible, relevant, and useful.

Acknowledgments

We would like to acknowledge with considerable appreciation those who have contributed to the publication of this book.

We would like to thank the individuals who made critical comments and suggestions for the tenth edition. In particular, we would like to thank Terrence Willyard, Baker College—Jackson Campus; Patricia H. Holmes, Des Moines Area Community College; Donald Benoit, Mitchell College; Harriet Maccracken, Arizona State University; Cynthia Peck, Anderson University; Matthew J. Haertzen, Northern Arizona University; Leslie B. Fletcher, Georgia Southern University; Michelle Lounsbery, Bellevue University; Ashwin M. Madia, Ph.D., North Hennepin Community College ; Metropolitan State University Carlson School of Management—University of Minnesota; Peggy James, Greenville Technical College; Bob Gregory, Bellevue University; Douglas E. Kulper, University of California Santa Barbara; Carole Weber-Brown, Alexandria Technical College; David J. Manifold, Caldwell Community College & Technical Institute; Richard Weldon, University of Florida; Linda Abernathy, Kirkwood Community College; Elaine Henry, University of Miami; Rick Johnston, Purdue University; and Chris Prestigiacomo, University of Missouri.

Many individuals have made critical comments and suggestions for the previous editions of the text. In particular, we would like to thank David K. Hensley, The University of Iowa; Robert Roller, LeTourneau University; Corolyn Clark, Saint Joseph's University; Dr. Elisa Muresan, School of Business, Long Island University; Dane Sheldon, University of Miami; Dan Dowdy, Mary Baldwin College; H. Francis Bush, Virginia Military Institute; Bob Gregory, Bellevue University; Patricia Doherty, Boston University School of Management; Wei He, University of Texas of the Permian Basin; Kenton Walker, University of Wyoming; Sean Salter, University of Southern Mississippi; Paul Fisher, Rogue Community College; Ray Whitmire, Texas A&M University–Corpus Christi; Micah Frankel, California State University, Hayward; Seok-Young Lee, The University of Texas at Dallas; Sadhana Alangar, Cleary University; Scott Pardee, Middlebury College; Jill Whitley, University of Sioux Falls; John Baber; Maurice Johnson, Fashion Institute of Technology/SUNY; Melanie Mogg, University of Minnesota, Carlson School of Management; Richard Fendler, Georgia State University; William Seltz, Harvard University; Robert Ewalt, Bergen Community College; Richard Frederics, Lasell College; Tom Geurts, Marist College; Jen Adkins, North Central State College; Irvin Morgan, Bentley College; Jack Cathey, University of North Carolina–Charlotte; and Glenda Levendowski, Arizona State University.

The authors would like to express grateful appreciation to Tim Carse for his careful and attentive proof-reading of the manuscript during the production process.

Special thanks go to Jacqui Ormiston for her excellent and creative work in preparing PowerPoints to accompany the book.

We would also like to thank the editorial, production, and marketing departments of Pearson for their assistance at each stage of the writing and production process. Taking a book through production once the writing is completed always presents challenges to the authors and to Pearson. This particular 10th edition had an urgency to get the book into print early in 2012 to provide timely updating of material that relates to turmoil in the financial markets and economy as well as to accounting fraud and financial reporting quality. Heather Johnson has been superb in meeting this schedule, and the authors are appreciative of her exceptionally efficient handling of the process in a patient and cordial manner.

The list would be incomplete without mentioning the pets in our households who helped keep us in good humor throughout the revision of this edition: Toot, AddieMae, Escalante, Mooli, Teddy, Toby, Torin, and Tisha.

Lyn M. Fraser

Aileen Ormiston

The publishers would like to thank Soumya Mukherjee of Maharaja Manindra Chandra College, Kolkata for reviewing the content of the International Edition.

About the Authors

Lyn M. Fraser has taught undergraduate and graduate classes in financial statement analysis at Texas A&M University and has conducted numerous seminars on the subject for executive development and continuing education courses. A Certified Public Accountant, she is the co-author with Aileen Ormiston of *Understanding the Corporate Annual Report: Nuts, Bolts, and a Few Loose Screws* (Prentice Hall, 2003) and has published articles in the *Journal of Accountancy*, the *Journal of Commercial Bank Lending*, the *Magazine of Bank Administration*, and the *Journal of Business Strategies*. She has been recognized for Distinguished Achievement in Teaching by the Former Students Association at Texas A&M University and is a member of Phi Beta Kappa.

Aileen Ormiston teaches accounting in the Business Department of Mesa Community College in Mesa, Arizona, and has taught in the MBA and honors programs at Arizona State University. She received her bachelor's degree in accounting from Michigan State University and a master's degree in finance from Texas A&M University. Prior to embarking on her teaching career, Aileen worked in cost accounting and also as an auditor in public accounting. Mesa Community College was one of 13 universities and colleges that received a grant from the Accounting Education Change Commission, and Aileen was actively involved in developing the new accounting curriculum. As a result of her pioneering work in changing accounting education, she was the recipient of the "Innovator of the Year" award from the League for Innovation in the Community College. For her service to honors students, Aileen has been named a Phi Theta Kappa mentor.

Financial Statements

An Overview

maze (māz), n. 1. An intricate, usually confusing network of passages, some blind and some leading to a goal. 2. Anything made up of many confused or conflicting elements. 3. A mental state of confusion or perplexity.

Map or Maze

A *map* helps its user reach a desired destination through clarity of representation. A *maze,* on the other hand, attempts to confuse its user by purposefully introducing conflicting elements and complexities that prevent reaching the desired goal. Business financial statements have the potential for being both map and maze.

As a map, financial statements form the basis for understanding the financial position of a business firm and for assessing its historical and prospective financial performance. Financial statements have the capability of presenting clear representations of a firm's financial health, leading to informed business decisions.

Unfortunately, there are mazelike interferences in financial statement data that hinder understanding the valuable information they contain. The sheer quantity of information contained in financial statements can be overwhelming and intimidating. Independent auditors attest to the fairness of financial statement presentation, but many lawsuits have been filed and won against accounting firms for issuing "clean" auditors' reports on companies that subsequently failed. The complexity of accounting policies underlying the preparation of financial statements can lead to confusion and variations in the quality of information presented. In addition, these rules are constantly evolving and changing. Management discretion in a number of areas influences financial statement content and presentation in ways that affect and even impede evaluation. Some key information needed to evaluate a company is not available in the financial statements, some is difficult to find, and much is impossible to measure.

Thinkstock

One of the main objectives of this book is to ensure that financial statements serve as a map, not a maze—that they lead to a determination of the financial health of a business enterprise that is as clear as possible for purposes of making sound business decisions about the firm.

Ongoing financial turmoil, major corporate failures, and the staggering collapse of financial markets underscore the need for financial analysts, financial advisors, creditors, investors, and individuals managing personal assets to have a basic understanding of financial statements. While this book focuses on firms operating primarily in nonfinancial industries, many of the underlying principles discussed in the book apply as well to the kinds of financial services and investment management firms—the Wall Street banks—that triggered the economic collapse of 2008, the most serious economic crisis in modern history.

One example of an essential "'map-like" principle conveyed in this book over all its editions is the importance of **cash flow from operations** as a key performance measure. This concept is fully discussed and illustrated in Chapter 4. Many firms have gone bankrupt while presenting rosy net income figures because of their inability to generate cash from operations. Lehman Brothers is a classic case.

In the three years prior to its bankruptcy in 2008, the largest in U.S. history, Lehman Brothers reported steadily increasing and robust net income figures of \$3.3 billion in 2005, \$4.0 billion in 2006, and \$4.2 billion in 2007. Cash flow from operations, however, which should have provided at least a hint of the financial disaster to come, was negative in those three years: \$12.2 billion in 2005, \$36.4 billion in 2006 and a whopping \$45.6 billion in 2007. As asset values tumbled, a company that already had staggering levels of debt had to borrow more and more to cover its failure to generate cash. The bankruptcies of the early 2000s such as Enron and WorldCom had similar map-like red flags. (See, for example, "I Told My Daughter Not to Invest in Enron" in *Understanding the Corporate Annual Report—Nuts, Bolts, and a Few Loose Screws*, Lyn M. Fraser and Aileen Ormiston, Prentice Hall, 2003).

The material in this book will convey information about how to read and evaluate business financial statements, and the authors will attempt to present the information in a straightforward manner, with relevant examples, that will be readily accessible to any reader, regardless of background or perspective. The book is intended for use by those who want to learn more about the content and interpretation of financial statements for such purposes as making sound investment and credit decisions about a company, evaluating a firm for current or prospective employment, surviving and advancing professionally in the current economic climate, and perhaps even passing an important examination or course. Throughout the book, the authors attempt to simplify and explain complex accounting and financial issues in a way that allows readers not only to understand the information presented in annual reports but to identify areas of potential strength and weakness—based on the reader's interpretation rather than on the "spin" provided by company management.

Shutterstock

The reader can expect more than a dull exposition of financial data and accounting rules. Throughout these pages we will attempt—using timely examples, illustrations, and explanations—to get behind the numbers, accounting policies, and tax laws to assess how well companies are actually performing. The chapters and appendixes in the book show how to approach financial statements to obtain practical, useful information from their content. Although the examples in the book are based on corporate financial statements, the discussion also applies to the financial statements of small business firms that use generally accepted accounting principles.

The emphasis throughout the book is on analysis. In the first four chapters of the book, we will look at the contents of an annual report and break the financial statements into parts for individual study to better understand the whole of their content as a map to intelligent decision making. To fully analyze a firm, it is important to assess the value of the information supplied by management. This material will be covered in Appendix 3A, on the quality of earnings. The final chapter of the book combines all parts learned in prior chapters with analytical tools and techniques to illustrate a comprehensive financial statement analysis.

Usefulness

Financial statements and their accompanying notes contain a wealth of useful information regarding the financial position of a company, the success of its operations, the policies and strategies of management, and insight into its future performance. The objective of the financial statement user is to find and interpret this information to answer questions about the company, such as the following:

- Would an investment generate attractive returns?
- What is the degree of risk inherent in the investment?

- Should existing investment holdings be liquidated?
- Will cash flows be sufficient to service interest and principal payments to support the firm's borrowing needs?
- Does the company provide a good opportunity for employment, future advancement, and employee benefits?
- How well does this company compete in its operating environment?
- Is this firm a good prospect as a customer?

The financial statements and other data generated by corporate financial reporting can help the user develop answers to these questions as well as many others. The remainder of this chapter will provide an approach to using effectively the information contained in a corporate annual report. Annual reports in this book will refer to the information package published by U.S. companies primarily for shareholders and the general public. The Securities and Exchange Commission (SEC) requires large, publicly held companies to file annually a 10-K report, which is generally a more detailed document and is used by regulators, analysts, and researchers. The basic set of financial statements and supplementary data is the same for both documents, and it is this basic set of information—financial statements, notes, and required supplementary data—that is explained and interpreted throughout this book.

Volume of Information

The user of a firm's annual report can expect to encounter a great quantity of information that encompasses the required information—financial statements, notes to the financial statements, the auditor's report, a five-year summary of key financial data, high and low stock prices, management's discussion and analysis of operations—as well as material that is included in the report at the imagination and discretion of management. To understand how to navigate the vast amount of information available to financial statement users, background on the accounting rule-making environment is necessary. Financial statements are currently prepared according to generally accepted accounting principles (GAAP) that have been adopted in order to achieve a presentation of financial information that is understandable by users as well as relevant and reliable for decision making. The accounting rules that have been issued in order to achieve these objectives can be complicated and sometimes confusing. The two authorities primarily responsible for establishing GAAP in the United States are the SEC, a public-sector organization, and the Financial Accounting Standards Board (FASB), a private-sector organization.

The SEC regulates U.S. companies that issue securities to the public and requires the issuance of a prospectus for any new security offering. The SEC also requires regular filing of

- Annual reports (10-K)
- Quarterly reports (10-Q)
- Other reports dependent on particular circumstances, such as a change in auditor, bankruptcy, financial restatements, or other important events (all filed as 8-K reports)

The SEC has congressional authority to set accounting policies and has issued rulings called Accounting Series Releases (ASRs) and Financial Reporting Rulings (FRRs). For the most part, however, accounting rule making has been delegated to the FASB.

Prior to September 15, 2009, FASB issued Statements of Financial Accounting Standards (SFASs) and interpretations. Effective September 15, 2009, the FASB Accounting Standards Codification™ became the source of authoritative GAAP. The FASB's three primary goals in developing the Codification were (1) to simplify user access by codifying in one source all authoritative GAAP in the United States; (2) to ensure that the codified content accurately represented authoritative U.S. GAAP as of July 1, 2009; and (3) to create a codification research system that is up to date for the released results of standard-setting activity.[1]

After 50-plus years and more than 2,000 standards, the FASB recognized the need for a better system to research accounting standards. The Codification includes not only SFASs, but also standards from other accounting organizations and relevant rules written by the SEC. The FASB Accounting Standards Codification™ Research System will be updated concurrently with the release of Accounting Standards Updates. Accounting Standards Updates will also be issued for amendments to the SEC content of the Codification. All updates and prior standards will be organized by related topics.[2]

The SEC and FASB have worked closely together in the development of accounting policy, with the SEC playing largely a supportive role. But at times the SEC has pressured the FASB to move on the issuance of accounting standards or to change its policies (inflation accounting, oil and gas accounting). Pressures on the FASB stem from the private sector and have been highly controversial at times. Figure 1.1 illustrates the relationship between the SEC and the FASB. An example of a measure that was vehemently opposed by the business sector was the FASB's proposal to require companies to deduct from profits compensation to executives in the form of stock options. The FASB first began exploring this issue in 1984, but it was not resolved until 1995 because of business and ultimately political intervention. Business lobbyists gained congressional support that effectively forced the FASB to compromise its stance on this issue.[3] As a result of the opposition, FASB Statement No. 123, "Accounting for Stock-Based Compensation," only required that companies disclose in the notes to the financial statements the effects on profits of new employee stock options based on the fair value at the date of grant. The controversy that arose with regard to stock-based compensation caused the SEC to take a closer look at the FASB's standard-setting process. In 1996, the SEC made public its concern that the standard-setting process is too slow; however, the SEC rejected suggestions from

---

[1] FASB Accounting Standards Codification: Notice to Constituents (v 4.1) About the Codification. Financial Accounting Foundation, 2010.

[2] The five topic areas of the Codification include the following: (1) General Principles (Topic Codes 105–199). These topics relate to broad conceptual matters. Topics include generally accepted accounting principles. (2) Presentation (Topic Codes 205–299). These topics relate only to presentation matters and do not address recognition, measurement, or derecognition matters. Topics include income statement, balance sheet, earnings per share, and so forth. (3) Financial Statement Accounts (Topic Codes 305–799). The Codification organizes topics in a financial statement order, including assets, liabilities, equity, revenue, and expenses. Topics include receivables, revenue recognition, inventory, and so forth. (4) Broad Transactions (Topic Codes 805–899). These topics relate to multiple financial statement accounts and are generally transaction oriented. Topics include business combinations, derivatives, nonmonetary transactions, and so forth. (5) Industry (Topic Codes 905–999). These topics relate to accounting that is unique to an industry or type of activity. Topics include airlines, software, real estate, and so forth.

[3] To learn more about this controversy see Stephen Barr, "FASB Under Siege," *CFO*, September 1994.

FIGURE 1.1 FASB/SEC Relationship

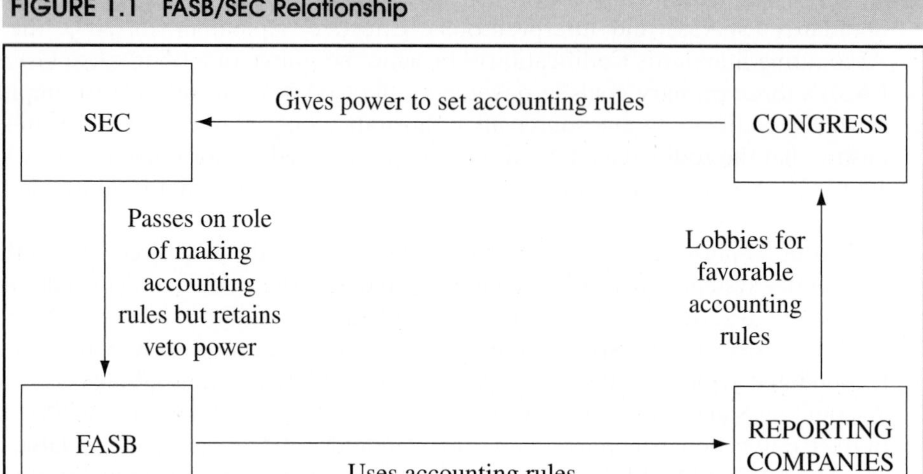

business executives that the private sector should have more influence in the process. The SEC vowed to maintain the FASB's effectiveness and independence.[4]

Corporate scandals such as Enron and WorldCom brought to the forefront the challenges and pressures the FASB faces when creating accounting rules. The issue of stock-based compensation was reopened by the FASB in 2002. A new FASB proposal adopted in December 2002 to force the expensing of all employee stock compensation from profits once again resulted in congressional interference, delaying the new rule from taking effect until after June 15, 2005. The SEC and the FASB continue to examine potential rule changes or new rules in a variety of areas such as off–balance-sheet financing and overhauling the financial statements; however, these changes will most likely evolve as a result of joint projects between the U.S. rule-making bodies and the International Accounting Standards Board (IASB).

The globalization of business activity has resulted in the need for a uniform set of accounting rules in all countries. Investors and creditors in international markets would benefit from financial statements that are consistent and comparable regardless of the firm's location. To address this need, the IASB, formerly the International Accounting Standards Committee, was formed in 1973. The eventual goal of the IASB is the adoption of uniform international accounting standards. Accomplishing this objective would allow companies to list securities in any market without having to prepare more than one set of financial statements. The need for international accounting standards has been underscored by global corporate scandals. While Enron was the catalyst for rethinking accounting standards in the United States, Europe also had a comparable scandal when Italian dairy food giant Parmalat filed for bankruptcy after committing financial fraud. Today the FASB and the IASB are working on a convergence of standards. Beginning in 2005, the European Union required publicly traded companies to use the international accounting rules, and it appears the United States could soon follow. The focus throughout this textbook will be on U.S. standards;

[4] "SEC Calls for More Efficient FASB but Rejects Stronger Outside Influence," *Journal of Accountancy*, May 1996.

however, recent changes in GAAP have been made as a beginning step in reconciling the U.S. rules to the international rules (IFRS). In 2006, the FASB and the IASB agreed to work on all major projects jointly. While no date has been set, as this book goes to print, it appears that U.S. companies could begin using IFRS as early as 2015.[5]

Where to Find a Company's Financial Statements

Corporate financial statements are available from several sources. First, all publicly held companies must file a Form 10-K annually with the SEC. The information in this document is mandated by the SEC and contains uniform content, presented in the same order for all filing companies. Figure 1.2 shows a sample of required 10-K items.

FIGURE 1.2 Form 10-K Components

Item #	Item Title
Item 1.	Business
Item 1A.	Risk Factors
Item 1B.	Unresolved Staff Comments
Item 2.	Properties
Item 3.	Legal Proceedings
Item 4.	Submission of Matters to a Vote of Security Holders
Item 5.	Market for Registrant's Common Equity and Related Stockholder Matters
Item 6.	Selected Financial Data
Item 7.	Management's Discussion and Analysis of Financial Condition and Results of Operations
Item 7A.	Quantitative and Qualitative Disclosures about Market Risk
Item 8.	Financial Statements and Supplementary Data
Item 9.	Changes in and Disagreements with Accountants on Accounting and Financial Disclosure
Item 9A.	Controls and Procedures
Item 9B.	Other Information
Item 10.	Directors and Executive Officers of the Registrant
Item 11.	Executive Compensation
Item 12.	Security Ownership of Certain Beneficial Owners and Management and Related Stockholder Matters
Item 13.	Certain Relationships and Related Transactions
Item 14.	Principal Accountant Fees and Services
Item 15.	Exhibits, Financial Statement Schedules, and Reports on Form 8-K

[5] Alexandra Defelice, "Schapiro, SEC Staff Want Companies to Have Ample Time for IFRS Adoption," *Journal of Accountancy*, December 6, 2010.

Documents filed with the SEC can usually be accessed through the Electronic Data Gathering, Analysis, and Retrieval (EDGAR) database at the SEC's Web site, www.sec.gov. Some companies mail the firm's 10-K report to shareholders, rather than producing a separate annual report. Other firms send a slickly prepared annual report that includes the financial statements as well as other public relations material to shareholders and prospective investors. Finally, most corporations now post their annual report (or provide a link to the EDGAR database) on their corporate Web site.

The Financial Statements

A corporate annual report contains four basic financial statements, illustrated in Appendix 1A for Sage Inc., pp. 40 to 52.

1. The *balance sheet or statement of financial position* shows the financial position—assets, liabilities, and stockholders' equity—of the firm on a particular date, such as the end of a quarter or a year.
2. The *income or earnings statement* presents the results of operations—revenues, expenses, net profit or loss, and net profit or loss per share—for the accounting period.

3. The *statement of stockholders' equity* reconciles the beginning and ending balances of all accounts that appear in the stockholders' equity section of the balance sheet. Some firms prepare a statement of retained earnings, frequently combined with the income statement, which reconciles the beginning and ending balances of the retained earnings account. Companies choosing the latter format will generally present the statement of stockholders' equity in a footnote disclosure.
4. The *statement of cash flows* provides information about the cash inflows and outflows from operating, financing, and investing activities during an accounting period.

Each of these statements will be illustrated, described, and discussed in detail in later chapters of the book.

Notes to the Financial Statements

Immediately following the four financial statements is the section entitled Notes to the Financial Statements (Appendix 1A, pp. 40 to 52). The notes are, in fact, an integral part of the statements and must be read in order to understand the presentation on the face of each financial statement.

The first note to the financial statements usually provides a summary of the firm's accounting policies. If there have been changes in any accounting policies during the reporting period, these changes will be explained and the impact quantified in a financial statement note. Other notes to the financial statements present details about particular accounts, such as

- Inventory
- Property, plant, and equipment
- Investments
- Long-term debt
- Equity accounts

The notes also include information about

- Any major acquisitions or divestitures that have occurred during the accounting period
- Officer and employee retirement, pension, and stock option plans
- Leasing arrangements
- The term, cost, and maturity of debt
- Pending legal proceedings
- Income taxes
- Contingencies and commitments
- Quarterly results of operations
- Operating segments

Certain supplementary information is also required by the governmental and accounting authorities—primarily the SEC and the FASB—that establish accounting policies. There are, for instance, supplementary disclosure requirements relating to reserves for companies operating in the oil, gas, or other areas of the extractive industries. Firms operating in foreign countries show the effect of foreign currency translations. If a firm has several lines of business, the notes will contain a section showing financial information for each reportable segment.

Auditor's Report

Related to the financial statements and notes is the report of an independent or external auditor (Appendix 1A, pp. 40 to 52.) Management is responsible for the preparation of financial statements, including the notes, and the auditor's report attests to the fairness of the presentation. In addition, beginning in 2005, the Sarbanes-Oxley Act of 2002, Section 404, requires that an internal control report be added to the annual report. In this report, management must state its responsibility for establishing and maintaining an adequate internal control structure so that accurate financial statements will be produced each year. Management must also include an assessment of the effectiveness of the internal control structure and procedures in the report. The external auditors are required to audit the internal control assessment of the company as well as the financial statements.

Sarbanes-Oxley, commonly shortened to SOX, has had a major impact on internal auditing. Section 404 of SOX requires companies to include in their annual reports a statement regarding the effectiveness of internal controls and the disclosure of any material weaknesses in a firm's internal controls system. This requirement has greatly boosted the need for internal auditors and SOX compliance specialists, but more important, has enhanced the value of the internal audit function within companies, as businesses have strengthened internal controls in response to SOX. Internal auditors have become the "rock stars" of the accounting industry.[6]

An *unqualified* report, illustrated for Sage. Inc. in Appendix 1A, states that the financial statements present fairly, in all material respects, the financial position, the results of operations, and the cash flows for the accounting period, in conformity with GAAP. Some circumstances warrant reports other than an unqualified opinion and are called *qualified* reports. A departure from GAAP will result in a qualified opinion and the use of the following language in the opinion sentence: "In our opinion, *except* for the (nature of the departure explained), the financial statements present fairly. . ." If the departure from GAAP affects numerous accounts and financial statement relationships, then an *adverse* opinion is rendered, which states that the financial statements have not been presented fairly in accordance with GAAP. A scope limitation means that the extent of the audit work has been limited. This will result in a qualified opinion unless the limitation is so material as to require a *disclaimer of opinion,* which means the auditor cannot evaluate the fairness of the statements and therefore expresses no opinion on them. Lack of independence by the auditor will also result in a disclaimer of opinion.

Many circumstances warrant an *unqualified opinion with explanatory language* such as: a consistency departure due to a change in accounting principle, uncertainty caused by future events such as contract disputes and lawsuits, or events that the auditor wishes to describe because they may present business risk and going-concern problems. Unqualified reports with explanatory language result in additional paragraphs to the standard report.

[6] Rachel Sams, "New Accounting Laws Make Internal Auditors 'Rock Stars,'" *Baltimore Business Journal,* June 2, 2006, and Peter Morton, "The New Rock Stars," *CA Magazine,* October 2006.

Financial Reporting Reforms

In theory, the auditing firm performing the audit and issuing the report is "independent" of the firm being audited. The annual report reader should be aware, however, that the auditor is hired by the firm whose financial statements are under review. Over time, a lack of independence and conflicts of interest between companies and their hired auditors led to a series of accounting scandals that eroded investors' confidence in the capital markets. The collapse of Enron and WorldCom was a catalyst for some of the most sweeping corporate reforms since the Securities Act of 1934 was passed. Congress was quick to pass the Sarbanes-Oxley Act of 2002 in hopes of ending future accounting scandals and renewing investor confidence in the marketplace. A discussion of the sections of SOX that directly impact the area of understanding financial reporting follows.[7]

Prior to SOX, auditors followed a self-regulatory model. Title I of the act established the Public Company Accounting Oversight Board (PCAOB), a private, nonprofit organization that has been given the authority to register, inspect, and discipline auditors of all publicly owned companies; however, the SEC appoints the board members and has ultimate oversight of the PCAOB. In addition, the PCAOB now has the authority to write auditing rules, and set quality control and ethics standards.

Title II of SOX addresses the area of auditor independence, prohibiting audit firms from providing certain nonaudit services when conducting an external audit of a firm. Prohibited services include bookkeeping; design and implementation of financial information systems; valuation and appraisal services; actuarial services; internal audit services; management or human resource functions; and broker, dealer, or investment banking services. Title II also encourages auditor independence by requiring the rotation of audit partners every five years if the audit partner is the primary partner responsible for a particular audit client. Another issue relating to auditor independence occurs when a company hires its chief financial officer (CFO) or other finance personnel from the ranks of the external audit firm. Section 206 of Title II inserts a one-year waiting period before an employee from the external audit firm may go to work for a client in the position of chief executive officer (CEO), CFO, or controller or any equivalent executive officer position; in any financial oversight role; or preparing any financial statements.

Titles III and IV of SOX focus on corporate responsibility; Title IX attaches harsher penalties for violations. Section 302 requires that the CEO and CFO of a publicly owned company certify the accuracy of the financial statements. An officer who certifies a report that is later found to be inaccurate could face up to $1 million in fines and/or a jail sentence of up to 10 years according to Section 906. These two sections work in conjunction with Section 404 (discussed previously) to encourage CEOs and CFOs to take responsibility for strong internal controls to prevent accounting fraud and financial statement misrepresentation.

Despite the enactment of SOX in 2002, corruption and unethical behavior continue. The subprime mortgage crisis surfaced in 2007, precipitating the demise of financial institutions such as Lehman Brothers and the eventual bailout that included AIG, Bank of America, Citigroup, Fannie Mae, and Freddie Mac. Just as Enron and

[7]Sarbanes-Oxley Act of 2002.

WorldCom were the catalysts for SOX, the crisis with financial institutions led to the passing of the Dodd-Frank Wall Street Reform and Consumer Protection Act in 2010. Sam Antar, convicted felon and the former CFO of the defunct consumer-electronics chain Crazy Eddie, helped mastermind one of the largest corporate frauds in the 1980s. In a 2011 interview with *CFO* magazine, Antar tells of his regret that he is no longer in the fraud game at a time when he claims corporate fraud is experiencing a resurgence. He states, "Nothing's changed. Wall Street analysts are just as gullible, internal controls remain weak, and the SEC is underfunded and, at best ineffective. Madoff only got caught because the economy tanked."[8] Based on such comments as well as recent history, the need for users of financial statements to gain a basic understanding of financial statement content and analysis for decision-making purposes is at an all-time high.

Management Discussion and Analysis

The *Management Discussion and Analysis* (MD&A) section, sometimes labeled "Financial Review," is of potential interest to the analyst because it contains information that cannot be found in the financial data. The content of this section includes coverage of any favorable or unfavorable trends and significant events or uncertainties in the areas of liquidity, capital resources, and results of operations. In particular, the analyst can expect to find a discussion of the following:

1. The internal and external sources of liquidity
2. Any material deficiencies in liquidity and how they will be remedied
3. Commitments for capital expenditures, the purpose of such commitments, and expected sources of funding
4. Anticipated changes in the mix and cost of financing resources
5. Unusual or infrequent transactions that affect income from continuing operations
6. Events that cause material changes in the relationship between costs and revenues (such as future labor or materials price increases or inventory adjustments)
7. A breakdown of sales increases into price and volume components

See Figure 1.3 for a more detailed explanation of these items.

Alas, there are problems as well with the usefulness of the MD&A section. One goal of the SEC in mandating this section was to make information about future events and trends that might affect future business operations publicly available. According to data compiled by Audit Analytics and analyzed by *CFO* magazine, the MD&A was the topic cited most frequently in 2009 by the SEC in its reviews of U.S. publicly traded companies' annual and quarterly filings. Based on a review of SEC comment letters, the SEC wants more than a historical description of operating results, liquidity, and capital resources and would like companies to disclose how they develop critical accounting estimates.[9]

The events of 2001, including the economic downturn, September 11, and the collapse of Enron, appear to have affected the quantity of precautionary and explanatory information companies have added to their MD&A sections of subsequent annual

[8]Laton McCartney, "Where There's Smoke, There's Fraud," *CFO*, March 2011.
[9]Sarah Johnson, "The SEC Has a Few Questions For You," *CFO*, May 2010.

FIGURE 1.3 MD&A Discussion Items: What Do They Mean?

Item	Translation
1. Internal and external sources of liquidity	From where does the company obtain cash—sales of products or services (internal source) or through borrowing and sales of stock (external sources)?
2. Material deficiencies in liquidity and how they will be remedied.	If the firm does not have enough cash to continue to operate in the long term, what is it doing to obtain cash and prevent bankruptcy?
3. Commitments for capital expenditures, the purpose of such commitments, and expected sources of funding.	How much is the company planning to spend next year for investments in property, plant, and equipment or acquisitions? Why? How will it pay for these items?
4. Anticipated changes in the mix and cost of financing resources.	Will the percentage of debt and equity change in the future relative to prior years—i.e., will the company borrow more or less, sell more stock, or generate significant profits or losses?
5. Unusual or infrequent transactions that affect income from continuing operations.	Will revenues or expenses be affected in the future by events not expected in the normal course of business operations?
6. Events that cause material changes in the relationship between costs and revenues.	Will significant changes occur that cause revenues (or expenses) to increase or decrease without a corresponding change in expenses (or revenues)?
7. Breakdown of sales increases into price and volume components.	Did the company's sales increase because it sold more products or services, or was the increase the result of price increases (with even a possible decrease in volume)?

reports. Some firms include a plethora of statements covering every possible negative event that could possibly occur, such as:

We may not be able to expand, causing sales to decrease.
We may be unable to successfully develop new products.
We may not be successful in our marketing efforts.
Our operating results may fluctuate, causing our stock price to decline.
Our suppliers may not meet our demand for materials.
Our products may have significant defects.

And on and on! These statements may be true, but an assessment of the probability that these events may occur would be more useful to the reader of this information.

More helpful has been the addition to the MD&A of explanations about why changes have occurred in profitability and liquidity. Many companies offer explanations of why certain accounts such as accounts receivable or inventories increased or decreased in its section on liquidity and capital resources. This change is welcome, but those companies still have not offered much in the way of forward-looking information in the MD&A.

The "Liquidity and Capital Resources" section of the MD&A for Sage Inc. (see Appendix 1A, pp. 40 to 52) reveals that the firm generates cash from operations (an internal source of liquidity) and also uses debt to fund operations (an external source of liquidity). Because cash from operations has been greater than the amounts borrowed in 2011 and 2013, no material deficiencies are indicated. Capital expenditures are predicted to be $15,900,000 in 2014, and it is anticipated that these funds will be used to open new stores. The funding sources will be cash from operations and borrowings. Based on the information given there is no indication that there will be a change in the mix and cost of financing resources.

The "Results of Operations" section of the MD&A for Sage Inc. does not include a discussion of any unusual or infrequent transactions, nor is any information given that would suggest a change in the relationship between revenues and expenses in the future. What can be determined from this section is that the 40.9% sales increase in 2013 resulted primarily from volume increases. In fact, the athletic footwear area contributed to a decline in comparable store sales due to both volume and selling price decreases. Other information that can be obtained from this section of the MD&A includes explanations of why gross profit, operating expenses, other income and expenses, and taxes have changed from one year to the next.

Five-Year Summary of Selected Financial Data and Market Data

A five-year summary of selected financial data required by the SEC includes net sales or operating revenues, income or loss from continuing operations, income or loss from continuing operations per common share, total assets, long-term obligations and redeemable preferred stock, and cash dividends per common share. Companies often choose to include more than five years of data and/or additional items. The summary offers the user of financial statements a quick look at some overall trends; however, the discussion in this book will focus on the financial statements themselves, not the summary data.

The market data required by the SEC contains two years of high and low common stock prices by quarter. Since the financial statements do not include market values of common stock, this item is useful when analyzing how well the firm does in the marketplace.

Pandora (a.k.a. "PR Fluff")

In addition to the material required for presentation, many companies add to the annual report an array of colored photographs, charts, a shareholders' letter from the CEO, and other items to make the report and the company attractive to current and prospective investors. Some of these creations also appear on corporate Web sites. Getting to what is needed through the "PR fluff" can be a challenge.

Public relations material, including the shareholders' letter, is often informative but can also be misleading. The chairman (and CEO) and president (and chief operating

DK Images

officer) of Lehman Brothers painted a positive picture for the future of Lehman Brothers in their jointly written 2007 letter to shareholders. They discussed that 2007 was "another year of record net revenues, net income, and earnings per share." They proudly shared how the Lehman team—with their "careful management of liquidity"—had built a bank able to survive the rapid shifts in liquidity that were occurring in the second half of 2007 as a result of the housing market, credit freeze, and repricing of credit-related securities. Toward the end of the letter, the two executives lamented that the marketplace did not reward them for their superb performance, as evidenced by their stock price declining "for the first time in five years."

Lehman Brothers declared bankruptcy the following year, 2008. As discussed in this chapter, red flags existed well before that event, including negative cash flow from operations and staggering levels of debt. It should also be noted that the 2007 Lehman Brothers Annual Report consisted of 129 pages, beginning with 40 glossy photographs and many pages before the reader could find any hard financial data.

Proxy Statement

The SEC requires companies to solicit shareholder votes in a document called the *proxy statement,* as many shareholders do not attend shareholder meetings. The proxy statement contains voting procedures and information, background information about the company's nominated directors, director compensation, executive compensation and any proposed changes in compensation plans, the audit committee report, and a breakdown of audit and nonaudit fees paid to the auditing firm. This information is important in assessing who manages the firm and how management is paid and potential conflict-of-interest issues.

The proxy material helps investors and creditors by providing information about the longevity and compensation of top management as well as corporate governance, audit-related matters, director and executive compensation including option grants, and related party transactions.

Missing and Hard-to-Find Information

Some of the facts needed to evaluate a company are not available in the financial statements. These include such intangibles as employee relations with management, the morale and efficiency of employees, the reputation of the firm with its customers, the firm's prestige in the community, the effectiveness of management, provisions for management succession, and potential exposure to changes in regulations—such as environmental or food and drug enforcement. These qualities impact the firm's operating success both directly and indirectly but are difficult to quantify.

Publicity in the media, which affects public perception of a firm, can also impact its financial performance. Pioneers in the "science of reputation management" are now selling their consulting services to firms to help them improve their reputation in the public's eye and thereby increase the firm's stock price. According to Communications Consulting Worldwide Inc., Walmart could improve its stock price by 4.9% or $9.7 billion if the company had the reputation of its competitor, Target. Target, while much smaller than Walmart, has been perceived by the public as a firm that adds value to the community in which it does business as a result of its charitable donations, the way it treats its employees, and the atmosphere Target creates in its stores. Walmart has been perceived as the bully that no one wants moving into their neighborhoods and an employer who treats employees poorly through low pay and discrimination.[10]

Some companies are identified with one primary leader or personality, and Apple Inc. is an example of that. Apple's share price was tied to its visionary leader Steve. Job's foresight in developing continued leadership for the company has had a positive impact. Following his death in October 2011, the share price fell initially but recovered almost immediately.

Although the reputation of a firm is difficult to measure, surveys each year offer insight into its importance. Johnson & Johnson historically maintained the number-one or number-two spot in surveys of the "most respected companies" until 2008.[11] The firm was often cited for its excellent handling of the 1982 Tylenol recall. Numerous recent recalls and quality concerns of Johnson & Johnson products, including a secret recall of Motrin, have seriously damaged the reputation of the firm as was evidenced by *Barron's* 2011 annual survey of the "world's most respected companies." Johnson & Johnson dropped to number 25 in the list of the largest 100 companies. Toyota's mishandling of the biggest quality crisis and recall in its history, related to gas pedal issues, resulted in its fall from the 3rd spot in 2008 to the 47th spot in *Barron's* 2011 survey. Apple Inc., which took over the number-one spot in the 2010 and 2011 survey, saw a rise in its stock price of 53% in 2010.[12]

Some relevant facts are available in the financial statements but may be difficult for an average user to find. For example, the amount of long-term debt a firm has outstanding is disclosed on the face of the balance sheet in the noncurrent liability section. However, "long-term" could apply to debt due in 12.5 months or 2 years or 15 years. To determine when cash resources will be required to meet debt principal payments, the user must find and analyze the note to the financial statements on long-term debt with its listing of principal, interest, and maturity of a firm's long-term debt instruments.

Another important form of supplementary information is that reported by diversified companies operating in several unrelated lines of business. These conglomerates report financial information for the consolidated entity on the face of its financial statements. For a breakdown of financial data by individual operating segments, the analyst must use information in notes to the financial statement.

---

[10]Pete Engardio and Michael Arndt, "What Price Reputation?" *Business Week,* July 9 and 16, 2007.
[11]Michael Santoli, "The Market's Finest," *Barron's*, September 8, 2008.
[12]Vito J. Racanelli, ". . . And the Award Goes to Apple!" *Barron's*, February 14, 2011.

The Enron collapse highlighted that some companies use complicated financing schemes that may or may not be completely revealed in the notes to the financial statements. Even with notes available, most average users may find these items beyond their comprehension unless they acquire a Ph.D. in accounting or finance or read the authors' discussion of Enron in their other book, *Understanding the Corporate Annual Report—Nuts, Bolts, and a Few Loose Screws*.

Complexities

Interpreting financial statements can be challenging because of the complexities inherent in the accounting rules that underlie financial reporting. GAAP, as established by the FASB and SEC, provide a measure of uniformity but also allow corporate management considerable discretion in applying the regulations.

Accounting Choices

Accounting choices and estimates can have a significant impact on the outcome of financial statement numbers. An example is the valuation of inventory (discussed in detail in Chapter 2). Companies can select from several acceptable methods that include, for instance, assuming that the oldest, lowest cost of goods are sold first, or that the most recent, highest cost of goods are sold first. The choice of inventory valuation methods affects both the amount of inventory on the balance sheet and the associated cost of selling inventory in the income statement. Because companies are allowed to select from several possible methods, comparability can be affected if companies within the same industry make different choices. And the quality of financial reporting can also be impacted if the accounting choice does not reflect economic reality.

GAAP-based financial statements are prepared according to the "accrual" rather than the "cash" basis of accounting. The accrual method means that the revenue is recognized in the accounting period when the sale is made rather than when the cash is received. The same principle applies to expense recognition; the expense associated with the product may occur before or after the cash is paid out. The purpose of the accrual method is to attempt to "match" expenses with revenues in appropriate accounting periods. If a firm sells goods on credit, there is a delay between the time the product is sold and the time the cash is collected. The process of matching expense and revenue to accounting periods involves considerable estimation and judgment and, like the inventory example, affects the outcome of the financial statement numbers.

Furthermore, financial statements are prepared on certain dates at the end of accounting periods, such as a year or a quarter. Whereas the firm's life is continuous, financial data must be appropriated to particular time periods.

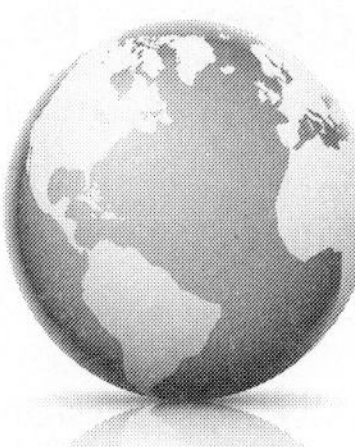

Shutterstock

The Future of Financial Statements

The accounting principles that underlie the preparation of financial statements have been complex historically. U.S. accounting rules established by the FASB have been perceived as being more complex than international standards developed by the IASB. The tendency of FASB has been to develop rules with a significant amount of detail, whereas the IASB has used a broader principles-based approach. As the FASB and the IASB work jointly toward one set of accounting standards, the set of rules that evolves may change significantly. The FASB and IASB have already agreed on some rule changes, but there are controversial issues yet to be resolved. Significant changes being worked on in 2011 (as the book goes to print) include lease accounting, classification of financial instruments, inventory accounting, and revenue recognition. Another important project is the reformatting of the financial statements. FASB has not yet decided on a new format for financial statements but has made public a proposed format that would require the income statement, balance sheet, and cash flow statement to show five general categories: business, discontinued operations, financing, income taxes, and equity. Each category would have its own subtotal. Within each of the categories, a breakdown of operating versus investing assets and liabilities is also being considered. These subcategories would also have their own subtotals.[13] Obviously, if these changes are agreed to and implemented, financial statements will look different from current GAAP-based statements. As of May 3, 2011, the FASB has classified the financial statement presentation project as a lower priority project and does not expect to take further action on this project before December 2011.

Quality of Financial Reporting

It has already been pointed out that management has considerable discretion within the overall framework of GAAP. As a result, the potential exists for management to "manipulate" the bottom line (profit or loss) and other accounts in financial statements. Ideally, financial statements should reflect an accurate picture of a company's financial condition and performance. The information should be useful both to assess the past and predict the future. The sharper and clearer the picture presented through the financial data and the closer that picture is to financial reality, the higher is the quality of the financial statements and reported earnings.

Many opportunities exist for management to affect the quality of financial statements. While financial reporting quality is covered throughout the textbook and Appendix 3A covers earnings quality in detail, some illustrations follow.

Timing of Revenue and Expense Recognition

One of the generally accepted accounting principles that provides the foundation for preparing financial statements is the matching principle: expenses are matched with the generation of revenues to determine net income for an accounting period.

[13] Marie Leone, "The Sums of All Parts: Redesigning Financials," *CFO.com,* November 14, 2007.

Reference was made earlier to the fact that published financial statements are based on the accrual rather than the cash basis of accounting, which means that revenues are recognized when earned and expenses are recognized when incurred, regardless of when the cash inflows and outflows occur. This matching process involves judgments by management regarding the timing of expense and revenue recognition. Although accounting rules provide guidelines helpful in making the necessary and appropriate allocations, these rules are not always precise.

For example, suppose that a company learns near the end of an accounting period that a material accounts receivable is probably uncollectible. When will the account be written off as a loss—currently, or in the next accounting period when a final determination is made? Pose the same question for obsolete inventory sitting on the warehouse shelves gathering dust. These are areas involving sometimes arbitrary managerial decisions. Generally speaking, the more conservative management is in making such judgments (conservatism usually implies the choice that is least favorable to the firm), the higher the quality of earnings resulting from the matching of revenues and expenses in a given accounting period.

Discretionary Items

Many expenditures made by a business firm are discretionary in nature. Management exercises control over the budget level and timing of expenditures for the repair and maintenance of machinery and equipment, marketing and advertising, research and development, and capital expansion. Policies are also flexible with respect to the replacement of plant assets, the development of new product lines, and the disposal of an operating division. Each choice regarding these discretionary items has both an immediate and a long-term impact on profitability, perhaps not in the same direction. A company might elect to defer plant maintenance in order to boost current period earnings; ultimately, the effect of such a policy could be detrimental.

For some industries, such as beverages and retail marketing, advertising and marketing expenditures are essential to gaining and maintaining market share. Research and development can be critical for ongoing success of industries such as computing and electronics, health, and auto.

The financial analyst should carefully scrutinize management's policies with respect to these discretionary items through an examination of expenditure trends (absolute and relative amounts) and comparison with industry competitors. Such an analysis can provide insight into a company's existing strengths and weaknesses and contribute to an assessment of its ability to perform successfully in the future.

The Journey Through the Maze Continues

Numerous other examples exist to illustrate the difficulty in finding and interpreting financial statement information. Many such examples are discussed in the chapters that follow. Annual reports provide a wealth of useful information, but finding what is relevant to financial decision making may involve overcoming mazelike challenges. The remaining chapters in this book are intended to help readers find and effectively use the information in financial statements and supplementary data.

Appendix 1A: Sage Inc.

Management's Discussion and Analysis of Financial Condition and Results of Operations

Net Sales

Net sales increased 40.9% in 2013 compared to 8.7% in 2012 due primarily to new store openings and the addition of e-commerce sales. Comparable store sales increased 10.4% and were attributable to sales increases in exercise apparel, athletic footwear, and golf equipment. Net sales increased 8.7% in 2012 compared to 2011 due primarily to new store sales. Comparable store sales decreased 1.8% mostly attributable to sales decreases in athletic footwear combined with a decrease in average unit retail price.

Three segments contribute to the Company's overall sales and include Sporting Apparel, Footwear, and Sporting Gear and Equipment. All three segments contributed significantly to the 40.9% overall sales increase from 2012 to 2013. From 2011 to 2012 the Sporting Apparel and Sporting Gear and Equipment contributed positively to the sales increase, 13.3% and 11.9%, respectively, while Footwear sales decreased 6.1%. Due to competition in the footwear industry, the Company lowered retail prices on footwear products in order to increase sales.

Gross Profit

Gross profit has decreased over the past three years. The gross profit margin decreased from 42.0% to 39.9% between fiscal year 2011 and 2012, due primarily to the lower margins resulting from realignment in the retail prices of athletic footwear. The gross profit margin increased slightly from fiscal year 2012 to fiscal year 2013 from 39.9% to 40.0%.

Operating Expenses

Although selling and administrative expenses increased over the past three years as a percentage of sales, the actual amount of selling and administrative expenses declined each year. The Company recognized expenses during fiscal 2013 related to the Company's e-commerce operations, while no expenses related to e-commerce were recorded in prior years. Higher costs associated with new store openings in all three years have been offset by lower payroll costs associated with cost-cutting efforts and closing of underperforming stores.

Advertising costs increased from $9,541,000 in 2011 to $10,792,000 in 2012 and $14,258,000 in 2013 as the Company began an advertising campaign to promote its new e-commerce unit.

Depreciation and amortization expenses have increased from $2,501,000 in 2011 to $3,998,000 in 2013 as a result of new store openings.

Impairment charges for the years ended 2013, 2012, and 2011 amounted to $3,015,000, $2,046,000, and $3,031,000, respectively and are mainly attributable to store relocations and store closings.

Other Income (Expense)

Interest income increased from 2011 to 2012 as a result of higher average interest rates, but decreased from 2012 to 2013 due to lower average balances in cash equivalents.

Interest expense increased from 2011 to 2013 as a result of higher interest rates and higher levels of corporate borrowings related to new store openings.

Income Tax

The Company's effective tax rate was 45%, 43%, and 45% for 2013, 2012, and 2011, respectively.

Liquidity and Capital Resources

Operating Activities

The following table provides information about the Company's cash flows:

(In Thousands)	2013	2012	2011
Net cash provided (used) by operating activities	$10,024	($3,767)	$5,629
Net cash used for investing activities	(13,805)	(4,773)	(3,982)
Net cash provided by financing activities	2,728	6,464	111

Cash flows from operations are seasonal, with the Christmas season being the peak selling season. Inventory is increased prior to peak selling seasons to meet increased demand for products and is subsequently reduced due to sales demand after the season is complete. After failing to generate cash from operations in 2012, the Company returned to a positive cash flow from operations in 2013, primarily due to the use of short-term supplier credit to finance increases in inventory levels in the fourth quarter. The significant increase in sales in 2013 resulted in higher accounts receivable at year-end compared to 2012 and 2011.

Investing Activities

Investing cash flows consist primarily of capital expenditures as a result of the Company's current expansion plans and the opening of new stores. Capital expenditures in 2013 were $14,100,000 and are expected to be approximately $15,900,000 in 2014. Funding sources for these expenditures will be cash flows from operating activities and borrowings, including the Company's credit line if necessary.

Financing Activities

Borrowings are the primary source of cash from financing activities. Cash used in financing activities consists mainly of debt repayments and dividends.

We believe that we have the financial resources needed to meet business requirements for the next 12 months, including capital expenditures.

Auditor's Report

Board of Directors and Stockholders

Sage Inc.

We have audited the accompanying consolidated balance sheets of Sage Inc., and subsidiaries as of December 31, 2013 and 2012, and the related consolidated statements of earnings, shareholders' equity, and cash flows for each of the three years in the period ended December 31, 2013. These financial statements are the responsibility of the Company's management. Our responsibility is to express an opinion on these financial statements based on our audits.

We conducted our audits in accordance with the standards of the Public Company Accounting Oversight Board (United States). Those standards require that we plan and perform the audits to obtain reasonable assurance about whether the financial statements are free of material misstatement. An audit includes examining, on a test basis, evidence supporting the amounts and disclosures in the financial statements. An audit also includes assessing the accounting principles used and significant estimates made by management, as well as evaluating the overall financial statement presentation. We believe that our audits provide a reasonable basis for our opinion.

In our opinion, the consolidated financial statements referred to above present fairly, in all material respects, the consolidated financial position of Sage Inc. and subsidiaries at December 31, 2013 and 2012, and the consolidated results of their operations and their cash flows for each of the three years in the period ended December 31, 2013, in conformity with accounting principles generally accepted in the United States of America.

We also have audited, in accordance with the standards of the Public Company Accounting Oversight Board (United States), the effectiveness of Sage Inc.'s internal control over financial reporting as of December 31, 2013, based on criteria established in Internal Control-Integrated Framework issued by the Committee of Sponsoring Organizations of the Treadway Commission, and our report dated February 15, 2014, expressed an unqualified opinion thereon.

J. J. Michaels and Company

Dime Box, TX

February 15, 2014

SAGE INC.
CONSOLIDATED BALANCE SHEETS
December 31, 2013 and 2012 (in Thousands)

	2013	2012
Assets		
Current Assets		
Cash and cash equivalents	$9,333	$10,386
Accounts receivable, less allowance for doubtful accounts of $448 in 2013 and $417 in 2012	8,960	8,350
Inventories	47,041	36,769
Prepaid expenses and other assets	512	759
Total current assets	65,846	56,264
Property, Plant, and Equipment		
Land	811	811
Buildings and leasehold improvements	18,273	11,928
Equipment	21,523	13,768
	40,607	26,507
Less accumulated depreciation and amortization	11,528	7,530
Net property, plant, and equipment	29,079	18,977
Goodwill	270	270
Other Assets	103	398
Total Assets	$95,298	$75,909
Liabilities and Stockholders' Equity		
Current Liabilities		
Accounts payable	$14,294	$ 7,591
Accrued liabilities	4,137	4,366
Income taxes payable	1,532	947
Short-term debt	5,614	6,012
Current maturities of long-term debt	1,884	1,516
Total current liabilities	27,461	20,432
Deferred Federal Income Taxes	843	635
Long-Term Debt	21,059	16,975
Commitments and Contingencies (See Notes 3 and 5)		
Total liabilities	49,363	38,042
Stockholders' Equity		
Common stock, par value $0.01, authorized, 10,000,000 shares; issued, 4,363,000 shares in 2013 and 4355,000 shares in 2012, and additional paid-in capital	5,760	5,504
Retained Earnings	40,175	32,363
Total stockholders' equity	45,935	37,867
Total Liabilities and Stockholders' Equity	$95,298	$75,909

The accompanying notes are an integral part of these statements.

SAGE INC.
CONSOLIDATED STATEMENTS OF EARNINGS
For the Years Ended December 31, 2013, 2012, and 2011
(in Thousands Except per Share Amounts)

	2013	**2012**	**2011**
Net sales	$215,600	$153,000	$140,700
Cost of goods sold	129,364	91,879	81,606
Gross profit	86,236	61,121	59,094
Selling and administrative expenses	45,722	33,493	32,765
Advertising	14,258	10,792	9,541
Depreciation and amortization	3,998	2,984	2,501
Impairment charges	3,015	2,046	3,031
Operating profit	19,243	11,806	11,256
Other income (expense)			
Interest income	422	838	738
Interest expense	(2,585)	(2,277)	(1,274)
Earnings before income taxes	17,080	10,367	10,720
Provision for income taxes	7,686	4,457	4,824
Net earnings	$ 9,394	$ 5,910	$ 5,896
Earnings per common share:			
Basic	$ 2.16	$ 1.36	$ 1.36
Diluted	$ 2.12	$ 1.33	$ 1.33
Weighted average common shares outstanding:			
Basic	4,359	4,350	4,342
Diluted	4,429	4,442	4,431

The accompanying notes are an integral part of these statements.

SAGE INC.
CONSOLIDATED STATEMENTS OF CASH FLOWS
For the Years Ended December 31, 2013, 2012, and 2011 (in Thousands)

	2013	2012	2011
Cash Flows from Operating Activities—Indirect Method			
Net income	$ 9,394	$ 5,910	$ 5,896
Adjustments to reconcile net income to cash provided (used) by operating activities			
Depreciation and amortization	3,998	2,984	2,501
Deferred income taxes	208	136	118
Cash provided (used) by current assets and liabilities			
Accounts receivable	(610)	(3,339)	(448)
Inventories	(10,272)	(7,006)	(2,331)
Prepaid expenses	247	295	(82)
Accounts payable	6,703	(1,051)	902
Accrued liabilities	(229)	(1,215)	(1,130)
Income taxes payable	585	(481)	203
Net cash provided (used) by operating activities	$ 10,024	($ 3,767)	$ 5,629
Cash Flows from Investing Activities			
Additions to property, plant, and equipment	(14,100)	(4,773)	(3,982)
Other investing activities	295	0	0
Net cash provided (used) by investing activities	($ 13,805)	($ 4,773)	($ 3,982)
Cash Flows from Financing Activities			
Sales of common stock	256	183	124
Increase (decrease) in short-term borrowings (includes current maturities of long-term debt)	(30)	1,854	1,326
Additions to long-term borrowings	5,600	7,882	629
Reductions of long-term borrowings	(1,516)	(1,593)	(127)
Dividends paid	(1,582)	(1,862)	(1,841)
Net cash provided (used) by financing activities	$ 2,728	$ 6,464	$ 111
Increase (decrease) in cash and cash equivalents	($ 1,053)	($ 2,076)	$ 1,758
Cash and cash equivalents, beginning of year	10,386	12,462	10,704
Cash and cash equivalents, end of year	9,333	10,386	12,462
Supplemental cash flow information:			
Cash paid for interest	$ 2,585	$ 2,277	$ 1,274
Cash paid for taxes	7,478	4,321	4,706

The accompanying notes are an integral part of these statements.

SAGE INC.
CONSOLIDATED STATEMENTS OF STOCKHOLDERS' EQUITY
For the Years Ended December 31, 2013, 2012, and 2011 (in Thousands)

	Common Stock and Additional Paid-in Capital			
	Shares	Amount	Retained Earnings	Total
Balance at December 31, 2010	4,340	$5,197	$24,260	$29,457
Net earnings			5,896	5,896
Proceeds from sale of shares from exercise of stock options, net of tax benefit	5	115		115
Stock-based compensation		9		9
Cash dividends			(1,841)	(1,841)
Balance at December 31, 2011	4,345	$5,321	$28,315	$33,636
Net earnings			5,910	5,910
Proceeds from sale of shares from exercise of stock options, net of tax benefit	10	176		176
Stock-based compensation		7		7
Cash dividends			(1,862)	(1,862)
Balance at December 31, 2012	4,355	$5,504	$32,363	$37,867
Net earnings			9,394	9,394
Proceeds from sale of shares from exercise of stock options, net of tax benefit	8	244		244
Stock-based compensation		12		12
Cash dividends			(1,582)	(1,582)
Balance at December 31, 2013	4,363	$5,760	$40,175	$45,935

Note 1—Basis of Presentation and Summary of Significant Accounting Policies

Operations: Sage Inc. is a retailer selling sporting apparel, footwear, gear, and equipment through its stores, which are located in the southwestern United States.

Fiscal Year: The Company's fiscal year ends on December 31. All fiscal years presented include 52 weeks of operation.

Principles of Consolidation: The consolidated financial statements include Sage Inc. and its wholly owned subsidiaries. All intercompany accounts and transactions have been eliminated in consolidation.

Use of Estimates in the Preparation of Financial Statements: The preparation of financial statements in conformity with GAAP requires management to make estimates and assumptions that affect the reported amounts of assets and liabilities at the date of the financial statements and the reported amounts of revenues and expenses during the reporting period. Actual results may differ materially from our estimates.

Cash and Cash Equivalents: Cash and cash equivalents consist of cash on hand and all highly liquid instruments purchased with a maturity of three months or less at the date of purchase.

Inventories: Inventories are stated at the lower of cost—last in, first out (LIFO)—or market. If the first in, first out (FIFO) method of inventory accounting had been used, inventories would have been approximately $2,681,000 and $2,096,000 higher than reported at December 31, 2013 and 2012.

Property, Plant, and Equipment: Property, plant, and equipment is stated at cost. Depreciation expense is calculated principally by the straight-line method based on estimated useful lives of 3 to 10 years for equipment, 3 to 30 years for leasehold improvements, and 40 years for buildings. Estimated useful lives of leasehold improvements represent the remaining term of the lease in effect at the time the improvements are made.

Impairment Charges: The Company evaluates its long-lived assets to assess whether the carrying values have been impaired whenever events and circumstances indicate that the carrying value of these assets may not be recoverable based on estimated undiscounted future cash flows. The amount of the impairment loss, if impairment exists, would be calculated based on the excess of the carrying amounts of the assets over their estimated fair value computed using discounted future cash flows.

Impairment charges for the years ended December 31, 2013, 2012, and 2011 related to store relocations and store closings amounted to $3,015,000, $2,046,000, and $3,031,000, respectively.

Goodwill: Goodwill represents the cost of acquiring a business over the fair values of the net assets received at the date of acquisition. Impairment of goodwill is evaluated each year or whenever events or circumstances indicate that the carrying value may not be recoverable.

Other Assets: Other assets are investments in properties not used in business operations.

Revenue Recognition: Revenue from retail sales is recognized at the point of sale, net of sales tax. A provision for anticipated sales returns is provided through a reduction of sales and cost of goods sold in the period that the related sales are recorded.

Expenses of New Stores: Expenses associated with the opening of new stores are charged to expense as incurred and include such items as rent, marketing, payroll, and recruiting costs.

Advertising Costs: Advertising costs are expensed the first time an advertisement takes place. Advertising expense was $14,258,000, $10,792,000, and $9,541,000 for fiscal years 2013, 2012, and 2011, respectively.

Selling and Administrative Expenses: Selling and administrative expenses include store payroll and fringe benefits, bank card charges, information systems, legal, accounting, repairs and maintenance and other expenses associated with the operations of stores and all corporate expenses. Repairs and maintenance expense was $2,946,000, $2,184,000, and $3,003,000, for fiscal years 2013, 2012, and 2011, respectively.

Stock-Based Compensation: The Company has the availability to grant stock options to purchase common stock under Sage Inc.'s Stock and Incentive Plan. The Company also has an employee stock purchase plan, which provides for eligible employees to purchase shares of the Company's common stock.

Note 2—Debt

Short-term Debt: The Company has a $10,000,000 bank line of credit. Interest is calculated at the prime rate plus 1% on any outstanding balance. Any balance on March 31, 2015, converts to a term note payable in quarterly installments over 5 years.

Long-term Debt: The Company's outstanding long-term debt at December 31, 2013, and December 31, 2012, was as follows (in thousands):

	2013	**2012**
Mortgage notes maturing in 15 to 25 years at 5.75–8.75%	$ 3,808	$ 4,174
Notes payable (unsecured) maturing in 2017 and 2019 at 9% and 6.5%	7,167	7,567
Notes payable (secured) maturing in 2021 and 2022 at 7% and 7.5%	11,968	6,750
	$22,943	$18,491
Less current maturities	1,884	1,516
	$21,059	$16,975

As of December 31, 2013, scheduled principal payments on long-term debt are as follows (in thousands):

Fiscal Year	
2014	$1,884
2015	1,516
2016	2,678
2017	2,678
2018	2,678
Thereafter	$11,509
Total	$22,943

Note 3—Commitments

The Company leases substantially all of its stores, office facilities, and distribution centers under noncancelable operating leases that expire at various dates through 2032. Certain of the store lease agreements contain renewal options for additional periods of five to ten years and contain rent escalation clauses. Rent expense was $13,058,000 in 2013, $7,111,000 in 2012, and $7,267,000 in 2011.

Minimum annual rental commitments as of December 31, 2013, are as follows (in thousands):

Fiscal Year	
2014	$14,561
2015	14,082
2016	13,673
2017	13,450
2018	13,003
Thereafter	$107,250
Total	$176,019

Note 4—Income Taxes

Components of the provision for income taxes are as follows (in thousands):

	2013	2012	2011
Current:			
Federal	$6,357	$3,759	$4,141
State	1,121	562	565
	7,478	4,321	4,706
Deferred:			
Federal	189	124	108
State	19	12	10
	208	136	118
Total Provision	$7,686	$4,457	$4,824

The difference between the tax provision at the statutory federal income tax rate and the tax provision as a percentage of income before taxes (effective tax rate) was as follows:

	2013	2012	2011
Federal statutory income tax rate	35.0%	35.0%	35.0%
State tax, net of federal benefit	5.2%	4.8%	4.7%
Other permanent items	4.8%	3.2%	5.3%
Effective tax rate	45.0%	43.0%	45.0%

Components of deferred tax assets (liabilities) consist of the following as of the fiscal years ended (in thousands):

	2013	**2012**
Store closing expense	$ 9	$ 15
Stock-based compensation	14	13
Total deferred tax assets*	23	28
Depreciation	628	430
Installment sales	215	205
Total deferred tax liabilities	(843)	(635)
Net deferred tax liabilities	($820)	($607)

*Included in Prepaid expenses and other assets on the balance sheet.

Note 5—Contingencies

The Company is involved in legal proceedings incidental to the normal conduct of its business. The outcome of these legal proceedings cannot be predicted with certainty; however, management believes that the ultimate resolution of these matters will not have a material adverse effect on the Company's liquidity, financial position, or results of operations.

Note 6—Segment Information

Sage Inc. has three reportable segments: sporting apparel, footwear, and sporting gear and equipment.

Sporting apparel includes men's, women's and children's sports clothing.

Footwear includes tennis, running, walking, aerobic, and golf shoes, as well as ski and hiking boots.

Sporting gear and equipment includes hunting and fishing gear, sporting goods equipment and an extensive line of golf, ski, and cycling equipment.

Segment information is as follows (in thousands):

	Year Ended December 31,		
	2013	2012	2011
Net sales:			
Sporting apparel	$ 62,524	$ 45,288	$ 39,959
Footwear	36,652	26,163	27,858
Sporting gear and equipment	116,424	81,549	72,883
Total	$215,600	$153,000	$140,700
Operating profit:			
Sporting apparel	$ 8,992	$ 6,443	$ 5,928
Footwear	518	(124)	98
Sporting gear and equipment	10,538	6,252	6,033
Corporate and other	(805)	(765)	(803)
Total	$ 19,243	$ 11,806	$ 11,256
Depreciation and amortization:			
Sporting apparel	$ 793	$ 681	$ 300
Footwear	1,202	1,190	1,200
Sporting gear and equipment	1,642	887	800
Corporate and other	361	226	201
Total	$ 3,998	$ 2,984	$ 2,501
Identifiable assets:			
Sporting apparel	$ 15,663	$ 13,463	$ 10,011
Footwear	23,760	29,444	30,893
Sporting gear and equipment	31,554	13,600	11,300
Corporate and other	24,321	19,402	18,116
Total	$ 95,298	$ 75,909	$ 70,320
Capital expenditures:			
Sporting apparel	$ 32	$ 24	$ 25
Footwear	35	75	78
Sporting gear and equipment	43	28	23
Corporate and other	28	16	18
Total	$ 138	$ 143	$ 144

SELF-TEST

Solutions are provided in Appendix B.

_______ **1.** Why should an individual learn to read and interpret financial statements?

(a) Understanding financial statements will guarantee at least a 20% return on investments.

(b) An individual need not learn to read and interpret financial statements because auditors offer a report indicating whether the company is financially sound or not.

(c) Learning to read and interpret financial statements will enable individuals to gain employment.

(d) Individuals cannot necessarily rely on auditors and management of firms to offer honest information about the financial well-being of firms.

______ **2.** Which of the following organizations write accounting rules for U.S. companies?
(a) FASB and Congress.
(b) EDGAR and IASB.
(c) FASB, SEC, and IASB.
(d) SEC and FASB.

______ **3.** Which accounting rules did the European Union require publicly traded companies to use since 2005?
(a) Financial Reporting Rulings (FRR).
(b) Accounting Series Releases (ASR).
(c) International Rules (IFRS).
(d) None of the above.

______ **4.** Which financial statement presents the results of operations for an accounting period?
(a) Balance sheet.
(b) Statement of cash flows.
(c) Income statement.
(d) Statement of stockholders' equity.

______ **5.** Which of the following is usually the first note to the financial statements?
(a) Summary of accounting policies.
(b) Changes in accounting policies, if any.
(c) Details of particular accounts.
(d) None of the above.

______ **6.** Which of the following statements is/are false?
(a) The FASB and the IASB agreed to work on all major projects independently.
(b) The financial statements present fairly the financial position, the results of operations, and the changes in cash flows for the company.
(c) The SOX has reduced the need for internal auditors.
(d) Management is responsible for the preparation of financial statements, including notes.

______ **7.** Which of the following statements is/are true?
(a) The Sarbanes-Oxley Act of 2002 was the cause of the demise of Enron.
(b) The Sarbanes-Oxley Act of 2002 has had a major impact on internal auditing.
(c) The Public Company Accounting Oversight Board has the authority to write auditing rules and set quality control and ethics standards.
(d) Titles II of SOX focus on corporate responsibility.

______ **8.** What does Section 404 of the Sarbanes-Oxley Act of 2002 require?
(a) A ten-year jail sentence and $1 million fine for violations of the act.
(b) Rotation of audit partners every five years.
(c) A statement by the company regarding the effectiveness of internal controls and a disclosure of any material weaknesses in a firm's internal control system.
(d) Auditor independence, which prohibits audit firms from offering any services other than audit services.

_____ **9.** Which of the following subjects should be discussed in the management discussion and analysis section?
(a) Profitability.
(b) Commitments for capital expenditures.
(c) Unusual or infrequent transactions
(d) None of the above.

_____ **10.** Which of the following statements is true?
(a) Annual reports only contain glossy pictures.
(b) Public relations material should be used cautiously.
(c) Market data refers to the advertising budget of a firm.
(d) The shareholders' letter should be ignored.

_____ **11.** The market data required by the SEC contains ____ years of high and low common stock prices by ______.
(a) two; month.
(b) two; quarter.
(c) five; quarter.
(d) five; month.

_____ **12.** What information does a proxy statement provide?
(a) Information on voting procedures.
(b) Information on worker compensation.
(c) Information on the breakdown of consultancy fees paid to a consultant.
(d) All of the above.

_____ **13.** What is the matching principle in accounting?
(a) Recognition of revenue when it is received in cash.
(b) Recognition of revenue in the accounting period when the sale is made rather than when cash is received.
(c) Matching expenses with revenue in the appropriate accounting period.
(d) Both (b) and (c).

_____ **14.** How many categories will be shown in the income statement, balance sheet, and cash flow statement of companies as per the proposed format of FASB?
(a) Three.
(b) Four.
(c) Five.
(d) Six.

_____ **15.** Where would you find the following information?
_____ (1) An attestation to the fairness of financial statements.
_____ (2) Summary of significant accounting policies.
_____ (3) Cash flow from operating, financing, and investing activities.
_____ (4) A qualified opinion.

______ (5) Information about principal, interest, and maturity of long-term debt.
______ (6) Financial position on a particular date.
______ (7) Discussion of the company's results of operations.
______ (8) Description of pension plans.
______ (9) Anticipated commitments for capital expenditures.
______(10) Reconciliation of beginning and ending balances of equity accounts.

(a) Financial statements.
(b) Notes to the financial statements.
(c) Auditor's report.
(d) Management discussion and analysis.

Study Questions and Problems

1.1. What types of questions can be answered by analyzing financial statements?

1.2. What are the different types of reports that a company is required to regularly file with the SEC?

1.3. What were the primary goals of the FASB in developing the Accounting Standards Codification?

1.4. What organization has legal authority to set accounting policies in the United States? Does this organization write most of the accounting rules in the United States? Explain.

1.5. Describe the financial statements that are contained in an annual report or Form 10-K.

1.6. Explain the impact of SOX on internal auditing.

1.7. What causes an auditor's report to be qualified? adverse? a disclaimer of opinion? unqualified with explanatory language?

1.8. Why is the management discussion and analysis useful to the financial analyst?

1.9. What is a proxy statement, and why is it important to the analyst?

1.10. What are the components of the five-year summary of selected financial data required by the SEC?

1.11. Writing Skills Problem

Staff members from the marketing department of your firm are doing a splendid job selling products to customers. Many of the customers are so pleased, in fact, they are also buying shares in the company's stock, which means that they receive a copy of the firm's annual report. Unfortunately, questions sometimes arise that the marketing staff members are woefully inadequate at answering. Technical questions about the firm's financial condition and performance are referred to the chief financial officer, but the director of marketing has asked you to write a memo in which you explain the key elements in an annual report so that marketing representatives are better prepared to respond to questions of a more general nature.

Required: Write a memo no longer than one page (single-spaced, double-spaced between paragraphs) in which you describe the contents of an annual report so that marketing personnel can understand the basic requirements. The memo should be dated and addressed to B. R. Neal, Director of Marketing, from you; the subject is "Contents of an Annual Report."

To the Student: In business writing, the primary elements are *clarity* and *conciseness*. You must keep in mind the audience you are addressing and the objective of the communication.

1.12. Research Problem

Research the joint FASB/IASB Financial Statement Presentation project. Write a short essay outlining the current status of the project and the expected changes to the financial statements.

1.13. Internet Problem

Access the SEC Web site: http://www.sec.gov/. Write a one-page summary explaining the items that a financial analyst might find useful at this Web site.

CASES

Case 1.1 Intel Case

The 2010 Intel Annual Report can be found at the following Web site: www.pearsoninternationaleditions.com/fraser. Using the annual report, answer the following questions:

a. Describe the type of business in which Intel operates.
b. Read the letters from the CEO and the chairman and discuss any information learned from this letter that might be useful to an analyst.
c. What type of audit opinion was given for the financial statements and the internal financial controls of Intel? Explain the key items discussed in the audit report.
d. Read the Management Discussion and Analysis (MD&A). Discuss whether the items that should be addressed in the MD&A are included. Support your answer with examples from the Intel MD&A.
e. After reading the MD&A, discuss the future prospects of Intel. Do you have any concerns? If so, describe those concerns.

Case 1.2 Avnet Comprehensive Analysis Case Using the Financial Statement Analysis Template

Each chapter in the textbook contains a continuation of this problem. The objective is to learn how to do a comprehensive financial statement analysis in steps as you learn the content of each chapter.

To complete this problem, access the Avnet 2010 Form 10-K and the financial statement analysis template at the following Web site: www.pearsoninternationaleditions.com/fraser.

a. Once you have linked to the template you should see a window that asks whether you want to enable the macros. You must click on "Enable Macros" to use the template. (You may have to change the security setting on your computer in order to use this feature.) Familiarize yourself with the instructions. The tab for the instructions is at the bottom of your screen and is labeled "ReadMe." Print out a copy of the instructions to be used for all Avnet problems in each chapter of the text. Click on the link at the bottom of the screen labeled "Cover." Enter all of the required data in the template for Avnet. Use the instructions to help you locate the necessary information. The amount for "Rent Expense" can be found in Note 11 under the heading "Long-Term Leases." Print the cover sheet when it is completed. Save the template on your computer or a disk in order to use it with subsequent problems in later chapters.
b. Access newspaper and periodical articles about Avnet to learn of any information that would be helpful in understanding the company's financial condition as well as future plans. Summarize what you learn in a short paper.
c. Use the 2010 Avnet Form 10-K to do the following:

   Review Items 1 and 3 of the Form 10-K as well as the Report of Independent Registered Public Accounting Firm found in Item 8. Write a concise summary of the important items learned from reading these items.

Note: Keep all information from this problem in a notebook or folder to be used with the Avnet problems in later chapters.

Case 1.3 Mattel Inc.

Required

Locate the Form 10-K for Mattel Inc. using the EDGAR database at the SEC Web site: www.sec.gov. Answer the following questions using Mattel's 2010 Form 10-K.

1. Briefly state the line of business within which Mattel Inc. operates.
2. Find the following items in Mattel's 2010 Form 10-K and indicate the page number(s) where the items can be found:
   a. Balance sheet
   b. Income statement
   c. Statement of cash flows
   d. Statement of stockholders' equity
   e. Notes to the financial statements
   f. Management Discussion and Analysis
   g. Summary of selected financial data
   h. Auditor's report
3. What public accounting firm conducted the audit for Mattel Inc.?
4. Using the information, for fiscal year 2010, fill in the amounts for the following items from the financial statements:
   a. Assets
   b. Liabilities
   c. Stockholders' equity
   d. Net sales or net revenues
   e. Net income or loss (specify if amount is income or loss)
   f. Change in cash (give dollar amount) and if change is an increase or decrease
   g. Retained earnings (ending balance)

Case 1.4 Apple Inc.

Excerpts from the Management Discussion and Analysis of Financial Condition and Results of Operations (MD&A) of the Apple Inc., 2010 Form 10-K are found on pages 59–66.

Required

1. Why is the MD&A section of the annual report useful to the financial analyst? What types of information can be found in this section?
2. Using the excerpts from the MD&A of the Apple Inc. 2010 Form 10-K, discuss whether each of the items that should be discussed in an MD&A are, in fact, presented in this section. Give examples to support your answer.
3. Evaluate the overall quality of the information presented by Apple Inc. in the MD&A.
4. Based on this section only, what is your assessment of the prospects for this company?

Executive Overview

The Company designs, manufactures, and markets a range of personal computers, mobile communication and media devices, and portable digital music players, and sells a variety of related software, services, peripherals, networking solutions, and third-party digital content and applications. The Company's products and services include Mac computers, iPhone, iPad, iPod, Apple TV, Xserve, a portfolio of consumer and professional software applications, the Mac OS X and iOS operating systems, third-party digital content and applications through the iTunes Store, and a variety of accessory, service, and support offerings. The Company sells its products worldwide through its retail stores, online stores, and direct sales force, and third-party cellular network carriers, wholesalers, retailers, and value-added resellers. In addition, the Company sells a variety of third-party Mac, iPhone, iPad and iPod compatible products, including application software, printers, storage devices, speakers, headphones, and various other accessories and peripherals through its online and retail stores. The Company sells to SMB, education, enterprise, government, and creative markets.

Fiscal Year 2010 versus 2009

Net sales during 2010 increased $22.3 billion or 52% compared to 2009. Several factors contributed positively to these increases, including the following:

- Net sales of iPhone and related products and services were $25.2 billion in 2010, representing an increase of $12.1 billion or 93% compared to 2009. Net sales of iPhone and related products and services accounted for 39% of the Company's total net sales for the year. iPhone unit sales totaled 40 million in 2010, which represents an increase of 19.3 million or 93% compared to 2009. iPhone year-over-year growth was attributable primarily to continued growth from existing carriers, expanded distribution with new international carriers and resellers, and strong demand for iPhone 4, which was released in the U.S. in June 2010 and in many other countries over the remainder of 2010. As of September 25, 2010, the Company distributed iPhone in 89 countries through 166 carriers.

- Net sales of iPad and related products and services were $5.0 billion and unit sales of iPad were 7.5 million during 2010. iPad was released in the U.S. in April 2010 and in various other countries over the remainder of 2010. As of September 25, 2010, the Company distributed iPad in 26 countries. The Company distributes iPad through its direct channels, certain cellular network carriers' distribution channels, and certain third-party resellers. Net sales of iPad and related products and services accounted for 8% of the Company's total net sales for 2010, reflecting the strong demand for iPad during the five months following its release.
- Mac net sales increased by $3.6 billion or 26% in 2010 compared to 2009, and Mac unit sales increased by 3.3 million or 31% in 2010 compared to 2009. Net sales per Mac unit sold decreased by 4% in 2010 compared to 2009 due primarily to lower average selling prices of Mac portable systems. Net sales of the Company's Macs accounted for 27% of the Company's total net sales in 2010 compared to 32% in 2009. During 2010, net sales and unit sales of the Company's Mac portable systems increased by 18% and 25%, respectively, primarily attributable to strong demand for MacBook Pro, which was updated in April 2010. Net sales and unit sales of the Company's Mac desktop systems increased by 43% and 45%, respectively, as a result of higher sales of iMac, which was updated in July 2010.
- Net sales of other music related products and services increased $912 million or 23% during 2010 compared to 2009. This increase was due primarily to growth of the iTunes Store which generated total net sales of $4.1 billion for 2010. The results of the iTunes Store reflect growth of the iTunes App Store, continued growth in the installed base of iPhone, iPad, and iPod customers, and the expansion of third-party audio and video content available for sale and rent via the iTunes Store. The Company continues to expand its iTunes content and applications offerings around the world. Net sales of other music related products and services accounted for 8% of the Company's total net sales for 2010.
- Net sales of iPods increased $183 million or 2% during 2010, while iPod unit sales declined by 7% during 2010 compared to 2009. Net sales per iPod unit sold increased by 10% to $164 in 2010 compared to 2009, due to a shift in product mix toward iPod touch. iPod touch had strong growth in each of the Company's reportable operating segments. Net sales of iPods accounted for 13% of the Company's total net sales for the year compared to 19% in 2009.

Fiscal Year 2009 versus 2008

Net sales during 2009 increased $5.4 billion or 14% compared to 2008. Several factors contributed positively to these increases, including the following:

- iPhone revenue and net sales of related products and services amounted to $13.0 billion in 2009, an increase of $6.3 billion or 93% compared to 2008. The year-over-year iPhone revenue growth is largely attributable to the year-over-year increase in iPhone handset unit sales. iPhone handset unit sales totaled 20.7 million during 2009, which represents an increase of 9.1 million or 78% during 2009 compared to 2008. This growth is attributed primarily to expanded distribution and strong overall demand for iPhones. iPhone 3GS was released in the U.S. on June 19, 2009, and in many other countries over the remainder of 2009.

- Net sales of other music-related products and services increased $696 million or 21% during 2009 compared to 2008. The increase was due predominantly to increased net sales of third-party digital content and applications from the iTunes Store, which experienced double-digit growth in each of the Company's geographic segments during 2009 compared to the same period in 2008. The Company believes this is attributable primarily to continued interest in and growth of the iTunes App Store, continued growth in the Company's base of iPhone, iPad, and iPod customers, and the expansion of third-party audio and video content available for sale and rent via the iTunes Store.

Partially offsetting the favorable factors discussed above, net sales during 2009 were negatively impacted by certain factors, including the following:

- Net sales of iPods decreased $1.1 billion or 12% during 2009 compared to 2008. iPod unit sales decreased by 1% during 2009 compared to 2008. Net sales per iPod unit sold decreased 11% to $149 in 2009 compared to 2008, resulting from lower average selling prices across all of the iPod product lines, due primarily to price reductions taken with the introduction of new iPods in September 2009 and September 2008 and a stronger U.S. dollar, offset partially by a higher mix of iPod touch sales.
- Mac net sales declined 3% during 2009 compared to 2008, while Mac unit sales increased by 7% over the same period. Net sales per Mac unit sold decreased by 10% during 2009 compared to 2008, due primarily to lower average selling prices across all Mac portable and desktop systems and a stronger U.S. dollar. Net sales of Macs accounted for 32% of the Company's total net sales for 2009. During 2009, Mac portable systems net sales and unit sales increased by 9% and 20%, respectively, compared to 2008. This growth was driven by strong demand for MacBook Pro, which was updated in June 2009 and October 2008, and which experienced double-digit net sales and unit growth in each of the Company's reportable operating segments compared to the same period in 2008. The Company also had a higher mix of Mac portable systems sales, which is consistent with overall personal computer market trends. Net sales and unit sales of the Company's Mac desktop systems decreased by 23% and 14%, respectively, during 2009 compared to 2008. The decrease in net sales of Mac desktop systems was due mainly to a shift in product mix towards lower-priced desktops, lower average selling prices across all Mac desktop systems and a stronger U.S. dollar.

Segment Operating Performance

The Company manages its business primarily on a geographic basis. The Company's reportable operating and reporting segments consist of the Americas, Europe, Japan, Asia-Pacific, and Retail operations. The Americas, Europe, Japan, and Asia-Pacific reportable segment results do not include the results of the Retail segment. The Americas segment includes both North and South America. The Europe segment includes European countries as well as the Middle East and Africa. The Asia-Pacific segment includes Australia and Asia, but does not include Japan. The Retail segment operates Apple retail stores in 11 countries, including the U.S. Each reportable operating segment provides similar hardware and software products and similar services. Further information regarding the Company's operating segments may be found in Note 9, "Segment Information and Geographic Data" in Notes to Consolidated Financial Statements of this Form 10-K.

Retail

Retail net sales increased $3.1 billion or 47% during 2010 compared to 2009. The increase in net sales was driven primarily by strong demand for iPad, increased sales of Mac desktop and portable systems, and a significant year-over-year increase in iPhone revenue. Mac net sales and unit sales grew in the Retail segment by 25% and 35%, respectively, during 2010. The Company opened 44 new retail stores during the year, 28 of which were international stores, ending the year with 317 stores open compared to 273 stores at the end of 2009. With an average of 288 stores and 254 stores opened during 2010 and 2009, respectively, average revenue per store increased to $34.1 million in 2010, compared to $26.2 million in 2009. The Retail segment represented 15% and 16% of the Company's total net sales in 2010 and 2009, respectively.

Retail net sales decreased $636 million or 9% during 2009 compared to 2008. The decline in net sales was driven largely by a decrease in net sales of iPhones, iPods and Mac desktop systems, offset partially by strong demand for Mac portable systems. The year-over-year decline in Retail net sales was attributable to continued third-party channel expansion, particularly in the U.S. where most of the Company's stores are located, and also reflects the challenging consumer-spending environment in 2009. The Company opened 26 new retail stores during 2009, including 14 international stores, ending the year with 273 stores open. This compares to 247 stores open as of September 27, 2008. With an average of 254 stores and 211 stores opened during 2009 and 2008, respectively, average revenue per store decreased to $26.2 million for 2009 from $34.6 million in 2008.

The Retail segment reported operating income of $2.4 billion during 2010 and $1.7 billion during both 2009 and 2008. The increase in Retail operating income during 2010 compared to 2009 was attributable to higher overall net sales. Despite the decline in Retail net sales during 2009 compared to 2008, the Retail segment's operating income was flat at $1.7 billion in 2009 compared to 2008 due primarily to a higher gross margin percentage in 2009 consistent with that experienced by the overall company.

Expansion of the Retail segment has required and will continue to require a substantial investment in fixed assets and related infrastructure, operating lease commitments, personnel, and other operating expenses. Capital asset purchases associated with the Retail segment since its inception totaled $2.2 billion through the end of 2010. As of September 25, 2010, the Retail segment had approximately 26,500 full-time equivalent employees and had outstanding lease commitments associated with retail space and related facilities of $1.7 billion. The Company would incur substantial costs if it were to close multiple retail stores and such costs could adversely affect the Company's financial condition and operating results.

Gross Margin

Gross margin for the three years ended September 25, 2010, are as follows (in millions, except gross margin percentages):

	2010	2009	2008
Net sales	$ 65,225	$ 42,905	$ 37,491
Cost of sales	39,541	25,683	24,294
Gross margin	$ 25,684	$ 17,222	$ 13,197
Gross margin percentage	39.4%	40.1%	35.2%

The gross margin percentage in 2010 was 39.4% compared to 40.1% in 2009. This decline in gross margin is primarily attributable to new products that have higher cost structures, including iPad, partially offset by a more favorable sales mix of iPhone, which has a higher gross margin than the Company average.

The gross margin percentage in 2009 was 40.1% compared to 35.2% in 2008. The primary contributors to the increase in 2009 as compared to 2008 were a favorable sales mix toward products with higher gross margins and lower commodity and other product costs, which were partially offset by product price reductions.

The Company expects its gross margin percentage to decrease in future periods compared to levels achieved during 2010 and anticipates gross margin levels of about 36% in the first quarter of 2011. This expected decline is largely due to a higher mix of new and innovative products that have higher cost structures and deliver greater value to customers, and expected and potential future component cost and other cost increases.

The foregoing statements regarding the Company's expected gross margin percentage are forward-looking and could differ from anticipated levels because of several factors, including but not limited to certain of those set forth below in Part I, Item 1A, "Risk Factors" under the subheading "*Future operating results depend upon the Company's ability to obtain key components including but not limited to microprocessors, NAND flash memory, DRAM and LCDs at favorable prices and in sufficient quantities*," which is incorporated herein by reference. There can be no assurance that targeted gross margin percentage levels will be achieved. In general, gross margins and margins on individual products will remain under downward pressure due to a variety of factors, including continued industry-wide global product pricing pressures, increased competition, compressed product life cycles, product transitions and expected and potential increases in the cost of key components including but not limited to microprocessors, NAND flash memory, DRAM and LCDs, as well as potential increases in the costs of outside manufacturing services and a potential shift in the Company's sales mix towards products with lower gross margins. In response to these competitive pressures, the Company expects it will continue to take product pricing actions, which would adversely affect gross margins. Gross margins could also be affected by the Company's ability to manage product quality and warranty costs effectively and to stimulate demand for certain of its products. Due to the Company's significant international operations, financial results can be significantly affected in the short-term by fluctuations in exchange rates.

Operating Expenses

Operating expenses for the three years ended September 25, 2010, are as follows (in millions, except for percentages):

	2010	2009	2008
Research and development	$ 1,782	$ 1,333	$ 1,109
Percentage of net sales	2.7%	3.1%	3.0%
Selling, general and administrative	$ 5,517	$ 4,149	$ 3,761
Percentage of net sales	8.5%	9.7%	10.0%

Research and Development Expense ("R&D")

R&D expense increased 34% or $449 million to $1.8 billion in 2010 compared to 2009. This increase was due primarily to an increase in headcount and related expenses in the current year to support expanded R&D activities. Also contributing to this increase in R&D expense in 2010 was the capitalization in 2009 of software development costs of $71 million related to Mac OS X Snow Leopard. Although total R&D expense increased 34% during 2010, it declined as a percentage of net sales given the 52% year-over-year increase in net sales in 2010. The Company continues to believe that focused investments in R&D are critical to its future growth and competitive position in the marketplace and are directly related to timely development of new and enhanced products that are central to the Company's core business strategy. As such, the Company expects to make further investments in R&D to remain competitive.

R&D expense increased 20% or $224 million to $1.3 billion in 2009 compared to 2008. This increase was due primarily to an increase in headcount in 2009 to support expanded R&D activities and higher stock-based compensation expenses. Additionally, $71 million of software development costs were capitalized related to Mac OS X Snow Leopard and excluded from R&D expense during 2009, compared to $11 million of software development costs capitalized during 2008. Although total R&D expense increased 20% during 2009, it remained relatively flat as a percentage of net sales given the 14% increase in revenue in 2009.

Selling, General and Administrative Expense ("SG&A")

SG&A expense increased $1.4 billion or 33% to $5.5 billion in 2010 compared to 2009. This increase was due primarily to the Company's continued expansion of its Retail segment, higher spending on marketing and advertising programs, increased stock-based compensation expenses and variable costs associated with the overall growth of the Company's net sales.

SG&A expenses increased $388 million or 10% to $4.1 billion in 2009 compared to 2008. This increase was due primarily to the Company's continued expansion of its Retail segment in both domestic and international markets, higher stock-based compensation expense and higher spending on marketing and advertising.

Other Income and Expense

Other income and expense for the three years ended September 25, 2010, are as follows (in millions):

	2010	2009	2008
Interest income	$ 311	$ 407	$ 653
Other income (expense), net	(156)	(81)	(33)
Total other income and expense	$ 155	$ 326	$ 620

Total other income and expense decreased $171 million or 52% to $155 million during 2010 compared to $326 million and $620 million in 2009 and 2008, respectively. The overall decrease in other income and expense is attributable to the significant declines in interest rates on a year-over-year basis, partially offset by the Company's higher cash, cash equivalents and marketable securities balances. The weighted average interest rate earned by the Company on its cash, cash equivalents and marketable securities was 0.75%, 1.43%, and 3.44% during 2010, 2009, and 2008, respectively. Additionally the Company incurred higher premium expenses on its foreign exchange option contracts, which further reduced the total other income and expense. During 2010, 2009, and 2008, the Company had no debt outstanding and accordingly did not incur any related interest expense.

Provision for Income Taxes

The Company's effective tax rates were 24%, 32%, and 32% for 2010, 2009, and 2008, respectively. The Company's effective rates for these periods differ from the statutory federal income tax rate of 35% due primarily to certain undistributed foreign earnings for which no U.S. taxes are provided because such earnings are intended to be indefinitely reinvested outside the U.S. The lower effective tax rate in 2010 as compared to 2009 is due primarily to an increase in foreign earnings on which U.S. income taxes have not been provided as such earnings are intended to be indefinitely reinvested outside the U.S.

Liquidity and Capital Resources

The following table presents selected financial information and statistics as of and for the three years ended September 25, 2010 (in millions):

	2010	2009	2008
Cash, cash equivalents and marketable securities	$51,011	$33,992	$24,490
Accounts receivable, net	$ 5,510	$ 3,361	$ 2,422
Inventories	$ 1,051	$ 455	$ 509
Working capital	$20,956	$20,049	$18,645
Annual operating cash flow	$18,595	$10,159	$ 9,596

As of September 25, 2010, the Company had $51 billion in cash, cash equivalents and marketable securities, an increase of $17 billion from September 26, 2009. The principal component of this net increase was the cash generated by operating activities of $18.6 billion, which was partially offset by payments for acquisition of property, plant and equipment of $2 billion and payments made in connection with business acquisitions, net of cash acquired, of $638 million.

The Company's marketable securities investment portfolio is invested primarily in highly rated securities, generally with a minimum rating of single-A or equivalent. As of September 25, 2010, and September 26, 2009, $30.8 billion and $17.4 billion, respectively, of the Company's cash, cash equivalents and marketable securities were held by foreign subsidiaries and are generally based in U.S. dollar-denominated holdings. The Company believes its existing balances of cash, cash equivalents and marketable securities will be sufficient to satisfy its working capital needs, capital asset purchases, outstanding commitments and other liquidity requirements associated with its existing operations over the next 12 months.

Capital Assets

The Company's capital expenditures were $2.6 billion during 2010, consisting of approximately $404 million for retail store facilities and $2.2 billion for other capital expenditures, including product tooling and manufacturing process equipment and corporate facilities and infrastructure. The Company's actual cash payments for capital expenditures during 2010 were $2 billion.

The Company anticipates utilizing approximately $4.0 billion for capital expenditures during 2011, including approximately $600 million for retail store facilities and approximately $3.4 billion for product tooling and manufacturing process equipment, and corporate facilities and infrastructure, including information systems hardware, software and enhancements.

Historically the Company has opened between 25 and 50 new retail stores per year. During 2011, the Company expects to open 40 to 50 new stores, over half of which are expected to be located outside the U.S.

The Balance Sheet

Old accountants never die; they just lose their balance.
—ANONYMOUS

A balance sheet, also called the *statement of condition* or *statement of financial position,* provides a wealth of valuable information about a business firm, particularly when examined over a period of several years and evaluated in relation to the other financial statements. A prerequisite to learning what the balance sheet can teach us, however, is a fundamental understanding of the accounts in the statement and the relationship of each account to the financial statements as a whole.

Consider, for example, the balance sheet *inventory* account. Inventory is an important component of liquidity analysis, which considers the ability of a firm to meet cash needs as they arise. (Liquidity analysis will be discussed in Chapter 5.) Any measure of liquidity that includes inventory as a component would be meaningless without a general understanding of how the balance sheet inventory amount is derived. This chapter will thus cover such issues as what inventories are, how the inventory balance is affected by accounting policies, why companies choose and sometimes change methods of inventory valuation, where to find disclosures regarding inventory accounting, and how this one account contributes to the overall measurement of a company's financial condition and operating performance. This step-by-step descriptive treatment of inventories and other balance sheet accounts will provide the background necessary to analyze and interpret balance sheet information.

Financial Condition

The balance sheet shows the financial condition or financial position of a company *on a particular date.* The statement is a summary of what the firm *owns* (assets) and what the firm *owes* to outsiders (liabilities) and to internal owners (stockholders' equity). By definition, the account balances on a balance sheet must balance; that is, the total of all assets must equal the sum of liabilities and stockholders' equity. The balancing equation is expressed as:

Assets = Liabilities + Stockholders' equity

This chapter will cover account by account the consolidated balance sheet of Sage Inc. (Exhibit 2.1). This particular firm sells recreational products through retail outlets, some owned and some leased, in cities located throughout the southwestern United States. Although the accounts on a balance sheet will vary somewhat by firm and by industry, those described in this chapter will be common to most companies.

Consolidation

Note first that the statements are "consolidated" for Sage Inc. and subsidiaries. When a parent owns more than 50% of the voting stock of a subsidiary, the financial statements are combined for the companies even though they are separate legal entities. The statements are consolidated because the companies are *in substance* one company, given the proportion of control by the parent. In the case of Sage Inc., the subsidiaries are wholly owned, which means that the parent controls 100% of the voting shares of the subsidiaries. Where less than 100% ownership exists, there are accounts in the consolidated balance sheet and income statement to reflect the minority or noncontrolling interest in net assets and income.

Balance Sheet Date

The balance sheet is prepared at a point in time at the end of an accounting period, a year, or a quarter. Most companies, like Sage Inc., use the calendar year with the accounting period ending on December 31. Interim statements would be prepared for each quarter, ending March 31, June 30, and September 30. Some companies adopt a fiscal year ending on a date other than December 31.

The fact that the balance sheet is prepared on a particular date is significant. For example, cash is the first account listed on the balance sheet and represents the amount of cash on December 31; the amount could be materially different on December 30 or January 2.

Comparative Data

Financial statements for only one accounting period would be of limited value because there would be no reference point for determining changes in a company's financial record over time. As part of an integrated disclosure system required by the SEC, the information presented in annual reports to shareholders includes two-year audited balance sheets and three-year audited statements of income and cash flows. The balance sheet for Sage Inc. thus shows the condition of the company at December 31, 2013 and 2012.

Common-Size Balance Sheet

A useful tool for analyzing the balance sheet is a common-size balance sheet. Common-size financial statements are a form of vertical ratio analysis that allows for comparison of firms with different levels of sales or total assets by introducing a common denominator. Common-size statements are also useful to evaluate trends within a firm and to make industry comparisons. The common-size balance sheet for Sage Inc. is presented in Exhibit 2.2. Information from the common-size balance sheet will be used throughout this chapter and also in Chapter 5. A common-size balance sheet expresses each item on the balance sheet as a percentage of total assets. Common-size statements facilitate the

EXHIBIT 2.1 Sage Inc. Consolidated Balance Sheets at December 31, 2013 and 2012 (in Thousands)

	2013	2012
Assets		
Current Assets		
Cash and cash equivalents	$9,333	$10,386
Accounts receivable, less allowance for doubtful accounts of $448 in 2013 and $417 in 2012	8,960	8,350
Inventories	47,041	36,769
Prepaid expenses and other assets	512	759
Total current assets	65,846	56,264
Property, Plant, and Equipment		
Land	811	811
Buildings and leasehold improvements	18,273	11,928
Equipment	21,523	13,768
	40,607	26,507
Less accumulated depreciation and amortization	11,528	7,530
Net property, plant, and equipment	29,079	18,977
Goodwill	270	270
Other Assets	103	398
Total Assets	$95,298	$75,909
Liabilities and Stockholders' Equity		
Current Liabilities		
Accounts payable	$14,294	$ 7,591
Accrued liabilities	4,137	4,366
Income taxes payable	1,532	947
Short-term debt	5,614	6,012
Current maturities of long-term debt	1,884	1,516
Total current liabilities	27,461	20,432
Deferred Federal Income Taxes	843	635
Long-Term Debt	21,059	16,975
Commitments and Contingencies (See Notes 3 and 5)		
Total liabilities	49,363	38,042
Stockholders' Equity		
Common stock, par value $0.01, authorized, 10,000,000 shares; issued, 4,363,000 shares in 2013 and 4355,000 shares in 2012, and additional paid-in capital	5,760	5,504
Retained Earnings	40,175	32,363
Total stockholders' equity	45,935	37,867
Total Liabilities and Stockholders' Equity	$95,298	$75,909

The accompanying notes are an integral part of these statements.

EXHIBIT 2.2 Sage Inc. Common-Size Balance Sheets (Percent)

	2013	2012	2011	2010	2009
Assets					
Current Assets					
Cash and cash equivalents	9.8	13.7	18.8	20.4	20.0
Accounts receivable, less allowance for doubtful accounts	9.4	11.0	7.6	6.6	6.8
Inventories	49.4	48.4	45.0	40.1	39.7
Prepaid expenses	0.5	1.0	1.6	2.4	2.6
Total current assets	69.1	74.1	73.0	69.5	69.1
Property, Plant, and Equipment					
Land	0.8	1.1	1.2	1.4	1.4
Buildings and leasehold improvements	19.2	15.7	14.4	14.1	14.5
Equipment	22.6	18.1	17.3	15.9	16.5
Less accumulated depreciation and amortization	(12.1)	(9.9)	(6.9)	(3.1)	(3.0)
Net property, plant, and equipment	30.5	25.0	26.0	28.3	29.4
Goodwill	0.3	0.4	0.4	0.5	0.5
Other Assets	0.1	0.5	0.6	1.7	1.0
Total Assets	100.0	100.0	100.0	100.0	100.0
Liabilities and Stockholders' Equity					
Current Liabilities					
Accounts payable	15.0	10.0	13.1	11.4	11.8
Accrued liabilities	4.3	5.8	9.2	6.4	4.5
Income taxes payable	1.6	1.2	1.4	1.3	1.2
Short-term debt	5.9	7.9	6.2	4.4	4.3
Current maturities of long-term debt	2.0	2.0	2.4	2.4	2.6
Total current liabilities	28.8	26.9	32.3	25.9	24.4
Deferred Federal Income Taxes	0.9	0.8	0.7	0.5	0.4
Long-Term Debt	22.1	22.4	16.2	14.4	14.9
Total liabilities	51.8	50.1	49.2	40.8	39.7
Stockholders' Equity					
Common stock and additional paid-in capital	6.0	7.3	8.0	8.9	9.3
Retained earnings	42.2	42.6	42.8	50.3	51.0
Total stockholders' equity	48.2	49.9	50.8	59.2	60.3
Total Liabilities and Stockholders' Equity	100.0	100.0	100.0	100.0	100.0

internal or structural analysis of a firm. The common-size balance sheet reveals the composition of assets within major categories, for example, cash and cash equivalents relative to other current assets, the distribution of assets in which funds are invested (current, long-lived, intangible), the capital structure of the firm (debt relative to equity), and the debt structure (long-term relative to short-term).

Assets

Current Assets

Assets are segregated on a balance sheet according to how they are utilized (Exhibit 2.3). Current assets include cash or those assets expected to be converted into cash within one year or one operating cycle, whichever is longer. The *operating cycle* is the time required to purchase or manufacture inventory, sell the product, and collect the cash. For most companies, the operating cycle is less than one year, but in some industries—such as tobacco and wine—it is longer. The designation "current" refers essentially to those assets that are continually used up and replenished in the ongoing operations of the business. The term *working capital* or *net working capital* is used to designate the amount by which current assets exceed current liabilities (current assets less current liabilities).

Shutterstock

Cash and Cash Equivalents

Two accounts, cash and cash equivalents, are generally combined on the balance sheet. The cash account is exactly that, cash in any form—cash awaiting deposit or in a bank account. Cash equivalents are short-term, highly liquid investments, easily turned into cash with maturities of three months or less. Money market funds, U.S. Treasury bills, and commercial paper (unsecured short-term corporate debt) generally qualify as cash equivalents. Sage Inc. has items that qualify as cash equivalents according to Note 1 of the Sage Inc. financial statements. As can be seen on the common-size balance sheet, there has been a proportionate change in the amount of cash and cash equivalents held by Sage Inc. from 20% in 2009 to less than 10% in 2013 as Sage Inc. has shifted holdings of cash to other asset accounts.

Marketable Securities

Marketable securities, also referred to as short-term investments, are highly liquid investments in debt and equity securities that can be readily converted into cash or mature in a year or less. Firms with excess cash that is not needed immediately in the business will often purchase marketable securities to earn a return.

EXHIBIT 2.3 Sage Inc. Consolidated Balance Sheets at December 31, 2013 and 2012 (in Thousands)

	2013	2012
Assets		
Current Assets		
Cash and cash equivalents	$9,333	$10,386
Accounts receivable, less allowance for doubtful accounts of $448 in 2013 and $417 in 2012	8,960	8,350
Inventories	47,041	36,769
Prepaid expenses and other assets	512	759
Total current assets	65,846	56,264
Property, Plant, and Equipment		
Land	811	811
Buildings and leasehold improvements	18,273	11,928
Equipment	21,523	13,768
	40,607	26,507
Less accumulated depreciation and amortization	11,528	7,530
Net property, plant, and equipment	29,079	18,977
Goodwill	270	270
Other Assets	103	398
Total Assets	$95,298	$75,909

The accompanying notes are an integral part of these statements.

The valuation of marketable securities on the balance sheet as well as other investments in debt and equity securities requires the separation of investment securities into three categories depending on the intent of the investment:

1. *Held to maturity* applies to those debt securities that the firm has the positive intent and ability to hold to maturity; these securities are reported at amortized cost. Debt securities are securities representing a creditor relationship, including U.S. Treasury securities, municipal securities, corporate bonds, convertible debt, and commercial paper.[1]
2. *Trading securities* are debt and equity securities that are held for resale in the short term, as opposed to being held to realize longer-term gains from capital appreciation. Equity securities represent an ownership interest in an entity, including common and preferred stock. These securities are reported at *fair value*

[1]Amortized cost refers to the fact that bonds (a debt security) may sell at a premium or discount because the stated rate of interest on the bonds is different from the market rate of interest; the premium or discount is amortized over the life of the bonds so that at maturity the cost equals the face amount.

with unrealized gains and losses included in earnings. Fair value is the price that would be received to sell an asset or the price paid to transfer a liability in an orderly transaction between market participants at the measurement date.[2]

3. *Securities available for sale* are debt and equity securities that are not classified as one of the other two categories, either held to maturity or trading securities. Securities available for sale are reported at fair value with unrealized gains and losses included in comprehensive income. The cumulative net unrealized gains or losses are reported in the accumulated other comprehensive income section of stockholders' equity.

Accounts Receivable

Accounts receivable are customer balances outstanding on credit sales and are reported on the balance sheet at their net realizable value, that is, the actual amount of the account less an *allowance for doubtful accounts.* Management must estimate—based on such factors as past experience, knowledge of customer quality, the state of the economy, the firm's collection policies—the dollar amount of accounts they expect will be uncollectible during an accounting period. Actual losses are written off against the allowance account, which is adjusted at the end of each accounting period.

The allowance for doubtful accounts can be important in assessing earnings quality. If, for instance, a company expands sales by lowering its credit standards, there should be a corresponding percentage increase in the allowance account. The estimation of this account will affect both the valuation of accounts receivable on the balance sheet and the recognition of bad debt expense on the income statement. The analyst should be alert to changes in the allowance account—both relative to the level of sales and the amount of accounts receivable outstanding—and to the justification for any variations from past practices.

The allowance account for Sage Inc. represents approximately 5% of total customer accounts receivable. To obtain the exact percentage figure, the amount of the allowance account must be added to the net accounts receivable balance shown on the face of the statement:

	2013	2012
$\dfrac{\text{Allowance for doubtful accounts}}{\text{Accounts receivable (net)} + \text{Allowance}}$	$\dfrac{448}{8{,}960 + 448} = 4.8\%$	$\dfrac{417}{8{,}350 + 417} = 4.8\%$

The allowance account, which is deducted from the balance sheet accounts receivable account, should reflect the volume of credit sales, the firm's past experience with customers, the customer base, the firm's credit policies, the firm's collection practices, economic conditions, and changes in any of these. There should be a consistent relationship between the rate of change or growth rates in sales, accounts receivable, and the allowance for doubtful accounts. If the amounts are changing at

[2]"Fair Value Measurements," Statement of Financial Accounting Standards No. 157, 2006.

significantly different rates or in different directions—for example, if sales and accounts receivable are increasing, but the allowance account is decreasing or is increasing at a much smaller rate—the analyst should be alert to the potential for manipulation using the allowance account. Of course, there could be a plausible reason for such a change.

The relevant items needed to relate sales growth with accounts receivable and the allowance for doubtful accounts are found on the income statement (sales) and balance sheet (accounts receivable and allowance for doubtful accounts). The following information is from the income statement and balance sheet of Sage Inc.

	2013	2012	Growth Rate*
	(In Thousands)		(% Change)
Net sales	$215,600	$153,000	40.9
Accounts receivable (total)	9,408	8,767	7.3
Allowance for doubtful accounts	448	417	7.4

*Growth rates are calculated using the following formula: $\dfrac{\text{Current amount} - \text{Prior amount}}{\text{Prior amount}}$

To analyze the preceding information consider the following:

- The relationship among changes in sales, accounts receivable, and the allowance for doubtful accounts—are all three accounts changing in the same directions and at consistent rates of change?
- If the direction and rates of change are not consistent, what are possible explanations for these differences?
- If there is not a normal relationship between the growth rates, what are possible reasons for the abnormal pattern?

For Sage Inc., sales, accounts receivable, and the allowance for doubtful accounts have all increased, but sales have grown at a much greater rate. The percentage increase in accounts receivable and the allowance account seems lower than expected relative to the change in sales. This relationship is probably a positive one for Sage Inc. because it means that the company has collected more sales in cash and thus will have potentially fewer defaults. The allowance account has increased appropriately in relation to accounts receivable, 7.4% and 7.3%, respectively; the allowance account, relative to accounts receivable, is constant at 4.8% in both years. Had the allowance account decreased, there would be concern that management might be manipulating the numbers to increase the earnings number.

Additional information helpful to the analysis of accounts receivable and the allowance account is provided in the schedule of "Valuation and Qualifying Accounts" required by the SEC in the Form 10-K. Companies sometimes include this schedule in the notes to the financial statements, but usually it is found under Item 15 of the Form 10-K. Sage Inc.'s schedule from the Form 10-K is shown here:

Sage Inc.
Schedule II—Valuation and Qualifying Accounts
December 31, 2013, 2012, and 2011
(in Thousands)

	Balance at Beginning of Year	Additions Charged to Costs and Expenses	Deductions	Balance at End of Year
Allowance for doubtful accounts				
2013	$417	$271	$240	$448
2012	$400	$217	$200	$417
2011	$391	$259	$250	$400

The column labeled "Additions Charged to Costs and Expenses" is the amount Sage Inc. has estimated and recorded as bad debt expense each year on the income statement. The "Deductions" column represents the actual amount that the firm has written off as accounts receivable they no longer expect to recover from customers. Because the expense is estimated each year, this amount also includes corrections of prior years' over- or underestimations. The analyst should use this schedule to assess the probability that the firm is intentionally over- or underestimating the allowance account to manipulate the net earnings number on the income statement. Sage Inc. appears to estimate an expense fairly close to the actual amount written off each year, although the firm has estimated slightly more expense than has actually been incurred. Further analysis of accounts receivable and its quality is covered in Appendix 3A and Chapter 5.

Inventories

Inventories are items held for sale or used in the manufacture of products that will be sold. A retail company, such as Sage Inc., lists only one type of inventory on the balance sheet: merchandise inventories purchased for resale to the public. A manufacturing firm, in contrast, would carry three different types of inventories: raw materials or supplies, work-in-process, and finished goods. For most firms, inventories are the firm's major revenue producer. Exceptions would be service-oriented companies that carry little or no inventory. Exhibit 2.4 illustrates the proportion of inventories at the manufacturing, wholesale, and retail levels. For these industries—drugs, household furniture, and sporting goods—the percentage of inventories to total assets ranges from 19.8% to 33.4% at the manufacturing stage to 32.6% to 58.0% for retail firms. The common-size balance sheet (Exhibit 2.2) for Sage Inc. reveals that inventories comprise 49.4% and 48.4% of total assets, respectively, in 2013 and 2012. As mentioned previously, from 2009 to 2013, cash and marketable securities have decreased by approximately 10%. Inventories have increased by almost 10% in this same time frame, indicating a shift in asset structure. Most likely, Sage Inc. has chosen to spend cash to expand. As new stores are opened, they must be stocked with inventory.

EXHIBIT 2.4

Inventories as a Percentage of Total Assets	%
Manufacturing	
Pharmaceutical preparations	19.8
Upholstered household furniture	32.3
Sporting and athletic goods	33.4
Wholesale	
Drugs	32.1
Furniture	30.2
Sporting and recreational goods	40.8
Retail	
Pharmacies and drug stores	32.6
Furniture stores	45.1
Sporting goods stores	58.0

Source: Based on The Risk Management Association, Annual Statement Studies 2010–2011, (c) 2010, Philadelphia, PA 2010.

Given the relative magnitude of inventory, the accounting method chosen to value inventory and the associated measurement of cost of goods sold have a considerable impact on a company's financial position and operating results. Understanding the fundamentals of inventory accounting and the effect various methods have on a company's financial statements is essential to the user of financial statement information.

Shutterstock

Inventory Accounting Methods

The method chosen by a company to account for inventory determines the value of inventory on the balance sheet and the amount of expense recognized for cost of goods sold on the income statement. The significance of inventory accounting is underlined by the presence of inflation and by the implications for tax payments and cash flow. Inventory valuation is based on an *assumption* regarding the flow of goods and has nothing whatever to do with the *actual* order in which products are sold. The cost flow assumption is made in order to *match* the cost of products sold during an accounting period to the revenue generated from the sales and to assign a dollar value to the inventory remaining for sale at the end of the accounting period.

The three cost flow assumptions most frequently used by U.S. companies are *FIFO* (first in, first out), *LIFO* (last in, first out), and *average cost*. As the terms imply, the FIFO method assumes the first units purchased are the first units sold during an accounting period, LIFO assumes that the items bought last are sold first, and the average cost method uses an average purchase price to determine the cost of products sold. A simple example should highlight the differences in the three methods. A new company in its first year of operations purchases five products for sale in the order and at the prices shown:

Item	**Purchase Price**
#1	$ 5
#2	$ 7
#3	$ 8
#4	$ 9
#5	$11

The company sells three of these items, all at the end of the year. The cost flow assumptions would be:

Accounting Method	**Goods Sold**	**Goods Remaining in Inventory**
FIFO	#1, #2, #3	#4, #5
LIFO	#5, #4, #3	#2, #1
Average cost	[Total cost/5] × 3	[Total cost/5] × 2

The resulting effect on the income statement and balance sheet would be:

Accounting Method	**Cost of Goods Sold (Income Statement)**	**Inventory Valuation (Balance Sheet)**
FIFO	$20	$20
LIFO	$28	$12
Average cost	$24	$16

It can be clearly seen that during a period of inflation, with product prices increasing, the LIFO method produces the highest cost of goods sold expense ($28) and the lowest ending valuation of inventory ($12). Further, cost of goods sold under the LIFO method most closely approximates the current cost of inventory items as they are the most recent purchases. On the other hand, inventories on the balance sheet are undervalued with respect to replacement cost because they reflect the older

FIGURE 2.1 Inventory Methods

Accounting Method	Cost of Goods Sold (Income Statement)	Inventory Valuation (Balance Sheet)
FIFO	First purchases	Last purchases (close to current cost)
LIFO	Last purchases (close to current cost)	First purchases
Average Cost	Average of all purchases	Average of all purchases

costs when prices were lower. If a firm uses LIFO to value inventory, no restatement is required to adjust cost of goods sold for inflation because LIFO matches current costs to current sales. Inventory on the balance sheet, however, would have to be revalued upward to account for inflation. FIFO has the opposite effect; during a period of rising prices, balance sheet inventory is valued at current cost, but cost of goods sold on the income statement is understated. (See Figure 2.1.)

In an annual survey of accounting practices followed by 600 industrial and merchandising corporations in the United States in the early 1970s, 146 companies surveyed reported using LIFO to account for all or part of inventory. By the 1990s, this number had increased to 326 but then fell to 228 by 2006.[3] Why did so many companies switch to LIFO in the 1990s? The answer is taxes.

Referring back to the example, note that when prices are rising (inflation), LIFO produces the largest cost of goods sold expense: the greater the expense deduction, the lower the taxable income. Use of LIFO thus reduces a company's tax bill during inflation. Unlike the case for some accounting rules—in which a firm is allowed to use one method for tax and another method for reporting purposes—a company that elects LIFO to figure taxable income must also use LIFO for reported income. The many companies that have switched to LIFO from other methods are apparently willing to trade lower reported earnings for the positive cash benefits resulting from LIFO's beneficial tax effect. The evidence, however, is that the trend toward LIFO is reversing and that the number of firms electing FIFO is gradually increasing. Reasons could include both a lower inflation rate and the desire to report higher accounting earnings.

In the earlier example, LIFO produced lower earnings than FIFO or average cost, but there can be exceptions. Obviously, in a *period of falling prices* (deflation) the results would reverse. Also, some firms experience price movements that are counter to the general trend—the high-technology industry, where prices on many products have declined, is a case in point.[4]

[3] *Accounting Trends and Techniques,* American Institute of Certified Public Accountants, 1971, 1998, 2007.

[4] Another exception that causes higher earnings when using LIFO during inflationary periods is a base LIFO layer liquidation. This occurs when a firm sells more goods than purchased or manufactured during an accounting period, resulting in the least expensive items being charged to cost of goods sold. To avoid the LIFO liquidation problem, some firms use the dollar-value LIFO method, which is applied to goods in designated pools and measures inventory changes in cost dollars—using a price index—rather than physical units.

Because the inventory cost flow assumption has a significant impact on financial statements—the amount of inventory reported on the balance sheet and the cost of goods sold expense in the income statement—it is important to know where to find its disclosure. The method used to value inventory will generally be shown in the note to the financial statements relating to inventory. Sage Inc. has the following explanation in Note 1: Inventories are stated at the lower of cost—last-in, first-out (LIFO)—or market. This statement indicates that the LIFO method is used to determine cost. The fact that inventories are valued at the lower of cost or market reflects the accounting convention of conservatism. If the actual market value of inventory falls below cost, as determined by the cost flow assumption (LIFO for Sage Inc.), then inventory will be written down to market price. Notice that the phrase is "lower" of cost or market. The carrying value of inventory would never be written up to market value—only down.

The inventory note for Sage Inc. also provides information regarding the value of inventory had FIFO been used, as the FIFO valuation would be higher than that recorded on the balance sheet and more closely approximates current value: "If the first-in, first-out (FIFO) method of inventory accounting had been used, inventories would have been approximately $2,681,000 and $2,096,000 higher than reported at December 31, 2013 and 2012."

Companies are allowed to use more than one inventory valuation method for inventories. For example, a multinational firm may choose to use the LIFO method for inventories in the United States, while using FIFO for inventories overseas. This would not be unusual: LIFO is actually an income tax concept, and the application of LIFO is set forth in the United States Internal Revenue Code, not in United States GAAP. Some countries do not recognize LIFO as an acceptable inventory valuation method and, as such, a firm may find it more convenient for reporting purposes to use methods acceptable in the country in which it operates. Diversified companies may also choose different inventory methods for different product lines. Using FIFO for high-technology products and LIFO for food products would make sense if the firm is trying to reduce taxes because the technology industry is usually deflationary, whereas the food industry is generally inflationary.

Prepaid Expenses

Certain expenses, such as insurance, rent, property taxes, and utilities, are sometimes paid in advance. They are included in current assets if they will expire within one year or one operating cycle, whichever is longer. Generally, prepayments are not material to the balance sheet as a whole. For Sage Inc., prepaid expenses represent less than 1% of total current assets in 2013.

Property, Plant, and Equipment

This category encompasses a company's fixed assets (also called *tangible, long-lived,* and *capital* assets)—those assets not used up in the ebb and flow of annual business operations. These assets produce economic benefits for more than one year, and they are considered "tangible" because they have a physical substance. Fixed assets other than land (which has a theoretically unlimited life span) are "depreciated" over the period of time they benefit the firm. The process of depreciation is a method of allocating the cost of long-lived assets. The original cost, less any estimated residual value at the end of the asset's life, is spread over the expected life of the asset. Cost is also considered to encompass any expenditures made to ready the asset for operating use. On any balance sheet date, property, plant, and equipment is shown at book value, which is the difference between original cost and any accumulated depreciation to date.

Management has considerable discretion with respect to fixed assets. Assume that Sage. Inc. purchases an artificial ski mountain, known as the "mythical mountain," for its Phoenix flagship store in order to demonstrate skis and allow prospective customers to test-run skis on a simulated black diamond course. The cost of the mountain is $50,000. Several choices and estimates must be made to determine the annual depreciation expense associated with the mountain. For example, Sage Inc. management must estimate how long the mountain will last and the amount, if any, of salvage value at the end of its useful life.

Furthermore, management must choose a method of depreciation: The straight-line method allocates an equal amount of expense to each year of the depreciation period, whereas an accelerated method apportions larger amounts of expense to the earlier years of the asset's depreciable life and lesser amounts to the later years.

If the $50,000 mountain is estimated to have a five-year useful life and $0 salvage value at the end of that period, annual depreciation expense would be calculated as follows for the first year.

Straight line

$$\frac{\text{Depreciable base (cost less salvage value)}}{\text{Depreciation period}} = \text{Depreciation expense}$$

$$\frac{\$50{,}000 - \$0}{5\text{ years}} = \$10{,}000$$

Accelerated[5]

Cost less accumulated depreciation × twice the straight-line rate = Depreciation expense

$$\$50{,}000 \times (2 \times 0.2) = \$20{,}000$$

The choices and estimates relating to the depreciation of equipment affect the amounts shown on the financial statements relating to the asset. The fixed asset account on the balance sheet is shown at historical cost less accumulated depreciation, and the annual depreciation expense is deducted on the income statement to determine net income. At the end of year 1, the accounts would be different according to the method chosen:

Straight line

Balance Sheet		*Income Statement*	
Fixed assets	$50,000	Depreciation expense	$10,000
Less accumulated depreciation	(10,000)		
Net fixed assets	$40,000		

Accelerated

Balance Sheet		*Income Statement*	
Fixed assets	$50,000	Depreciation expense	$20,000
Less accumulated depreciation	(20,000)		
Net fixed assets	$30,000		

The amounts would also vary if the estimates were different regarding useful life or salvage value. For example, if Sage Inc. management concludes the mountain could be sold to Denver Mountaineering Co. at the end of five years for use in testing snowshoes, the mountain would then have an expected salvage value that would enter into the calculations.

The total amount of depreciation over the asset's life is the same regardless of method, although the rate of depreciation varies. The straight-line method spreads the expense evenly by periods, and the accelerated methods yield higher depreciation

[5]The example uses the double-declining balance method of figuring accelerated depreciation, which is twice the straight-line rate times the net book value (cost less accumulated depreciation) of the asset. Depreciation for year 2 would be:

Straight line $50,000/5 = $10,000 Accelerated $30,000 × 0.4 = $12,000

expense in the early years of an asset's useful life, and lower depreciation expense in the later years. Another depreciation choice is the units-of-production method, which bases depreciation expense for a given period on actual use. According to *Accounting Trends and Techniques*, the vast majority of companies use the straight-line method for financial reporting:[6]

Straight line	488
Accelerated	30
Units of production	16

Refer now to the property, plant, and equipment section of the Sage Inc. balance sheet. First note that there are three categories listed separately: land, buildings and leasehold improvements, and equipment. *Land,* as designated in the fixed asset section, refers to property used in the business; this would be land on which there are corporate offices and retail stores. Any land held for investment purposes would be segregated from property used in the business. (For Sage Inc., see the "Other Assets" section.)

Sage Inc. owns some of its retail outlets, and others are leased. *Buildings* would include those stores owned by the company as well as its corporate offices. *Leasehold improvements* are additions or improvements made to leased structures. Because leasehold improvements revert to the property owner when the lease term expires, they are amortized by the lessee over the economic life of the improvement or the life of the lease, whichever is shorter.[7]

Some companies may also have an account called *construction in progress*. These are the costs of constructing new buildings that are not yet complete. Sage Inc. does not include this account on its balance sheet.

Equipment represents the original cost, including delivery and installation charges, of the machinery and equipment used in business operations. Included are a variety of items such as the centralized computer system; equipment and furnishings for offices, stores, and warehouses; and delivery trucks. The final two lines under the property, plant, and equipment section for Sage Inc. show the amount of accumulated depreciation and amortization (for all items except land) and the amount of net property, plant, and equipment after the deduction of accumulated depreciation and amortization.

The relative proportion of fixed assets in a company's asset structure will largely be determined by the nature of the business. A firm that manufactures products would likely be more heavily invested in capital equipment than a retailer or wholesaler. Exhibit 2.5 shows the relative percentage of net fixed assets to total assets for the same three industries identified in Exhibit 2.4. Realize, however, that firms with newly purchased fixed assets will have a higher percentage than firms with older, and hence lower, net fixed asset numbers.

[6] *Accounting Trends and Techniques,* American Institute of Certified Public Accountants, 2010.

[7] *Amortization* is the term used to designate the cost allocation process for assets other than buildings, machinery, and equipment—such as leasehold improvements and intangible assets, discussed later in the chapter.

EXHIBIT 2.5

Net Fixed Assets as a Percentage of Total Assets	**%**
Manufacturing	
Pharmaceutical preparations	24.9
Household furniture	19.6
Sporting and athletic goods	16.4
Wholesale	
Drugs	10.0
Furniture	12.2
Sporting and recreational goods	10.0
Retail	
Pharmacies and drug stores	12.4
Furniture stores	22.2
Sporting goods stores	16.0

Source: Based on The Risk Management Association, Annual Statement Studies 2010–2011, © 2010 Philadelphia, PA 2010.

Fixed assets are most prominent at the manufacturing level; retailers are next, probably because retailers require stores and buildings in which to sell products; and the wholesale segment requires the least investment in fixed assets.

For Sage Inc., net fixed assets have increased in proportion to total assets between 2012 and 2013 from 25.0% to 30.5% as can be seen on the common-size balance sheet (Exhibit 2.2). Chapter 5 covers the financial ratios used to measure the efficiency of managing these assets.

Goodwill

Goodwill arises when one company acquires another company (in a business combination accounted for as a purchase) for a price in excess of the fair market value of the net identifiable assets (identifiable assets less liabilities assumed) acquired. This excess price is recorded on the books of the acquiring company as goodwill. Goodwill must be evaluated annually to determine whether there has been a loss of value. If there is no loss of value, goodwill remains on the balance sheet at the recorded cost indefinitely. If it is determined that the book value or carrying value of goodwill exceeds the fair value, the excess book value must be written off as an impairment expense. For Sage Inc. goodwill represents less than 1% of assets; however, for many firms, goodwill is a material item on the balance sheet and should be assessed when analyzing the financial statements. If impairment charges are related to goodwill, it is important to read the footnote disclosures to determine why goodwill was impaired.

Other Assets

Other assets on a firm's balance sheet can include a multitude of other noncurrent items such as property held for sale, start-up costs in connection with a new business, the cash surrender value of life insurance policies, and long-term advance payments.

For Sage Inc., other assets represent minor holdings of property not used in business operations (as explained in Note 1 to the financial statements found in Appendix 1A). Additional categories of noncurrent assets frequently encountered (but not present for Sage Inc.) are long-term investments and intangible assets (other than goodwill), such as patents, copyrights, trademarks, brand names, and franchises.

Liabilities

Current Liabilities

Liabilities represent claims against assets, and current liabilities are those that must be satisfied in one year or one operating cycle, whichever is longer. Current liabilities include accounts and notes payable, the current portion of long-term debt, accrued liabilities, unearned revenue, and deferred taxes.

Accounts Payable

Accounts payable are short-term obligations that arise from credit extended by suppliers for the purchase of goods and services. For example, when Sage Inc. buys inventory on credit from a wholesaler for eventual sale to its own customers, the transaction creates an account payable.

This account is eliminated when the bill is satisfied. The ongoing process of operating a business results in the spontaneous generation of accounts payable, which increase and decrease depending on the credit policies available to the firm from its suppliers, economic conditions, and the cyclical nature of the firm's own business operations. Note that Sage Inc. has almost doubled the amount of accounts payable between 2012 and 2013 (Exhibit 2.6). Part of the balance sheet analysis should include an exploration of the causes for this increase. To jump briefly ahead, the reader might also note that the income statement reveals a significant sales increase in 2013. Perhaps the increase in accounts payable is at least partially explained by this sales growth.

Short-Term Debt

Short-term debt (also referred to as notes payable) consists of obligations in the form of promissory notes to suppliers or financial institutions due in one year or less. For Sage. Inc. the short-term debt (explained in Note 2 to the financial statements) is comprised of a bank line of credit. A line of credit permits borrowing from a financial institution up to a maximum amount. The total amount that can be borrowed under Sage Inc.'s line of credit is $10 million, of which about half ($5,614,000) was outstanding debt at the end of 2013.

Current Maturities of Long-Term Debt

When a firm has bonds, mortgages, or other forms of long-term debt outstanding, the portion of the principal that will be repaid during the upcoming year is classified as a current liability. The currently maturing debt for Sage Inc. occurs as the result of several long-term obligations, described in Note 2 to the financial statements. The note lists the amount of long-term debt outstanding, less the portion due currently, and also provides the schedule of current maturities for the next five years.

EXHIBIT 2.6 Sage Inc. Consolidated Balance Sheets at December 31, 2013 and 2012 (in Thousands)

	2013	**2012**
Liabilities and Stockholders' Equity		
Current Liabilities		
Accounts payable	$14,294	$ 7,591
Accrued liabilities	4,137	4,366
Income taxes payable	1,532	947
Short-term debt	5,614	6,012
Current maturities of long-term debt	1,884	1,516
Total current liabilities	27,461	20,432
Deferred Federal Income Taxes	843	635
Long-Term Debt	21,059	16,975
Commitments and Contingencies (See Notes 3 and 5)		
Total liabilities	49,363	38,042
Stockholders' Equity		
Common stock, par value $0.01, authorized, 10,000,000 shares; issued, 4,363,000 shares in 2013 and 4355,000 shares in 2012, and additional paid-in capital	5,760	5,504
Retained Earnings	40,175	32,363
Total stockholders' equity	45,935	37,867
Total Liabilities and Stockholders' Equity	$95,298	$75,909

The accompanying notes are an integral part of these statements.

Accrued Liabilities

Like most large corporations, Sage Inc. uses the accrual rather than the cash basis of accounting: Revenue is recognized when it is earned, and expenses are recorded when they are incurred, regardless of when the cash is received or paid. Accrued liabilities result from the recognition of an expense in the accounting records prior to the actual payment of cash. Thus, they are liabilities because there will be an eventual cash outflow to satisfy the obligations.

Assume that a company has a $100,000 note outstanding, with 12% annual interest due in semiannual installments on March 31 and September 30. For a balance sheet prepared on December 31, interest will be accrued for three months (October, November, and December):

$$\$100{,}000 \times 0.12 = \$12{,}000 \text{ annual interest}$$
$$\$12{,}000/12 = \$1{,}000 \text{ monthly intereset}$$
$$\$1{,}000 \times 3 = \$3{,}000 \text{ accrued interest for three months}$$

The December 31 balance sheet would include an accrued liability of $3,000. Accruals also arise from salaries, rent, insurance, taxes, and other expenses.

Reserve accounts are often set up for the purpose of estimating obligations for items such as warranty costs, sales returns, or restructuring charges, and are recorded as accrued liabilities. Generally, the only way to determine whether a company has set up a reserve account is to read the notes to the financial statements carefully. Reserve accounts are also set up to record declines in asset values; the allowance for doubtful accounts explained earlier in the chapter is an example.

The potential for manipulation exists whenever a firm is estimating amounts to be recorded on financial statements. Reserve accounts are discussed in more detail in Appendix 3A.

Unearned Revenue or Deferred Credits

Companies that are paid in advance for services or products record a liability on the receipt of cash. The liability account is referred to as *unearned revenue* or *deferred credits*. The amounts in this account will be transferred to a revenue account when the service is performed or the product delivered as required by the matching concept of accounting. Sage Inc. does not have unearned revenue because it is a retail company that does not generally receive payment in advance of selling its products. However, companies in high-technology, publishing, or manufacturing industries are apt to have unearned revenue accounts on their balance sheets. For example, Intel Corporation shows $622 million on its 2010 balance sheet for "Deferred income on shipments to distributors." In the footnotes to the financial statements, this account is explained as follows under the heading "Revenue recognition": "We recognize net product revenue when the earnings process is complete, as evidenced by an agreement with the customer, transfer of title, and acceptance, if applicable, as well as fixed pricing and probable collectability. We record pricing allowances, including discounts based on contractual arrangements with customers, when we recognize revenue as a reduction to both accounts receivable and net revenue. Because of frequent sales price reductions and rapid technology obsolescence in the industry, we defer product revenue and related costs of sales from sales made to distributors under agreements allowing price protection or right of return until the distributors sell the merchandise. The right of return granted generally consists of a stock rotation program in which distributors are able to exchange certain products based on the number of qualified purchases made by the distributor. Under the price protection program, we give distributors credits for the difference between the original price paid and the current price that we offer. We record the net deferred income from product sales to distributors on our balance sheet as deferred income on shipments to distributors. We include shipping charges billed to customers in net revenue, and include the related shipping costs in cost of sales.

"Sales of software, primarily through our Wind River Software Group, are made through term licenses that are generally 12 months in length, or perpetual licenses. Revenue is generally deferred and recognized ratably over the course of the license."[8]

[8]Intel, 2010 Form 10-K, p. 56.

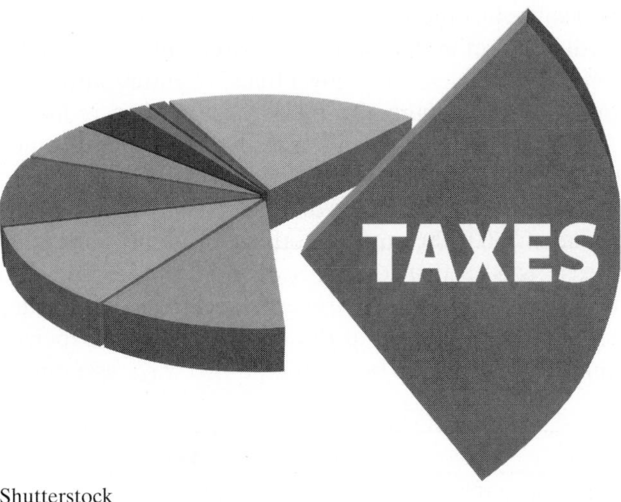

Shutterstock

Deferred Federal Income Taxes

Deferred taxes are the result of temporary differences in the recognition of revenue and expense for taxable income relative to reported income. Most large companies use one set of rules for calculating income tax expense, paid to the IRS, and another set for figuring income reported in the financial statements. The objective is to take advantage of all available tax deferrals to reduce actual tax payments, while showing the highest possible amount of reported net income. There are many areas in which firms are permitted to use different procedures for tax and reporting purposes. Most firms use an accelerated method of depreciation (the Modified Accelerated Cost Recovery System) to figure taxable income and the straight-line method for reporting purposes. The effect is to recognize more depreciation expense in the early years of an asset's useful life for tax calculations.

Although depreciation methods are the most common source, other temporary differences arise from the methods used to account for installment sales, long-term contracts, leases, warranties and service contracts, pensions and other employee benefits, and subsidiary investment earnings. They are called *temporary differences* (or timing differences) because, in theory, the total amount of expense and revenue recognized will eventually be the same for tax and reporting purposes. There are also *permanent differences* in income tax accounting. Municipal bond revenue, for example, is recognized as income for reporting purposes but not for tax purposes; life insurance premiums on officers are recognized as expense for financial reporting purposes but are not deductible for income tax purposes. These permanent differences do not affect deferred taxes because a tax will never be paid on the income or the expense will never be deducted on the tax return.

The deferred tax account reconciles the temporary differences in expense and revenue recognition for any accounting period. Business firms recognize deferred tax liabilities for all temporary differences when the item causes financial income to exceed taxable income with an expectation that the difference will be offset in future accounting periods. Deferred tax assets are reported for deductible temporary differences and operating loss and tax credit carryforwards. A deductible temporary difference is one that causes taxable income to exceed financial income, with the expectation that the difference will be offset in the future. Measurement of tax liabilities and assets is based on provisions of the enacted tax law; effects of future anticipated changes in tax law are not considered. A *valuation allowance* is used to reduce deferred tax assets to expected realizable amounts when it is determined that it is more likely than not that some of the deferred tax assets will not be realized.

To illustrate the accounting for deferred taxes, assume that a company has a total annual revenue of $500,000; expenses other than depreciation are $250,000; and depreciation expense is $100,000 for tax accounting and $50,000 for financial reporting (eventually this difference would reverse and the reported depreciation expense in later years would be greater than the tax depreciation expense). The income for tax and reporting purposes would be computed two ways, assuming a 34% tax rate:

	Tax	**Reporting**
Revenue	$500,000	$500,000
Expenses	(350,000)	(300,000)
Earnings before tax	$150,000	$200,000
Tax expense (× 0.34)	(51,000)	(68,000)
Net income	$ 99,000	$132,000

Taxes actually paid ($51,000) are less than the tax expense ($68,000) reported in the financial statements. To reconcile the $17,000 difference between the expense recorded and the cash outflow, there is a deferred tax liability of $17,000:

Reported tax expense	$68,000
Cash paid for taxes	51,000
Deferred tax liability	$17,000

For an additional example of deferred taxes, including the ultimate reversal of the temporary difference, see Figure 2.2.

Deferred taxes are classified as current or noncurrent on the balance sheet, corresponding to the classification of related assets and liabilities underlying the temporary difference. For example, a deferred tax asset arising from accounting for 90-day warranties would be considered current. On the other hand, a temporary difference based on five-year warranties would be noncurrent; depreciation accounting would also result in a noncurrent deferred tax because of the noncurrent classification of the underlying plant and equipment account. A deferred tax asset or liability that is not related to an asset or liability for financial reporting, including deferred tax assets related to carryforwards, is classified according to anticipated reversal or benefit. At the end of the accounting period, the firm will report one net current amount and one net noncurrent amount unless the liabilities and assets are attributable to different tax-paying components of the enterprise or to different tax jurisdictions. Thus, the deferred tax account can conceivably appear on the balance sheet as a current asset, current liability, noncurrent asset, or noncurrent liability.

FIGURE 2.2 Deferred Taxes—An Example

A company purchases a piece of equipment for $30,000. The equipment is expected to last three years and have no salvage value at the end of the three-year period. Straight-line depreciation is used for financial reporting purposes and an accelerated method is used for tax purposes. The following table shows the amounts of depreciation that would be recorded for both sets of books over the three-year life of the equipment:

Year	Depreciation expense (Financial reporting)	Depreciation expense (Tax reporting)
1	$10,000	$20,000
2	$10,000	$ 6,667
3	$10,000	$ 3,333

Assume that revenues are $90,000 and all expenses other than depreciation are $20,000 each year, the tax rate is 30%, and depreciation is the only temporary difference that creates the deferred tax account. Calculations to determine tax expense for reporting purposes and tax paid are below:

Year 1	Income Statement		Tax Return
Revenues	$90,000		$90,000
Expenses:			
Depreciation	(10,000)		(20,000)
Other	(20,000)		(20,000)
Earnings before taxes	$60,000	Taxable income	$50,000
Tax rate	× 0.30		× 0.30
Tax expense	$18,000		$15,000

The recording of taxes at the end of year 1 will involve a decrease in the cash account of $15,000; an increase in tax expense of $18,000; and an increase in the deferred tax liability account of the difference, $3,000.

Year 2	Income Statement		Tax Return
Revenues	$90,000		$90,000
Expenses:			
Depreciation	(10,000)		(6,667)
Other	(20,000)		(20,000)
Earnings before taxes	$60,000	Taxable income	$63,333
Tax rate	× 0.30		× 0.30
Tax expense	$18,000		$19,000

The recording of taxes at the end of year 2 will involve a decrease in the cash account of $19,000; an increase in tax expense of $18,000; and a decrease in the deferred tax liability account of the difference, $1,000. The deferred tax liability account will now have a balance of $2,000 at the end of year 2.

Year 3	Income Statement		Tax Return
Revenues	$90,000		$90,000
Expenses:			
Depreciation	(10,000)		(3,333)
Other	(20,000)		(20,000)
Earnings before taxes	$60,000	Taxable income	$66,667
Tax rate	× 0.30		× 0.30
Tax expense	$18,000		$20,000

The recording of taxes at the end of year 3 will involve a decrease in the cash account of $20,000; an increase in tax expense of $18,000; and a decrease in the deferred tax liability account of the difference, $2,000. The deferred tax liability account will now have a balance of $0 at the end of year 3, as the temporary difference has completely reversed.

Notice that the total amount of income tax expense ($54,000) recorded for reporting purposes is exactly equal to the tax paid ($54,000) over the three-year period.

Sage Inc. reports deferred federal income taxes as a current asset as well as a noncurrent liability. The temporary differences are based on store closing expenses, stock-based compensation, depreciation methods, and long-term installment sales as reported in Note 4—Income Taxes in the Sage Inc. annual report.

Long-Term Debt

Obligations with maturities beyond one year are designated on the balance sheet as noncurrent liabilities. This category can include bonds payable, long-term notes payable, mortgages, obligations under leases, pension liabilities, and long-term warranties. In Note 2 to the financial statements, Sage Inc. specifies the nature, maturity, and interest rate of each long-term obligation. Even though long-term debt increased by over $4,000 from 2012 to 2013, notice that on the common-size balance sheet (Exhibit 2.2), the percentage of long-term debt relative to total assets has declined.

Capital Lease Obligations

A commonly used type of leasing arrangement is a capital lease. Capital leases are, in substance, a "purchase" rather than a "lease." If a lease contract meets any one of four criteria—transfers ownership to the lessee, contains a bargain purchase option, has a lease term of 75% or more of the leased property's economic life, or has minimum lease payments with a present value of 90% or more of the property's fair value—the lease must be capitalized by the lessee according to the requirements of FASB. Leases not meeting one of the four criteria are treated as operating leases, discussed under commitments and contingencies later in the chapter. Sage Inc. uses only operating leases.

A capital lease affects both the balance sheet and the income statement. An asset and a liability are recorded on the lessee's balance sheet equal to the present value of the lease payments to be made under the contract. The asset account reflects what is, in essence, the purchase of an asset, and the liability is the obligation incurred in financing the purchase. Each lease payment is apportioned partly to reduce the outstanding liability and partly to interest expense. The asset account is amortized with amortization expense recognized on the income statement, just as a purchased asset would be depreciated. Disclosures about capital leases can be found in the notes to the financial statements, often under both the property, plant, and equipment note and the commitments and contingencies note.

Pensions and Postretirement Benefits

Other liability accounts (not present for Sage Inc.) can appear under the liability section of the balance sheet. Pensions are cash compensation paid to retired employees. Employers that offer employees a defined benefit plan are promising the employee a monthly cash amount upon retirement. The amount of the monthly payment is determined by such factors as the age of the employee, number of years the employee has worked for the firm, and the salary earned by the employee. Accounting for defined benefit plans is beyond the scope of this book; however, the concept of pension liabilities is the same as accrued liabilities. A firm pays into the employees' pension fund an amount that will hopefully cover the ultimate benefits that will be paid to employees in the future. The amount paid into the fund plus the earnings on the fund's assets may be less than the estimated pension obligation. In this case, a net pension liability would be included in the liability section of the balance sheet.

Postretirement benefits are benefits other than pensions that employers promise to pay for retired employees. These benefits might include health and life insurance costs. While the obligation for these benefits must be estimated and reported in the balance sheet, firms often do not set aside cash to fund these obligations, causing the firms to report significant postretirement benefit liabilities.

Sage Inc. has a defined contribution plan rather than a defined benefit plan. Defined contribution plans require the employer to contribute a defined amount to employees' pension funds. At retirement the employee receives the amount contributed plus whatever has been earned on the pension fund. Once the employer has made the contribution to the fund, no obligation exists.

Commitments and Contingencies

Many companies will list an account titled "Commitments and Contingencies" on the balance sheet even though no dollar amount will appear. This disclosure is intended to draw attention to the fact that required disclosures can be found in the notes to the financial statements. *Commitments* refer to contractual agreements that will have a significant financial impact on the company in the future. Sage Inc. reports commitments in Note 3 that describe the company's operating leases.

If the leasing contract does not meet one of the four criteria required to record the lease as a capital lease, the lessee will record "rent expense" on the income statement and a corresponding reduction to cash. Operating leases are a form of *off–balance sheet financing.* In fact, the lessee is contractually obligated to make lease payments but is not required by generally accepted accounting principles (GAAP) to record this obligation as a debt on the balance sheet. Companies could purposely negotiate a lease as an operating lease so that the long-term commitment does not have to be shown on the balance sheet; however, astute users of financial statements will know to look at the notes to the financial statements to determine any commitment the company may have with regard to operating leases. For Sage Inc., Note 3 indicates that the company will be required to make lease payments in the amount of $176,019,000 in the future.

Many firms use complicated financing schemes—product financing arrangements, sales of receivables with recourse, limited partnerships, joint ventures—that do not have to be recorded on balance sheets. Disclosures about the extent, nature, and terms of off–balance sheet financing arrangements are in the notes to the financial statements, but they may be very complex and difficult to understand, and require putting pieces together from several different sections.

Contingencies refer to potential liabilities of the firm such as possible damage awards assessed in lawsuits. Generally, the firm cannot reasonably predict the outcome and/or the amount of the future liability; however, information about the contingency must be disclosed in the notes to the financial statements.

Stockholders' Equity

The ownership interests in the company are represented in the final section of the balance sheet, stockholders' equity or shareholders' equity. Ownership equity is the residual interest in assets that remains after deducting liabilities. The owners bear the greatest risk because their claims are subordinate to creditors in the event of liquidation, but owners also benefit from the rewards of a successful enterprise. The relationship between the amount of debt and equity in a firm's capital structure and the concept of financial leverage, by which shareholder returns are magnified, is explored in Chapter 5.

"The good news, sir, is that Harris was able to sell off our losing stocks. The bad news is that Simpson here bought them from Harris."

Cartoon Features Syndicate

Common Stock

Sage Inc. has only common stock shares outstanding. Common shareholders do not ordinarily receive a fixed return but do have voting privileges in proportion to ownership interest. Dividends on common stock are declared at the discretion of a company's board of directors. Further, common shareholders can benefit from stock ownership through potential price appreciation (or the reverse can occur if the share price declines).

The amount listed under the common stock account is based on the par or stated value of the shares issued. The par or stated value usually bears no relationship to actual market price but rather is a floor price below which the stock cannot be sold initially. At year-end 2013, Sage Inc. had 4,363,000 shares outstanding of $0.01 par value stock, rendering a total of $43,630, which is included in the common stock account.

Additional Paid-In Capital

This account reflects the amount by which the original sales price of the stock shares exceeded par value. If, for example, a company sold 1,000 shares of $1 par value stock for $3 per share, the common stock account would be $1,000, and additional paid-in capital would total $2,000.

Sage Inc. combines the additional paid-in capital account with the common stock account for reporting purposes on the balance sheet. The total amount in these combined accounts is $5,760,000 at the end of 2013 for Sage Inc. Because $43,630 of this amount is the par value of the shares, the balance is the additional amount paid above par value for shares of Sage's common stock. On average, the firm's common stock has sold at a price of $1.32 per share ($5,760,000 divided by 4,363,000 shares). The additional paid-in capital account is not affected by the price changes resulting from stock trading subsequent to its original issue.[9]

Retained Earnings

The retained earnings account is the sum of every dollar a company has earned since its inception, less any payments made to shareholders in the form of cash or stock dividends. Retained earnings do not represent a pile of unused cash stashed away in corporate vaults; retained earnings are funds a company has elected to reinvest in the operations of the business rather than pay out to stockholders in dividends. Retained earnings should not be confused with cash or other financial resources currently or prospectively available to satisfy financial obligations. Rather, the retained earnings account is the measurement of all undistributed earnings. The retained earnings account is a key link between the income statement and the balance sheet. Unless there are unusual transactions affecting the retained earnings account, the following equation illustrates this link:

Beginning retained earnings ± Net income (loss) − Dividends = Ending retained earnings

Other Equity Accounts

In addition to the stockholders' equity accounts shown on the Sage Inc. balance sheet, there are other accounts that can appear in the equity section. These include preferred stock, accumulated other comprehensive income, and treasury stock. Exhibit 2.7 illustrates these additional items for Pfizer, Inc.

Preferred stock usually carries a fixed annual dividend payment but no voting rights. Pfizer, Inc. issued preferred stock in connection with an acquisition.

Companies must report comprehensive income or loss for the accounting period. Comprehensive income consists of two parts, net income and other comprehensive income. Other comprehensive income is reported in a separate equity account on the balance sheet generally referred to as *accumulated other comprehensive income/(expense)*. This account includes up to four items: (1) unrealized gains or losses in the market value of investments in available-for-sale securities (2) any change in the excess of additional pension liability over unrecognized prior service cost, (3) certain gains and losses on derivative financial instruments, and (4) foreign currency translation adjustments resulting from converting financial statements from a foreign currency into U.S. dollars. (Comprehensive income and the four items noted above are discussed in Chapter 3.)

[9]The paid-in capital account can be affected by treasury stock transactions, preferred stock, retirement of stock, stock dividends, and warrants and by the conversion of debt into stock.

EXHIBIT 2.7 Pfizer, Inc. Shareholders' Equity at December 31 (in Millions, except preferred stock issued)

	2010	2009
Shareholders' Equity		
Preferred stock, without par value, at stated value; 27 shares authorized; issued: 2010—1,279; 2009—1,511	52	61
Common stock, $.05 par value; 12,000 shares authorized; issued: 2010—8,876; 2009—8,869	444	443
Additional paid-in capital	70,760	70,497
Employee benefit trusts	(7)	(333)
Treasury stock, shares at cost; 2010—864; 2009—799	(22,712)	(21,632)
Retained earnings	42,716	40,426
Accumulated other comprehensive (loss)/income	(3,440)	552
Total Pfizer, Inc. shareholders' equity	87,813	90,014
Equity attributable to noncontrolling interests	452	432
Total shareholders' equity	88,265	90,446

Firms often repurchase shares of their own stock for a variety of reasons that include meeting requirements for employee stock option and retirement plans, building shareholdings for potential merger needs, increasing earnings per share by reducing the number of shares outstanding in order to build investor confidence, preventing takeover attempts by reducing the number of shareholders, and as an investment use of excess cash holdings. If the repurchased shares are not retired, they are designated as *treasury stock* and are shown as an offsetting account in the stockholders' equity section of the balance sheet. Pfizer, Inc. held 864 million shares of treasury stock at the end of 2010. The cost of the shares is shown as a reduction of stockholders' equity.[10]

Employee benefit trusts, an account shown in the Pfizer, Inc. shareholders' equity section, is explained as follows:

> The Pfizer, Inc. Employee Benefit Trust (EBT) was established in 1999 to fund our employee benefit plans through the use of its holdings of Pfizer, Inc. stock. Our consolidated balance sheet reflects the fair value of the shares owned by the EBT as a reduction of Shareholders' Equity. Beginning in May, 2009, the Company began using the shares held in the EBT to help fund the Company's matching contributions in the Pfizer Savings Plan.[11]

Equity attributable to noncontrolling interests represents the equity interest Pfizer has in companies whose financial statements have been consolidated with Pfizer's financial statements but are not 100% owned by Pfizer.

[10]The two methods used to account for treasury stock transactions are the cost method (deducting the cost of the purchased shares from equity) and the par value method (deducting the par or stated value of the shares from equity). Most companies use the cost method.

[11]Pfizer, Inc., 2010 Annual Report, p. 93.

Quality of Financial Reporting—The Balance Sheet

An extensive discussion of financial reporting quality and its impact on financial performance is provided as an Appendix to Chapter 3, but it is important to introduce here some of the qualitative issues that relate to the balance sheet. As has been documented in earlier sections of the book, the economic recession of 2008 and many of the market gyrations since then can be traced directly to the overvaluation of balance sheet assets, such as the subprime mortgages carried by financial institutions. When financial reporting does not reflect economic reality, the quality, and thus the usefulness, of that information is significantly impaired.

In addition to the overvaluation of assets, other examples of balance sheet items that relate directly to the quality of financial reporting include the type of debt used to finance assets, commitments and contingencies, and the classification of leases. In general, a firm should strive for a matching of debt to the type of asset being financed; that is, short term debt should be used to finance current assets, and long-term debt (or equity) should be used to finance long-term assets. A mismatching of debt to assets could indicate that the firm may be having trouble finding financing sources.

As discussed earlier in the chapter, the "Commitments and Contingencies" disclosure in the notes to the financial statements should be read and evaluated carefully because these disclosures can provide important information about off-balance sheet financing and other complex financing arrangements. Enron is a prime example of a company that had enormous activity, leading ultimately to its downfall, reported in these notes to its financial statement presentation. Enron's notes included extensive discussions of financial information that was relevant to the firm's current and future operations but that was not quantified on the balance sheet, such as balance sheet partnerships, a proposed merger, price risk management and financial instruments, unconsolidated subsidiaries, regulatory issues, and litigation.

The twelve pages of notes to the financial statements related to the commitments and contingencies of Pfizer Inc. in 2010 may help the financial statement user understand potential liabilities that can affect the firm in the future. Besides operating lease commitments and guarantees, Pfizer is involved in many legal proceedings. Some of the lawsuits Pfizer is party to involve patents, product litigation, commercial matters, and government investigations, among other legal proceedings. Though most of the information in the notes cannot be quantified on a financial statement, the notes do allow readers to determine that there are significant litigation issues.

Also included in the commitments note is information relating to capital and operating leases. While capital leases are included on the balance sheet, the financial statement user should consider the effects on debt ratios (discussed in Chapter 5) if operating leases are extensive because the firm is committed to making lease payments, similar to payments involved in servicing debt. If such leases had been negotiated as capital leases, there would be a higher amount of debt on the balance sheet. The consumer goods retailer Walmart provides a good example. Walmart reported long-term debt in the amount of $40.7 million and capital lease obligations of $3.2 million in 2010. In addition, Walmart had $14.1 million of operating lease commitments, reported in the notes to the financial statements, and the analyst would want to be aware of the increased risk associated with this off–balance sheet item.

The appendix on financial reporting quality following Chapter 3 will include further discussion of such balance sheet issues as the allowance for doubtful accounts, inventory valuation, inventory write-downs, asset impairment, and gains (losses) from sales of assets.

Other Balance Sheet Items

Corporate balance sheets are not limited to the accounts described in this chapter for Sage Inc. and other companies. The reader of annual reports will encounter additional accounts and will also find many of the same accounts listed under a variety of different titles. Those discussed in this chapter, however, should be generally sufficient for understanding the basics of most balance sheet presentations in a set of published financial statements. The balance sheet will recur throughout the remaining chapters of this book given the interrelationship among the financial statements and its important role in the analysis of financial data.

SELF-TEST

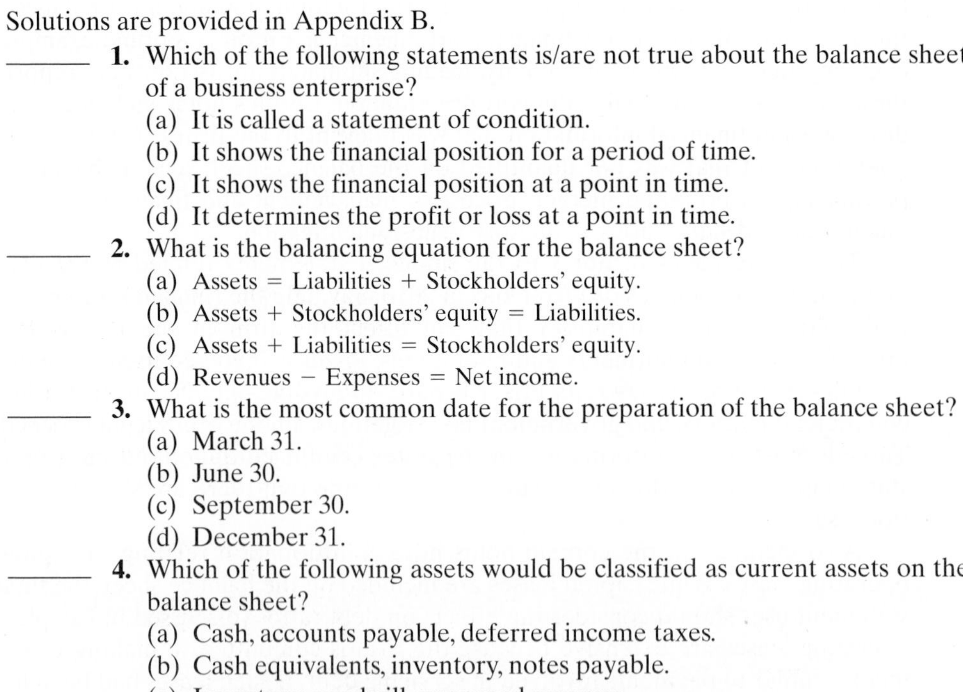

Solutions are provided in Appendix B.

______ **1.** Which of the following statements is/are not true about the balance sheet of a business enterprise?
(a) It is called a statement of condition.
(b) It shows the financial position for a period of time.
(c) It shows the financial position at a point in time.
(d) It determines the profit or loss at a point in time.

______ **2.** What is the balancing equation for the balance sheet?
(a) Assets = Liabilities + Stockholders' equity.
(b) Assets + Stockholders' equity = Liabilities.
(c) Assets + Liabilities = Stockholders' equity.
(d) Revenues − Expenses = Net income.

______ **3.** What is the most common date for the preparation of the balance sheet?
(a) March 31.
(b) June 30.
(c) September 30.
(d) December 31.

______ **4.** Which of the following assets would be classified as current assets on the balance sheet?
(a) Cash, accounts payable, deferred income taxes.
(b) Cash equivalents, inventory, notes payable.
(c) Inventory, goodwill, unearned revenue.
(d) Accounts receivable, prepaid expenses, inventory.

______ **5.** Which of the following statements is/are true for held to maturity marketable securities?
(a) These are the debt securities that the firm has the positive intent and ability to hold to maturity.
(b) These securities are reported at fair value with unrealized gains and losses included in earnings.
(c) These securities are reported at amortized cost.
(d) All of the above.

______ **6.** What type of firm generally has the highest proportion of inventory to total assets?
(a) Retailers.
(b) Wholesalers.
(c) Manufacturers.
(d) Service-oriented firms.

______ **7.** Why is the method of valuing inventory important?
(a) Inventory valuation is based on the actual flow of goods.
(b) Inventories always account for more than 50% of total assets and therefore have a considerable impact on a company's financial position.
(c) Companies desire to use the inventory valuation method that minimizes the cost of goods sold expense.
(d) The inventory valuation method chosen determines the value of inventory on the balance sheet and the cost of goods sold expense on the income statement, two items having considerable impact on the financial position of a company.

______ **8.** What are three major cost flow assumptions used by U.S. companies in valuing inventory?
(a) LIFO, FIFO, average market.
(b) LIFO, FIFO, actual cost.
(c) LIFO, FIFO, average cost.
(d) LIFO, FIFO, double-declining balance.

______ **9.** Assuming a period of inflation, which method of inventory cost flow assumption would be suitable?
(a) LIFO.
(b) FIFO.
(c) Simple average.
(d) Weighted average.

______ **10.** Why would a company switch to the LIFO method of inventory valuation?
(a) By switching to LIFO, reported earnings will be higher.
(b) A new tax law requires companies using LIFO for reporting purposes also to use LIFO for figuring taxable income.
(c) LIFO produces the largest cost of goods sold expense in a period of inflation and thereby lowers taxable income and taxes.
(d) A survey by *Accounting Trends and Techniques* revealed that the switch to LIFO is a current accounting "fad."

______ **11.** Where can one most typically find the cost flow assumption used for inventory valuation for a specific company?
(a) In The Risk Management Association, *Annual Statement Studies*.
(b) In the statement of retained earnings.
(c) On the face of the balance sheet with the total current asset amount.
(d) In the notes to the financial statements.

______ **12.** What type of firm generally has the lowest proportion of fixed assets to total assets?
(a) Manufacturers.
(b) Retailers.
(c) Wholesalers.
(d) Retailers and wholesalers.

______ **13.** How is goodwill evaluated?
(a) Goodwill must be amortized over a 40-year period.
(b) Goodwill should be written up each year.
(c) Companies should determine whether goodwill has lost value, and if so, the loss in value should be written off as an impairment expense.
(d) Goodwill is to be written off at the end of the tenth year.

______ **14.** Which of the following liabilities would be included in the current liabilities section on the balance sheet?
(a) Capital lease obligations, notes payable, common stock.
(b) Accounts payable, short-term debt, unearned revenues.
(c) Accrued liabilities, deferred credits, retained earnings.
(d) Current maturities of long-term debt, additional paid-in capital, pension obligations.

______ **15.** What do current liabilities and current assets have in common?
(a) Current assets are claims against current liabilities.
(b) If current assets increase, then there will be a corresponding increase in current liabilities.
(c) Current liabilities and current assets are converted into cash.
(d) Current liabilities and current assets are those items that will be satisfied and converted into cash, respectively, in one year or one operating cycle, whichever is longer.

______ **16.** Which of the following items could cause the recognition of accrued liabilities?
(a) Sales, interest expense, rent.
(b) Sales, taxes, interest income.
(c) Salaries, rent, insurance.
(d) Salaries, interest expense, interest income.

______ **17.** Which statement is false?

(a) Deferred taxes are the product of temporary differences in the recognition of revenue and expense for taxable income relative to reported income.

(b) Deferred taxes arise from the use of the same method of depreciation for tax and reporting purposes.

(c) Deferred taxes arise when taxes actually paid are less than tax expense reported in the financial statements.

(d) Temporary differences causing the recognition of deferred taxes may arise from the methods used to account for items such as depreciation, installment sales, leases, and pensions.

______ **18.** Which of the following would be classified as long-term debt?

(a) Mortgages, current maturities of long-term debt, bonds.

(b) Mortgages, long-term notes payable, bonds due in 10 years.

(c) Accounts payable, bonds, obligations under leases.

(d) Accounts payable, long-term notes payable, long-term warranties.

______ **19.** What accounts are most likely to be found in the stockholders' equity section of the balance sheet?

(a) Common stock, long-term debt, preferred stock.

(b) Common stock, additional paid-in capital, liabilities.

(c) Common stock, retained earnings, dividends payable.

(d) Common stock, additional paid-in capital, retained earnings.

______ **20.** What does the additional paid-in capital account represent?

(a) The difference between the par and the stated value of common stock.

(b) The price changes that result for stock trading subsequent to its original issue.

(c) The market price of all common stock issued.

(d) The amount by which the original sales price of stock exceeds the par value.

______ **21.** What does the retained earnings account measure?

(a) Cash held by the company since its inception.

(b) Payments made to shareholders in the form of cash or stock dividends.

(c) All undistributed earnings.

(d) Financial resources currently available to satisfy financial obligations.

______ **22.** Listed below are balance sheet accounts for Elf's Gift Shop. Mark current accounts with "C" and noncurrent accounts with "NC."

______ (a) Long-term debt.

______ (b) Inventories.

______ (c) Accounts payable.

______ (d) Prepaid expenses.

______ (e) Equipment.

______ (f) Accrued liabilities.

______ (g) Accounts receivable.

______ (h) Cash.

______ (i) Bonds payable.

______ (j) Patents.

_____ **23.** Dot's Delicious Donuts has the following accounts on its balance sheet:

(1) Current assets.
(2) Property, plant, and equipment.
(3) Intangible assets.
(4) Other assets.
(5) Current liabilities.
(6) Deferred federal income taxes.
(7) Long-term debt.
(8) Stockholders' equity.

How would each of the following items be classified?

_____ (a) Land held for speculation.
_____ (b) Current maturities on mortgage.
_____ (c) Common stock.
_____ (d) Mortgage payable.
_____ (e) Balances outstanding on credit sales to customers.
_____ (f) Accumulated depreciation.
_____ (g) Buildings used in business.
_____ (h) Accrued payroll.
_____ (i) Preferred stock.
_____ (j) Debt outstanding from credit extended by suppliers.
_____ (k) Patents.
_____ (l) Land on which warehouse is located.
_____ (m) Allowance for doubtful accounts.
_____ (n) Liability due to difference in taxes paid and taxes reported.
_____ (o) Additional paid-in capital.

_____ **24.** Match the following terms to the correct definitions.

_____ (a) Consolidated financial statements.
_____ (b) Current assets.
_____ (c) Depreciation.
_____ (d) Deferred taxes.
_____ (e) Allowance for doubtful accounts.
_____ (f) Prepaid expenses.
_____ (g) Current maturities.
_____ (h) Accrued expenses.
_____ (i) Capital lease.
_____ (j) Market value of stock.

(1) Used up within one year or operating cycle, whichever is longer.
(2) Expenses incurred prior to cash outflow.
(3) An agreement to use assets that is in substance a purchase.
(4) Estimation of uncollectible accounts receivable.
(5) Cost allocation of fixed assets other than land.
(6) Expenses paid in advance.
(7) Combined statements of parent company and controlled subsidiary companies.
(8) Price at which stock trades.
(9) Difference in taxes reported and taxes paid.
(10) Portion of debt to be repaid during the upcoming year.

Study Questions and Problems

2.1. When are the financial statements consolidated?

2.2. Why are comparative data provided in financial statements?

2.3. What benefits are derived by preparing the common-size balance sheet?

2.4. How are marketable securities valued when they are categorized as "available for sale"?

2.5. Why is cost flow assumption made during accounting for inventory?

2.6. Why would a company switch to the LIFO method of inventory valuation in an inflationary period?

2.7. Which inventory valuation method, FIFO or LIFO, will generally produce an ending inventory value on the balance sheet that is closest to current cost?

2.8. Discuss the difference between the straight-line method of depreciation and the accelerated methods. Why do companies use different depreciation methods for tax reporting and financial reporting?

2.9. What is the purpose of listing the account "Commitments and contingencies" on the balance sheet even though no dollar amounts appear?

2.10. How is it possible for a company with positive retained earnings to be unable to pay a cash dividend?

2.11. The King Corporation has a total annual revenue of $900,000; expenses other than depreciation of $550,000; depreciation expense of $200,000 for tax purposes; and depreciation expense of $130,000 for reporting purposes. The tax rate is 30%. Calculate the net income for reporting purposes and for tax purposes. What is the deferred tax liability?

2.12. Explain how treasury stock affects the stockholders' equity section of the balance sheet and the calculation of earnings per share.

2.13. Using the following amounts (in thousands) reported in ABC Inc.'s consolidated balance sheets and statements of income at December 31, 2012 and 2011, and the valuation schedule, analyze the accounts receivable and allowance accounts for all years.

	2012	2011
Net Revenues	$395,684	$387,546
Accounts receivable, net of allowances for doubtful accounts of $1,206 in 2012 and $3,001 in 2011	$ 93,233	$ 89,135

Schedule II—Valuation and Qualifying Accounts Years Ended December 31, 2012 and 2011

		Balance at Beginning of Period	Charged (Credited) to Expenses	Deductions	Balance at End of Period
2012	Allowance for doubtful accounts	$3,001	$(890)	$(905)	$1,206
2011	Allowance for doubtful accounts	$2,658	$ 798	$(455)	$3,001
2010	Allowance for doubtful accounts	$3,422	$(550)	$(214)	$2,658

2.14. Tisha's Toys had the following goods available for sale in the last accounting period:

Beginning inventory	600 units @ $10
Purchases (in order from first to last):	1,000 units @ $11
	900 units @ $12
	700 units @ $14
Sales for the period were 1,900 units.	

(a) Compute the inventory balance and the cost of goods sold at the end of the accounting period using average cost, FIFO, and LIFO.
(b) Which method shows the highest ending inventory?
(c) Which method shows the highest cost of goods sold?
(d) Explain why ending inventory and cost of goods sold differ under the three methods of inventory valuation.

2.15. The F.L.A.C. Corporation sells a single product. The following is information on inventory, purchase, and sales for the current year:

		Number of Units	Unit Cost	Sale Price
January 1	Inventory	10,000	$ 3.00	
January 10	Purchase	4,000	3.50	
January 1–March 31	Sales	8,000		$ 5.00
April 25	Purchase	10,000	4.00	
April 1–June 30	Sales	11,000		5.50
July 10	Purchase	6,000	4.50	
July 1–September 30	Sales	3,000		6.00
October 15	Purchase	8,000	5.00	
October 1–December 31	Sales	9,000		6.50

(a) Compute the inventory balance and the cost of goods sold expense reported at the end of the year using the following methods: FIFO, LIFO, and average cost.
(b) Discuss the effect of each method on the balance sheet and income statement during periods of inflation.

2.16. The following information is available for Chemco Inc's inventories as of June 30, 2012:

(in Thousands)	2012	2011
Finished goods	$382,925	$303,249
Work in process	76,524	60,588
Raw materials and supplies	72,246	49,844
Inventories at current cost	531,695	413,681
Less LIFO valuation	(83,829)	(88,368)
Total inventories	$447,886	$325,313

We used the LIFO method of valuing our inventories for approximately 40% and 44% of total inventories at June 30, 2012 and 2011, respectively.

(a) What method of inventory is used for the other 60% and 56% of total inventories?
(b) Explain the meaning of each of the numbers listed in the table.

2.17. The Lazy O Ranch just purchased equipment costing $80,000. The equipment is expected to last five years and have no salvage value.

(a) Calculate the depreciation expense using the straight-line method for the first two years the equipment is owned.

(b) Calculate the depreciation expense using the double-declining balance method for the first two years the equipment is owned.

2.18. Using the information below for Dean Corporation, calculate the amount of dividends Dean most likely paid to common stockholders in 2008, 2009, and 2010.

Retained Earnings Balances		**Year**	**Net Income**
January 1, 2008	$ 600		
December 31, 2008	790	2008	$350
December 31, 2009	1,095	2009	425
December 31, 2010	1,050	2010	150

2.19. From the following accounts, prepare a balance sheet for Chester Co. for the current calendar year.

Accrued interest payable	$ 1,400
Property, plant, and equipment	34,000
Inventory	12,400
Additional paid-in capital	7,000
Deferred taxes payable (noncurrent)	1,600
Cash	1,500
Accumulated depreciation	10,500
Bonds payable	14,500
Accounts payable	4,300
Common stock	2,500
Prepaid expenses	700
Land held for sale	9,200
Retained earnings	?
Current portion of long-term debt	1,700
Accounts receivable	6,200
Notes payable	8,700

2.20. **Writing Skills Problem.** At fiscal year-end December 31, 2012, ShopWorld had the following assets and liabilities on its balance sheet (in millions):

Current liabilities	$9,459
Long-term debt	12,330
Other liabilities	1,180
Total assets	37,411

ShopWorld reported the following information on leases in the notes to the financial statements:

Total rent expense was $195 million in 2012, $189 million in 2011, and $188 million in 2010. Most of the long-term leases include options to renew, with terms varying from 1 to 50 years. Certain leases also include options to purchase the property.

Future minimum lease payments required under noncancelable lease agreements existing at December 31, 2012, were:

Future Minimum Lease Payments (in millions)	Operating Leases	Capital Leases
2013	$224	$ 7
2014	201	9
2015	193	9
2016	168	10
2017	142	10
After 2017	3,935	138
Total future minimum lease payments	$4,863	$183
Less: Interest		(70)
Present value of minimum capital lease payments		$113

Required: Your friend, Liz, loves to shop at ShopWorld and is now interested in investing in the company. Tom, another friend of Liz, has told her that ShopWorld's debt structure is risky, with obligations nearly 74% of total assets. Liz sees that debt on the balance sheet is 61% of total assets and is confused by Tom's comment. Write an explanation to Liz discussing the debt structure of ShopWorld and why Tom thinks ShopWorld is risky. Be sure to explain clearly to Liz what information appears on financial statements, as well as what information does not appear directly on the financial statements.

2.21. Research Problem

Locate a library that carries "The Risk Management Association, Annual Statement Studies." Choose three industries from Annual Statement Studies (different from those illustrated in Exhibits 2.4 and 2.5 presented earlier in this chapter) and create a table with the percentages for the following items: accounts receivable, inventories, fixed assets, accounts payable, and long-term debt as a percentage of total assets.

2.22. Internet Problem

Choose a publicly held corporation (unless your teacher assigns a particular corporation for this assignment) and find the balance sheet and notes to the financial statements in the most recent Form 10-K. The Form 10-K can be located by going to the home page of the Securities and Exchange Commission and locating the SEC EDGAR Database. The address for the home page is www.sec.gov.

Using the information you find, answer the following questions:

(a) What current assets are included on the balance sheet?

(b) If the company lists accounts receivable and an allowance account, analyze these accounts.

(c) What method does the company use to value inventory?

(d) What depreciation method does the company use?

(e) What assets other than current assets and property, plant, and equipment are included on the balance sheet?

(f) What current liabilities are included on the balance sheet?

(g) How many deferred tax accounts are included on the balance sheet? Under which classification(s) are deferred taxes found? What temporary differences caused the creation of the deferred tax account(s)?

(h) Does the company have long-term debt? How much?

(i) Does the company have commitments and contingencies? If so, what commitments does the company have and for what amount is the company committed? Explain any contingencies.

(j) What stockholders' equity accounts are included on the balance sheet?

CASES

Case 2.1 Intel Case

The 2010 Intel Annual Report can be found at the following Web site: www .pearsoninternationaleditions.com/fraser. Using the annual report, answer the following questions:

(a) Prepare a common-size balance sheet for Intel for all years presented.

(b) Describe the types of assets Intel owns. Which assets are the most significant to the company? Using the notes to the financial statements, discuss the accounting methods used to value assets. What other information can be learned about the asset accounts from the notes? Have there been significant changes to the asset structure from 2009 to 2010?

(c) Analyze the accounts receivable and allowance accounts.

(d) Describe the types of liabilities Intel has incurred. Which liabilities are the most significant to the company? Have there been significant changes to the liability and equity structure from 2009 to 2010?

(e) Describe the commitments and contingencies of Intel.

(f) Under which classification(s) are deferred taxes listed? What item is the most significant component of deferred taxes?

(g) What equity accounts are included on the balance sheet of Intel?

Case 2.2 Avnet Comprehensive Analysis Case Using the Financial Statement Analysis Template

Each chapter in the textbook contains a continuation of this problem. The objective is to learn how to do a comprehensive financial statement analysis in steps as the content of each chapter is learned. Using the 2010 Avnet Form 10-K that can be found at www.pearsoninternationaleditions.com/fraser, complete the following requirements:

(a) Open the financial statement analysis template that you saved from the Chapter 1 Avnet problem and input the data from the Avnet balance sheet. Be sure to read the notes to the financial statements to determine the correct numbers to input on the template. For example, the company has combined income taxes payable with another liability account and property, plant and equipment has been recorded net of accumulated depreciation. When you have finished inputting the data, review the balance sheet to make sure there are no red blocks indicating that your numbers do not match the cover sheet information you input from the Chapter 1 problem. Make any necessary corrections before printing out both your input and the common-size balance sheet that the template automatically creates for you.

(b) Analyze the balance sheet. Write a summary that includes important points that an analyst would use in assessing the financial condition of Avnet.

Case 2.3 Logitech International S.A.

The following are excerpts from the 2010 Logitech International S.A. Form 10-K:

LOGITECH INTERNATIONAL S.A.
CONSOLIDATED BALANCE SHEETS
(In thousands, except share and per share amounts)

	March 31,	
	2010	**2009**
Assets		
Current assets:		
Cash and cash equivalents	$ 319,944	$ 492,759
Short-term investments	—	1,637
Accounts receivable	195,247	213,929
Inventories	219,593	233,467
Other current assets	58,877	56,884
Total current assets	793,661	998,676
Property, plant, and equipment	91,229	104,132
Goodwill	553,462	242,909
Other intangible assets	95,396	32,109
Other assets	65,930	43,704
Total assets	$ 1,599,678	$ 1,421,530
Liabilities and shareholders' equity		
Current liabilities:		
Accounts payable	$ 257,955	$ 157,798
Accrued liabilities	182,336	131,496
Total current liabilities	440,291	289,294
Other liabilities	159,672	134,528
Total liabilities	599,963	423,822
Commitments and contingencies		
Shareholders' equity:		
Shares, par value CHF 0.25—191,606,620 issued and authorized and 50,000,000 conditionally authorized at March 31, 2010 and 2009	33,370	33,370
Additional paid-in capital	14,880	45,012
Shares in treasury, at cost, 16,435,528 at March 31, 2010 and 12,124,078 at March 31, 2009	(382,512)	(341,454)
Retained earnings	1,406,618	1,341,661
Accumulated other comprehensive loss	(72,641)	(80,881)
Total shareholders' equity	999,715	997,708
Total liabilities and shareholders' equity	$ 1,599,678	$ 1,421,530

The accompanying notes are an integral part of these consolidated financial statements.

Logitech International S.A.
Notes to Consolidated Financial Statements

Note 1—The Company

Logitech is a world leader in personal peripherals for computers and other digital platforms. We develop and market innovative products in PC navigation, Internet communications, digital music, home-entertainment control, gaming and wireless devices. For the PC, our products include mice, trackballs, keyboards, interactive gaming controllers, multimedia speakers, headsets, webcams, 3D control devices, and lapdesks. Our Internet communications products include webcams, headsets, video communications services, and digital video security systems for a home or small business. Our LifeSize division offers scalable high-definition video communications products, support, and services. Our digital music products include speakers, earphones, and custom in-ear monitors. For home entertainment systems, we offer the Harmony line of advanced remote controls and the Squeezebox and Transporter wireless music solutions for the home. For gaming consoles, we offer a range of gaming controllers, including racing wheels, wireless guitar and drum controllers, and microphones, as well as other accessories.

Note 2—Summary of Significant Accounting Policies

Concentration of Credit Risk

Financial instruments that potentially subject the Company to concentrations of credit risk consist principally of cash and cash equivalents and accounts receivable. The Company maintains cash and cash equivalents with various financial institutions to limit exposure with any one financial institution.

The Company sells to large OEMs, distributors and key retailers and, as a result, maintains individually significant receivable balances with such customers. As of March 31, 2010, one customer represented 14% of total accounts receivable. As of March 31, 2009, two customers represented 18% and 10% of total accounts receivable. Typical payment terms require customers to pay for product sales generally within 30 to 60 days; however, terms may vary by customer type, by country, and by selling season. Extended payment terms are sometimes offered to a limited number of customers during the second and third fiscal quarters. The Company does not modify payment terms on existing receivables.

The Company's OEM customers tend to be well-capitalized, multi-national companies, while distributors and key retailers may be less well-capitalized. The Company manages its accounts receivable credit risk through ongoing credit evaluation of its customers' financial condition. The Company generally does not require collateral from its customers.

Allowances for Doubtful Accounts

Allowances for doubtful accounts are maintained for estimated losses resulting from the inability of the Company's customers to make required payments. The allowances are based on the Company's regular assessment of the creditworthiness and financial condition of specific customers, as well as its historical experience with bad debts and customer deductions, receivables aging, current economic trends, geographic or country-specific risks and the financial condition of its distribution channels.

Inventories

Inventories are stated at the lower of cost or market. Cost is computed on a first-in, first-out basis. The Company records write-downs of inventories which are obsolete or in excess of anticipated demand or market value based on a consideration of marketability and product life cycle stage, product development plans, component cost trends, demand forecasts, historical sales, and assumptions about future demand and market conditions.

Note 7—Balance Sheet Components

The following provides the components of certain balance sheet amounts (in thousands):

	March 31,	
	2010	**2009**
Long-term liabilities:		
Income taxes payable—noncurrent	$ 116,456	$ 101,463
Obligation for management deferred compensation	10,307	10,499
Defined benefit pension plan liability	19,343	19,822
Other long-term liabilities	13,566	2,744
	$ 159,672	$ 134,528

Note 8—Goodwill and Other Intangible Assets

The following table summarizes the activity in the Company's goodwill account during fiscal years ended March 31, 2010 and 2009 (in thousands):

	March 31,	
	2010	**2009**
Beginning balance	$ 242,909	$ 194,383
Additions	313,041	48,526
Other adjustments	(2,488)	–
Ending balance	$ 553,462	$ 242,909

Additions to goodwill during fiscal year 2010 primarily related to our acquisitions of LifeSize and TV Compass. Logitech will maintain discrete financial information for LifeSize and accordingly, the acquired goodwill related to the LifeSize acquisition will be separately evaluated for impairment. TV Compass's business was fully integrated into the Company's existing operations, and discrete financial information for TV Compass is not maintained. Accordingly, the acquired goodwill related to TV Compass is evaluated for impairment at the total enterprise level. The adjustment to goodwill represents an adjustment of the deferred tax asset recognized in connection with the acquisitions of SightSpeed, Inc. and the Ultimate Ears companies.

Additions to goodwill during fiscal year 2009 were primarily related to our acquisitions of SightSpeed and Ultimate Ears, as well as a $2.0 million pre-acquisition contingency related to our WiLife acquisition.

Note 9—Financing Arrangements

The Company had several uncommitted, unsecured bank lines of credit aggregating $151.9 million at March 31, 2010. There are no financial covenants under these lines of credit with which the Company must comply. At March 31, 2010, the Company had no outstanding borrowings under these lines of credit.

Note 16—Commitments and Contingencies

The Company leases facilities under operating leases, certain of which require it to pay property taxes, insurance, and maintenance costs. Operating leases for facilities are generally renewable at the Company's option and usually include escalation clauses linked to inflation. Future minimum annual rentals under non-cancelable operating leases at March 31, 2010, are as follows (in thousands):

Year ending March 31,	
2011	$ 13,679
2012	9,666
2013	8,204
2014	4,171
2015	3,473
Thereafter	7,503
	$ 46,696

Rent expense was $16.3 million, $15.5 million, and $13.8 million for the years ended March 31, 2010, 2009, and 2008. The Company's asset retirement obligations for its leased facilities as of March 31, 2010, were not material.

At March 31, 2010, fixed purchase commitments for capital expenditures amounted to $12.9 million, and primarily related to commitments for manufacturing equipment, tooling, computer software, and computer hardware. Also, the Company has commitments for inventory purchases made in the normal course of business to original design manufacturers, contract manufacturers, and other suppliers. At March 31, 2010, fixed purchase commitments for inventory amounted to $183.6 million, which are expected to be fulfilled by December 31, 2010. The Company also had other commitments totaling $33.3 million for consulting services, marketing arrangements, advertising, and other services. Although open purchase orders are considered enforceable and legally binding, the terms generally allow the Company the option to reschedule and adjust its requirements based on the business needs prior to delivery of goods or performance of services.

The Company has guaranteed the purchase obligations of some of its contract manufacturers and original design manufacturers to certain component suppliers. These guarantees generally have a term of one year and are automatically extended for one or more years as long as a liability exists. The amount of the purchase obligations of these manufacturers varies over time, and therefore the amounts subject to Logitech's guarantees similarly vary. At March 31, 2010, there were no outstanding guaranteed purchase obligations. The maximum total potential future payments under three of the five guarantee arrangements is limited to $30.8 million. The remaining two guarantees are limited to purchases of specified components from the named suppliers. The Company does not believe, based on historical experience and information currently available, that it is probable that any amounts will be required to be paid under these guarantee arrangements.

Logitech International S.A., the parent holding company, has guaranteed certain contingent liabilities of various subsidiaries related to specific transactions occurring in the normal course of business. The maximum amount of the guarantees was $8.2 million as of March 31, 2010. As of March 31, 2010, $7.6 million was outstanding under these guarantees. The parent holding company has also guaranteed the purchases of one of its subsidiaries under two guarantee agreements. These guarantees do not specify a maximum amount. As of March 31, 2010, $8.7 million was outstanding under these guarantees.

Logitech indemnifies some of its suppliers and customers for losses arising from matters such as intellectual property rights and product safety defects, subject to certain restrictions. The scope of these indemnities varies, but in some instances, includes indemnification for damages and expenses, including reasonable attorneys' fees. No amounts have been accrued for indemnification provisions at March 31, 2010. The Company does not believe, based on historical experience and information currently available, that it is probable that any amounts will be required to be paid under its indemnification arrangements.

The Company provides various third parties with irrevocable letters of credit in the normal course of business to secure its obligations to pay or perform pursuant to the requirements of an underlying agreement or the provision of goods and services. These standby letters of credit are cancelable only at the option of the beneficiary who is authorized to draw drafts on the issuing bank up to the face amount of the standby letter of credit in accordance with its terms. At March 31, 2010, the Company had $3.4 million of letters of credit in place, of which $0.3 million was outstanding. These letters of credit relate primarily to equipment purchases by a subsidiary in China, and expire between April and June 2010. At March 31, 2009, the Company had $0.4 million of letters of credit in place, with no balance outstanding.

In November 2007, the Company acquired WiLife Inc., a privately held company offering PC-based video cameras for self-monitoring a home or a small business. The purchase agreement provides for a possible performance-based payment, payable in the first calendar quarter of 2011. The performance-based payment is based on net revenues attributed to WiLife during calendar year 2010. No payment is due if the applicable net revenues total $40.0 million or less. The maximum performance-based payment is $64.0 million. The total performance-based payment amount, if any, will be recorded in goodwill and will not be known until the end of calendar year 2010. As of March 31, 2010, no amounts were payable towards performance-based payments under the WiLife acquisition agreement.

The Company is involved in a number of lawsuits and claims relating to commercial matters that arise in the normal course of business. The Company believes these lawsuits and claims are without merit and intends to vigorously defend against them. However, there can be no assurances that its defenses will be successful, or that any judgment or settlement in any of these lawsuits would not have a material adverse impact on the Company's business, financial condition, cash flows and results of operations. The Company's accruals for lawsuits and claims as of March 31, 2010, were not material.

LOGITECH INTERNATIONAL S.A.
VALUATION AND QUALIFYING ACCOUNTS
For the Fiscal Years Ended March 31, 2010, 2009, and 2008 (in thousands)

Fiscal Year	Description	Balance at beginning of period	Charged (credited) to Income Statement	Write-offs charged to (recovered against) allowance	Balance at end of period
2010	Allowance for doubtful accounts	$ 6,705	$ (72)	$ (763)	$ 5,870
2009	Allowance for doubtful accounts	$ 2,497	$ 5,102	$ (894)	$ 6,705
2008	Allowance for doubtful accounts	$ 3,322	$ 603	$ (1,428)	$ 2,497

LOGITECH INTERNATIONAL S.A.
INFORMATION FROM CONSOLIDATED INCOME STATEMENTS
For the Fiscal Years Ending March 31, 2010, 2009, and 2008
(in thousands)

	2010	2009	2008
Sales	$1,966,748	$2,208,832	$2,370,496
Net income	$ 64,597	$ 107,032	$ 231,026

Required:

1. Using the Consolidated Balance Sheets for Logitech International S.A. (Logitech) for March 31, 2010 and 2009, prepare a common-size balance sheet.
2. Evaluate the asset, debt, and equity structure of Logitech, and explain trends and changes found on the common-size balance sheet.
3. Analyze accounts receivable and allowance for doubtful accounts.
4. What inventory method is used to value inventories? Does this method reflect current cost at year-end?
5. Based on the inventory valuation method used, would you expect Logitech to have tax savings or pay more in taxes? Explain your answer. (You do not need to do any calculations.)
6. Discuss the commitments and contingencies of Logitech and the significance of these items.
7. Explain what has caused the change in the retained earnings account from March 31, 2009, to March 31, 2010.
8. Discuss any positive items learned about Logitech from the balance sheet and excerpts from the Form 10-K.
9. What concerns would investors and creditors have based on only this information?
10. What additional financial and nonfinancial information would investors and creditors need to make good investing and lending decisions for Logitech?

Case 2.4 Walgreen Co. and Subsidiaries

The following excerpts are from the 2010 Walgreen Co. Form 10-K:

CONSOLIDATED BALANCE SHEETS

Walgreen Co. and Subsidiaries at August 31, 2010 and 2009 (in millions, except shares and per share amounts)

Assets		2010	2009
Current Assets	Cash and cash equivalents	$ 1,880	$ 2,087
	Short-term investments	—	500
	Accounts receivable, net	2,450	2,496
	Inventories	7,378	6,789
	Other current assets	214	177
	Total Current Assets	11,922	12,049
Noncurrent Assets	Property and equipment, at cost, less accumulated depreciation and amortization	11,184	10,802
	Goodwill	1,887	1,461
	Other noncurrent assets	1,282	830
	Total Noncurrent Assets	14,353	13,093
	Total Assets	$ 26,275	$ 25,142
Liabilities and Shareholders' Equity			
Current Liabilities	Short-term borrowings	$ 12	$ 15
	Trade accounts payable	4,585	4,308
	Accrued expenses and other liabilities	2,763	2,406
	Income taxes	73	40
	Total Current Liabilities	7,433	6,769
NonCurrent Liabilities	Long-term debt	2,389	2,336
	Deferred income taxes	318	265
	Other noncurrent liabilities	1,735	1,396
	Total Noncurrent Liabilities	4,442	3,997
	Commitments and Contingencies (see Note 10)		
Shareholders' Equity	Preferred stock, $.0625 par value; authorized 32 million shares; none issued	—	—
	Common stock, $.078125 par value; authorized 3.2 billion shares; issued 1,025,400,000 shares in 2010 and 2009	80	80
	Paid-in capital	684	605
	Employee stock loan receivable	(87)	(140)
	Retained earnings	16,848	15,327
	Accumulated other comprehensive (loss) income	(24)	37
	Treasury stock at cost, 86,794,947 shares in 2010 and 36,838,610 shares in 2009	(3,101)	(1,533)
	Total Shareholders' Equity	14,400	14,376
	Total Liabilities and Shareholders' Equity	$ 26,275	$ 25,142

The accompanying Notes to Consolidated Financial Statements are integral parts of these statements.

Notes to Consolidated Financial Statements

1. Summary of Major Accounting Policies

Description of Business

The Company is principally in the retail drugstore business and its operations are within one reportable segment. At August 31, 2010, there were 8,046 drugstore and other locations in 50 states, the District of Columbia, Guam, and Puerto Rico. Prescription sales were 65.2% of total sales for fiscal 2010 compared to 65.3% in 2009 and 64.9% in 2008.

Inventories

Inventories are valued on a lower of last-in, first-out (LIFO) cost or market basis. At August 31, 2010 and 2009, inventories would have been greater by $1,379 million and $1,239 million, respectively, if they had been valued on a lower of first-in, first-out (FIFO) cost or market basis. Inventory includes product costs, inbound freight, warehousing costs, and vendor allowances.

3. Leases

The Company owns 20.2% of its operating locations; the remaining locations are leased premises. Initial terms are typically 20 to 25 years, followed by additional terms containing cancellation options at five-year intervals, and may include rent escalation clauses. The commencement date of all lease terms is the earlier of the date the Company becomes legally obligated to make rent payments or the date the Company has the right to control the property. Additionally, the Company recognizes rent expense on a straight-line basis over the term of the lease. In addition to minimum fixed rentals, most leases provide for contingent rentals based upon a portion of sales.

Minimum rental commitments at August 31, 2010, under all leases having an initial or remaining noncancelable term of more than one year are shown below *(In millions)*:

	Capital Lease	Operating Lease
2011	$ 8	$ 2,301
2012	7	2,329
2013	6	2,296
2014	7	2,248
2015	6	2,188
Later	89	25,428
Total minimum lease payments	$ 123	$ 36,790

WALGREEN CO. INFORMATION FROM CONSOLIDATED STATEMENTS OF EARNINGS
For the Years Ended August 31, 2010 and 2009
(in millions)

	2010	2009
Sales	$67,420	$63,335
Net income	$ 2,091	$ 2,006

Required:

1. Using the Consolidated Balance Sheets for Walgreen Co. for August 31, 2010 and 2009, prepare a common-size balance sheet.
2. Which current asset is the most significant? Which noncurrent asset is the most significant? Are the relative proportions of current and noncurrent assets what you would expect for a drug store?
3. What inventory method is used to value inventories? Has Walgreen experienced inflation or deflation? Explain your answer.
4. Assess the level of debt and risk that Walgreen has by looking only at the balance sheet.
5. Estimate the dollar amount of dividends Walgreen paid in 2010.
6. Does Walgreen use off–balance sheet financing? Explain your answer.
7. Evaluate the creditworthiness of Walgreen based on the balance sheet and the excerpts from the notes.

CHAPTER 3

Income Statement and Statement of Stockholders' Equity

Learning about earnings, the bottom line,
Is very important most of the time.
A phony number
Just may encumber
Those folks trying to make more than a dime.

—A. ORMISTON

The operating performance of a business firm has traditionally been measured by its success in generating earnings—the "bottom line." Investors, creditors, and analysts eagerly await companies' earnings reports. One objective of this book is to broaden the reader's perspective of operating success to consider such yardsticks as "cash flow from operations" as well as net income. In this chapter, however, the focus will be on the income statement and how a company arrives at its "bottom line." Appendix 3A presents examples of ways in which companies manipulate their "bottom line" and what readers can look for to detect and adjust for these strategies.

The *income statement,* also called the *statement of earnings,* presents revenues, expenses, net income, and earnings per share for an accounting period, generally a year or a quarter. (The terms *income, earnings,* and *profit* are used interchangeably throughout the book.) The statement of stockholders' equity is an important link between the balance sheet and the income statement. This statement documents the changes in the balance sheet equity accounts from one accounting period to the next. Companies may choose to report the information on the statement of stockholders' equity in a supplementary schedule or in a note to the financial statements rather than preparing a formal financial statement. Annual reports include three years of income statements and stockholders' equity information.

Sage Inc. prepares a formal statement of stockholders' equity. Both the income statement and statement of stockholders' equity will be discussed in this chapter using the Sage Inc. statements as the basis for a description of each statement and the accounts that typically appear in the statements.

The Income Statement

Regardless of the perspective of the financial statement user—investor, creditor, employee, competitor, supplier, regulator—it is essential to understand and analyze the earnings statement. But it is also important that the analyst realize that a company's report of earnings and other information presented on the income statement are not complete and sufficient barometers of financial performance. The income statement is one of many pieces of a financial statement package, and, like the other pieces, the income statement is partially the product of a wide range of accounting choices, estimates, and judgments that affect reported results, just as business policies, economic conditions, and many other variables affect results.

It has previously been explained that earnings are measured on an accrual rather than a cash basis, which means that income reported on the income statement is not the same as cash generated during the accounting period. Cash flow from operations and its importance to analysis are covered in Chapter 4. The purpose of this chapter is not to minimize the importance of the income statement, however, but to provide a clear context for its interpretation.

The income statement comes in two basic formats and with considerable variation in the degree of detail presented. The earnings statement for Sage Inc. is presented in a *multiple-step* format, which provides several intermediate profit measures—gross profit, operating profit, and earnings before income tax—prior to the amount of net earnings for the period. (See Exhibit 3.1.) The *single-step* version of the income statement groups all items of revenue together, then deducts all categories of expense to arrive at a figure for net income. Exhibit 3.2 illustrates the single-step approach if Sage Inc. used that method to report earnings. For purposes of analysis, the multiple-step format should be used. If a company presents income statement information in single-step or a modified multiple-step format, the user of the financial statements should redo the income statement in multiple-step format before beginning an analysis.

Certain special items, if they occur during an accounting period, must be disclosed separately on an income statement, regardless of format. These include *discontinued operations* and *extraordinary transactions* discussed later in this chapter.

As noted in Chapter 2, most companies report *comprehensive income.* Comprehensive income is the change in equity of a company during a period from transactions, other events, and circumstances relating to nonowner sources. It includes all changes in equity during a period except those resulting from investments by owners and distributions to owners. Companies are required to report total comprehensive income in one of three ways:

- on the face of its income statement,
- in a separate statement of comprehensive income, or
- in its statement of stockholders' equity.

Data are presented in corporate income statements for three years to facilitate comparison and to provide evidence regarding trends of revenues, expenses, and net earnings. Because Sage Inc. has only net earnings and no other comprehensive income,

EXHIBIT 3.1 Sage Inc. Consolidated Statements of Earnings for the Years Ended December 31, 2013, 2012, and 2011 (in Thousands Except per Share Amounts)

	2013	2012	2011
Net sales	$215,600	$153,000	$140,700
Cost of goods sold	129,364	91,879	81,606
Gross profit	86,236	61,121	59,094
Selling and administrative expenses	45,722	33,493	32,765
Advertising	14,258	10,792	9,541
Depreciation and amortization	3,998	2,984	2,501
Impairment charges	3,015	2,046	3,031
Operating profit	19,243	11,806	11,256
Other income (expense)			
Interest income	422	838	738
Interest expense	(2,585)	(2,277)	(1,274)
Earnings before income taxes	17,080	10,367	10,720
Provision for income taxes	7,686	4,457	4,824
Net earnings	$ 9,394	$ 5,910	$ 5,896
Earnings per common share:			
Basic	$ 2.16	$ 1.36	$ 1.36
Diluted	$ 2.12	$ 1.33	$ 1.33
Weighted average common shares outstanding:			
Basic	4,359	4,350	4,342
Diluted	4,429	4,442	4,431

The accompanying notes are an integral part of these statements.

EXHIBIT 3.2 Sage Inc. Consolidated Statements of Earnings for Years Ended December 31, 2013, 2012, and 2011 (in Thousands Except per Share Amounts)

	2013	2012	2011
Income			
Net sales	$215,600	$153,000	$140,700
Interest income	422	838	738
	216,022	153,838	141,438
Costs and Expenses			
Cost of goods sold	129,364	91,879	81,606
Marketing, administrative, and other expenses	66,993	49,315	47,838
Interest expense	2,585	2,277	1,274
Income taxes	7,686	4,457	4,824
Net Earnings	$ 9,394	$ 5,910	$ 5,896
Basic Earnings per Common Share	$ 2.16	$ 1.36	$ 1.36
Diluted Earnings per Common Share	$ 2.12	$ 1.33	$ 1.33

the company does not have a statement of comprehensive income. The statements for Sage Inc. are consolidated, which means that the information presented is a combination of the results for Sage Inc. and its wholly owned subsidiaries. The disclosure of comprehensive income and the accounting methods used for subsidiary investments will be discussed later in the chapter under the headings "Comprehensive Income" and "Equity Earnings."

Common-Size Income Statement

As discussed in Chapter 2, common-size financial statements are a useful analytical tool to compare firms with different levels of sales or total assets, facilitate internal or structural analysis of a firm, evaluate trends, and make industry comparisons. The common-size income statement expresses each income statement item as a percentage of net sales. The common-size income statement shows the relative magnitude of various expenses relative to sales, the profit percentages (gross profit, operating profit, and net profit margins), and the relative importance of "other" revenues and expenses. Exhibit 3.3 presents the common-size income statement for Sage Inc. that will be used in this chapter and Chapter 5 to analyze the firm's profitability.

Net Sales

Total sales revenue for each year of the three-year period is shown net of returns and allowances. A *sales return* is a cancellation of a sale, and a *sales allowance* is a deduction from the original sales invoice price. Sales are the major revenue source for most companies; therefore, the trend of this figure is a key element in performance measurement. Although most of the analysis of Sage Inc.'s financial statements will be conducted in Chapter 5, the reader can look for clues on the income statement.

EXHIBIT 3.3 Sage Inc. Common-Size Income Statements (Percent)

	2013	2012	2011	2010	2009
Net Sales	100.0	100.0	100.0	100.0	100.0
Cost of Goods Sold	60.0	60.1	58.0	58.2	58.2
Gross Profit	40.0	39.9	42.0	41.8	41.8
Operating Expenses					
Selling and administrative expenses	21.2	21.8	23.2	20.3	20.0
Advertising	6.6	7.1	6.8	6.4	6.3
Depreciation and amortization	1.9	2.0	1.8	1.4	1.2
Impairment Charges	1.4	1.3	2.2	2.7	2.7
Operating Profit	8.9	7.7	8.0	11.0	11.6
Other Income (Expense)					
Interest income	0.2	0.5	0.5	0.3	0.3
Interest expense	(1.2)	(1.5)	(0.9)	(0.9)	(1.0)
Earnings before income taxes	7.9	6.7	7.6	10.4	10.9
Provision for income taxes	3.6	2.9	3.4	5.4	5.7
Net Earnings	4.3	3.8	4.2	5.0	5.2

It would appear, for instance, that Sage Inc. had a much better sales year in 2013 than 2012: Sales increased 40.9% ($62.6 million) between 2012 and 2013, compared with an 8.7% ($12.3 million) growth between 2011 and 2012. If a company's sales are increasing (or decreasing), it is important to determine whether the change is a result of price, volume, or a combination of both. Are sales growing because the firm is increasing prices or because more units are being sold, or both? It would seem that, in general, higher-quality earnings would be the product of both volume and price increases (during inflation). The firm would want to sell more units and keep prices increasing at least in line with the rate of inflation. The reasons for sales growth (or decline) are covered in a firm's Management Discussion and Analysis section of the annual or 10-K report (see Chapter 1).

A related issue is whether sales are growing in "real" (inflation-adjusted) as well as "nominal" (as reported) terms. The change in sales in nominal terms can be readily calculated from the figures reported on the income statement. An adjustment of the reported sales figure with the Consumer Price Index (CPI) (or some other measure of general inflation) will enable the analyst to make a comparison of the changes in real and nominal terms. To make the calculation to compare real with nominal sales, begin with the sales figures reported in the income statement, and adjust years prior to the current year with the CPI or some other price index. For Sage Inc., the nominal growth rate was already calculated to be 40.9%. Assuming the CPIs for 2013 and 2012 are 207.3 and 201.6, respectively, the adjusted or real sales figure for 2012 is $157,326, (207.3/201.6) × $153,000. Sales when adjusted for inflation still increased 37.0% from 2012 to 2013, but at a smaller rate. Note 1 (see Appendix 1A) to the Sage Inc. financial statements indicates that new store openings have occurred that could explain the large sales growth in the past year.

The remainder of the income statement reveals management's ability to translate sales dollars into profits. The sales or revenue number is the common denominator in the common-size income statement (Exhibit 3.3) and is, therefore, 100% for all companies when preparing this statement. The calculations are shown for other important items on the common-size income statement as they are discussed in this chapter.

Cost of Goods Sold

The first expense deduction from sales is the cost to the seller of products or services sold to customers. This expense is called *cost of goods sold* or *cost of sales.* The amount of cost of goods sold for any accounting period, as explained in Chapter 2, will be affected by the cost flow assumption used to value inventory. Sage Inc. uses the last-in, first-out (LIFO) method, which means that the last purchases made during the year have been charged to expense. The LIFO method generally results in the matching of current costs with current revenues and therefore produces higher-quality earnings than either first-in, first-out (FIFO) or average cost.

The relationship between cost of goods sold and net sales—called the *cost of goods sold percentage*—is an important one for profit determination because cost of goods sold is the largest expense item for many firms.

	2013	2012	2011
$\frac{\text{Cost of goods sold}}{\text{Net sales}}$	$\frac{129{,}364}{215{,}600} = 60.0\%$	$\frac{91{,}879}{153{,}000} = 60.1\%$	$\frac{81{,}606}{140{,}700} = 58.0\%$

The cost of goods sold percentage for Sage Inc. increased between 2011 and 2012. This is a result of the firm lowering prices or increasing costs. The MD&A for Sage Inc. (see Appendix 1A, page 41) explains that lower prices on athletic footwear have resulted in lower margins. See Figure 3.1 for a more detailed explanation. Since then, the firm either has controlled costs more effectively and/or has been able to pass along price increases to customers. The cost of goods sold percentage will vary significantly by industry, according to markup policies and other factors. For example, the cost of goods sold percentage for jewelry retailers averages 57.3%, compared with 73.4% for retailers of groceries.[1]

Gross Profit

The difference between net sales and cost of goods sold is called *gross profit* or *gross margin.* Gross profit is the first step of profit measurement on the multiple-step income statement and is a key analytical tool in assessing a firm's operating performance. The gross profit figure indicates how much profit the firm is generating after deducting the cost of products or services sold. Gross profit, expressed as a percentage of net sales, is the gross profit margin.

	2013	2012	2011
$\frac{\text{Gross profit}}{\text{Net sales}}$	$\frac{86{,}236}{215{,}600} = 40.0\%$	$\frac{61{,}121}{153{,}000} = 39.9\%$	$\frac{59{,}094}{140{,}700} = 42.0\%$

FIGURE 3.1 Understand the Math!

If the cost of goods sold (COGS) percentage increases or decreases, this does not necessarily mean that costs have increased or decreased. The change in the percentage may be caused by decreases or increases in the selling price. Here's an example:

Assume it costs a company $4 to make a toy that sells for $10 in year 1. In year 2, competition is fierce, and the company must drop the selling price to $8 to sell the toy.

	Year 1		Year 2	
Sales	$10	100%	$8	100%
COGS	4	40%	4	50%
Gross Profit	$ 6	60%	$4	50%

Notice that the COGS percentage has increased, but the cost to manufacture the toy has not. The decrease in selling price is the cause of the higher COGS percentage and lower gross profit margin.

Always pay attention to the numbers—know the difference between raw dollars and percentages!

[1]The Risk Management Association, *Annual Statement Studies,* Philadelphia, PA, 2010.

"We found the accounting error. Somebody printed all the zeroes upside down."

The gross profit margin and cost of goods sold percentage are complements of each other (the two percentages always add to 100%); therefore, the analysis of these ratios will be the same. Generally, firms want to maintain the relationship between gross profit and sales, or, if possible, increase gross profit margin. In stable industries, such as groceries, one can expect to find the same gross profit margin from year to year because companies will raise prices proportionately as cost of goods sold increases. In volatile industries such as high technology, gross profit margin may increase or decrease significantly from year to year. For example, Target Corporation's gross profit margin for 2008, 2009, and 2010 was 30% whereas Applied Materials Inc. had a 42.4%, 28.5%, and 38.9% gross profit margin, respectively, in the same three years. In capital intensive industries such as manufacturing, sales volume changes will cause volatility in the gross profit margin because there are fixed costs included in cost of goods sold. Fixed costs do not vary proportionately with volume changes but remain the same within a relevant range of activity.

Companies having more than one revenue source will show each revenue line separately and also show the corresponding cost of goods sold or cost of sales for each revenue source. An illustration of how to calculate and analyze gross profit margin when there are multiple revenue sources is shown in Figure 3.2.

FIGURE 3.2 Gross Profit Margin for Multiple Revenue Sources

ABC Company has two distinct revenue sources, food and tobacco. The following information is from ABC Company's income statement:

	2013	%	2012	%
Food sales	$ 800		$ 750	
Tobacco sales	900		900	
Total sales	$1,700	100.0	$1,650	100.0
Cost of goods sold—food	$ 560		$ 525	
Cost of goods sold—tobacco	450		360	
Total cost of goods sold	$1,010	59.4	$ 885	53.6
Gross profit	$ 690	40.6	$ 765	46.4

To analyze the overall gross profit margin change from 46.4% to 40.6%, the gross profit margins of each revenue source should be calculated as follows:

	2013	%	2012	%
Food sales	$800	100.0	$750	100.0
Less: Cost of goods sold—food	(560)	70.0	(525)	70.0
Gross profit—food	$240	30.0	$225	30.0
Tobacco sales	$900	100.0	$900	100.0
Less: Cost of goods sold—tobacco	(450)	50.0	(360)	40.0
Gross profit—tobacco	$450	50.0	$540	60.0

The overall decline in gross profit margin has been caused by the tobacco product line, not the food product line. By analyzing each revenue source individually, the analyst can better understand which divisions of a company are successful and which may be facing challenges.

Operating Expense

Sage Inc. discloses four categories of operating expense: selling and administrative, advertising, depreciation and amortization, and impairment charges. In addition, details of advertising expense, repairs and maintenance expense, and operating lease payments (rent expense) are disclosed in Notes 1 and 3. These are all areas over which management exercises discretion and that have considerable impact on the firm's current and future profitability. Thus, it is important to track these accounts carefully in terms of trends, absolute amounts, relationship to sales, and relationship to industry competitors.

Selling and administrative expenses are expenses relating to the sale of products or services and to the management of the business. They include salaries, rent, insurance, utilities, supplies, and sometimes depreciation and advertising expense. Sage Inc. provides separate disclosures for advertising and for depreciation and amortization. Note 1 to the Sage Inc. financial statements indicates that the firm includes the expenses related to the opening of new stores in selling and administrative expense.

Advertising costs are or should be a major expense in the budgets of companies for which marketing is an important element of success. This topic was discussed in Chapter 1. As a retail firm operating in a competitive industry, sporting apparel and equipment, Sage Inc. spends 6 to 7 cents of every sales dollar for advertising, as indicated by the ratio of advertising to net sales:

	2013	**2012**	**2011**
Advertising / Net sales	14,258 / 215,600 = 6.6%	10,792 / 153,000 = 7.1%	9,541 / 140,700 = 6.8%

Lease payments include the costs associated with operating rentals of leased facilities for retail outlets. Note 3 to the financial statements explains the agreements that apply to the rental arrangements and presents a schedule of minimum annual rental commitments. Observation of the sharp rise in lease payments for Sage Inc. between 2012 and 2013, from $7.1 million to $13.1 million—an increase of 84%—would indicate an expansion of the firm's use of leased space.

Depreciation and amortization represent the cost of assets other than land that will benefit a business enterprise for more than a year is allocated over the asset's service life rather than expensed in the year of purchase. Land is an exception to the rule because land is considered to have an unlimited useful life. The cost allocation procedure is determined by the nature of the long-lived asset. *Depreciation* is used to allocate the cost of tangible fixed assets such as buildings, machinery, equipment, furniture and fixtures, and motor vehicles. *Amortization* is the process applied to capital leases, leasehold improvements, and the cost expiration of intangible assets such as patents, copyrights, trademarks, and franchises. The cost of acquiring and developing natural resources—oil and gas, other minerals, and standing timber—is allocated through *depletion.* The amount of expense recognized in any accounting period will depend on the level of investment in the relevant asset; estimates with regard to the asset's service life and residual value; and for depreciation, the method used.

Sage Inc. recognizes annual depreciation expense for the firm's buildings and equipment and amortization expense for the leasehold improvements on rental property. Note 1 to the Sage Inc. financial statements explains the company's procedures relating to depreciation and amortization: "Property, plant, and equipment is stated at cost. Depreciation expense is calculated principally by the straight-line method based on estimated useful lives of 3 to 10 years for equipment, 3 to 30 years for leasehold improvements, and 40 years for buildings. Estimated useful lives of leasehold improvements represent the remaining term of the lease in effect at the time the improvements are made."

With any expense on the income statement, the analyst should evaluate the amount and trend of the expenditure as well as its relationship to the volume of firm activity that is relevant to the expense. For a firm like Sage Inc., one would expect a fairly constant relationship between the investment in buildings, leasehold improvements, and equipment on the balance sheet and the annual expense recorded for depreciation and amortization on the income statement.

	2013	**2012**
Depreciation and amortization / Buildings, leasehold improvements, equipment	3,998 / 39,796 = 10.0%	2,984 / 25,696 = 11.6%

The percentage of depreciation and amortization expense has decreased somewhat, possibly due to the fact that new assets were placed in service during 2013 for only a part of the year, rendering less than a full year's depreciation and amortization.

Repairs and maintenance are the annual costs of repairing and maintaining the firm's property, plant, and equipment. Sage Inc. includes amounts for repairs and maintenance in Note 1 under Selling and Administrative Expenses. Expenditures in this area should correspond to the level of investment in capital equipment and to the age and condition of the company's fixed assets. Similar to research and development and advertising and marketing expenses, inadequate allowance for repair and maintenance can impair the ongoing success of an organization. This category, like depreciation, should be evaluated in relation to the firm's investments in fixed assets. The percentage decrease in this account for Sage Inc. could be a result of having newer fixed assets needing fewer repairs, or it could be a choice to delay repairs in order to increase operating profit in the short-term.

	2013	**2012**
$\frac{\text{Repairs and maintenance}}{\text{Buildings, leasehold improvements, equipment}}$	$\frac{2{,}946}{39{,}796} = 7.4\%$	$\frac{2{,}184}{25{,}696} = 8.5\%$

Firms in industries other than retail will have different expenses that should also be evaluated. For example, the trend of research and development expenses relative to net sales is an important measurement to evaluate for high-technology and pharmaceutical companies. By preparing a common-size income statement, each operating expense can be easily analyzed for any company. When evaluating operating expenses, good judgment must be used to decide whether increases or decreases in expenses are warranted. For example, reducing advertising or research and development may be detrimental in the long term if sales decrease; however, unnecessary increases in operating expense accounts could indicate inefficiencies in the company's operations.

Impairment charges are the expenses recognized to record a decline in value of a long-term asset. As discussed in Chapter 2, impairment charges may occur in connection with goodwill but can also be recognized when asset values of property, plant, and equipment decrease below book value. According to Note 1 of the Sage Inc. financial statements, impairment charges have been recorded each year as a result of store relocations and store closings.

Operating Profit

Operating profit (also called *EBIT* or *earnings before interest and taxes*) is the second step of profit determination on the Sage Inc. earnings statement and measures the overall performance of the company's operations: sales revenue less the expenses associated with generating sales. The figure for operating profit provides a basis for assessing the success of a company apart from its financing and investing activities and separate from tax considerations. The *operating profit margin* is calculated as the relationship between operating profit and net sales:

	2013	2012	2011
$\frac{\text{Operating profit}}{\text{Net sales}}$	$\frac{19{,}243}{215{,}600} = 8.9\%$	$\frac{11{,}806}{153{,}000} = 7.7\%$	$\frac{11{,}256}{140{,}700} = 8.0\%$

The ratio indicates that Sage Inc. strengthened its return on operations in 2013 after a dip in 2012. Looking at the common-size income statement (Exhibit 3.3), it is easy to see that despite the percentage increase in cost of goods sold over the past two years, Sage Inc. has reduced the percentage of selling and administrative and advertising expenses enough to increase operating profit. It should be noted that even though the percentages have decreased, the dollar amounts of selling and administrative and advertising expenses have actually increased. This mathematical anomaly is a result of the common denominator, net sales, increasing 40.9% between 2012 and 2013. The MD&A discusses the reasons for the increases in dollars. Expenses related to the e-commerce operations first appear in 2013; higher costs of new store openings have been offset by lower payroll costs associated with cost-cutting efforts and closing of underperforming stores. Sage Inc. has chosen to increase advertising dollars all three years and the increased amounts are being used to promote the firm's new e-commerce unit.

Other Income (Expense)

This category includes revenues and costs other than from operations, such as dividend and interest income, interest expense, gains (losses) from investments, equity earnings (losses), and gains (losses) from the sale of fixed assets. Equity earnings (losses) are discussed in the next section. Sage Inc. recognizes as other income the interest earned on its investments in cash equivalents and as other expense the interest paid on its debt. The relative amounts will be dependent on the level of investments and the amount of debt outstanding, as well as the prevailing level of interest rates.

Firms (primarily financial institutions and insurance companies) that carry debt and equity securities classified as "trading securities" report these investments on the balance sheet at market value with any unrealized gains and losses included in earnings.

In the assessment of earnings quality (discussed in Appendix 3A), it is important that the analyst consider the materiality and the variability of the nonoperating items of income—for example, gains and losses on the sale of major capital assets, accounting changes, extraordinary items, investment income from temporary investments in cash equivalents, and investment income recognized under the equity method.

Equity Earnings

An additional issue that users sometimes encounter in attempting to evaluate financial statement data is the method—cost or equity—employed to account for investments in the voting stock of other companies. This method is not an issue for Sage Inc. because the parent owns 100% of the voting stock in its subsidiaries; Sage Inc. and its subsidiaries are, in substance, one consolidated entity. Where one firm owns more than 50% of the voting stock of another company, the parent company can obviously control the business operations, financial policies, and dividend declarations of the subsidiary, and consolidated financial statements are prepared with the disclosures relating to consolidation policies provided in the financial statement notes. The accounting rules underlying the preparation of consolidated financial statements, though similar to the equity method, are extremely complicated and beyond the scope of this book.[2] Questions regarding use of cost or equity come into play for stock investments of less than 50%, where consolidated financial statements are not prepared.

Accounting rules permit two different methods to account for stock investments of less than 50%. The equity method allows the investor proportionate recognition of the investee's net income, irrespective of the payment or nonpayment of cash dividends; under the cost method, the investor recognizes investment income only to the extent of any cash dividends received. At issue in the choice of accounting methods is whether the investor exercises control over the investee.

The equity method of accounting should be used when the investor can exercise significant influence over the investee's operating and financing policies. No problem exists where there is ownership of 50% or more because, clearly, one company can control the other. But at what level below 50% ownership can one firm substantially influence the affairs of another firm? Although there can be exceptions, 20% ownership of voting stock is generally considered to be evidence of substantial influence. There are, however, circumstances in which less than 20% ownership reflects control and cases in which more than 20% does not. Such factors as the extent of representation on the

[2]Accounting for consolidated financial statements is fully discussed and explained in advanced accounting textbooks.

investee's board of directors, major intercompany transactions, technological dependence, and other relationships would be considered in the determination.

Use of the equity method is justified on a theoretical basis because it fits the requirements of the accrual basis of accounting. The investor's share in investee income is recorded by the investor in the period in which it is earned, rather than as cash is received. Analysts, however, should be aware of whether a company uses the cost or the equity method. What difference does it make whether a company uses the cost or equity method? An illustration should help provide the answer.

Assume that Company A acquires exactly 20% of the voting common stock of Company B for $400,000. Company B reports $100,000 earnings for the year and pays $25,000 in cash dividends. For Company A, the income recognition in the earnings statement and the noncurrent investment account on the balance sheet would be entirely different depending on the accounting method used for the investment.

	Cost	**Equity**
Income statement: investment income	$ 5,000	$ 20,000
Balance sheet: investment account	$400,000	$415,000

The cost method allows recognition of investment income only to the extent of any cash dividends actually received ($25,000 × 0.20), and the investment account is carried at cost.[3] The equity method permits the investor to count as income the percentage interest in the investee's earnings.

Company B's earnings	$100,000
Company A's percent ownership	×0.20
Company A's investment income	$ 20,000

Under the equity method, the investment account is increased by the amount of investment income recognized and is reduced by the amount of cash dividends received.

Investment at cost	$400,000
Investment income	+20,000
Cash dividends received	−5,000
Investment account	$415,000

Use of the equity method somewhat distorts earnings in the sense that income is recognized even though no cash may ever be received. The theoretical justification for the equity method is that it is presumed that the investor (Company A), through its control of voting shares, could cause Company B to pay dividends. In reality, this may not be true, and Company A is permitted to recognize more income than is received in cash.

One adjustment to net income (illustrated in Chapter 4) to calculate cash flow from operations is to deduct the amount by which income recognized under the equity

[3]Or market, depending on the provisions of the FASB rules that relate to this area; this statement does not apply to investments accounted for under the equity method.

method of accounting exceeds cash received from dividends. For Company A this amount would be $15,000 (investment income $20,000 less cash dividends $5,000). It is also equal to the increase in the balance sheet investment account (ending balance $415,000 less original cost $400,000). For comparative purposes it would be appropriate to eliminate this noncash portion of earnings.

Earnings Before Income Taxes/Effective Tax Rate

Earnings before income taxes is the profit recognized before the deduction of income tax expense. Income taxes are discussed in notes to the financial statements describing the difference between the reported figure for income taxes and the actual amount of income taxes paid (see the discussion of deferred income taxes in Chapter 2). For Sage Inc., refer to Note 4, which explains why the differences occur and which quantifies the reconciliation between taxes paid and tax expense reported on the income statement. Sage Inc.'s *effective tax rate* would be calculated by dividing income taxes on the income statement by earnings before taxes.

	2013	2012	2011
$\frac{\text{Income taxes}}{\text{Earnings before income taxes}}$	$\frac{7{,}686}{17{,}080} = 45.0\%$	$\frac{4{,}457}{10{,}367} = 43.0\%$	$\frac{4{,}824}{10{,}720} = 45.0\%$

In recent years, as revenues have been sluggish or decreasing, some companies have resorted to techniques to reduce taxes in order to increase earnings. Legitimately cutting taxes should always be applauded; however, firms cannot rely on tax-cutting techniques to continually increase earnings. Users of financial statements need to distinguish between earnings increasing due to core operations versus items such as tax rate deductions. (See Appendix 3A for more on this topic.)

Noteworthy items that may affect the effective tax rate are net operating losses (NOLs) and foreign taxes. Companies operating at a loss are allowed to carry back the loss two years and/or carry forward the loss 20 years, offsetting prior or future tax payments. If the NOL is carried back, the company may receive a refund of taxes previously paid.

Companies often have operations in foreign countries and must pay taxes based on that country's tax law. By reading the notes to the financial statements, the user can determine the effect foreign taxes have on the overall effective tax rate. General Electric Company (GE) reported growth in earnings before income taxes from 2009 to 2010 of 42%, yet its provision for income taxes declined from 11.5% to a tax benefit of 7.4%. GE has one of the lowest effective tax rates in the United States (the U.S. federal statutory income tax rate for corporations was 35% in 2010). How has GE accomplished this? GE primarily was able to reduce its statutory tax rate through lower foreign tax rates.

Special Items

If companies are affected by the following two items, they must be disclosed separately on the income statement, net of income tax effects:

- Discontinued operations
- Extraordinary items

Special items are often one-time items that will not recur in the future. Because of the special disclosure requirements, it is easier for the analyst to determine whether these items should be included when predicting future earnings amounts. Sage Inc. is not affected by any special items; however, each item will be explained in this chapter and examples are discussed further in Appendix 3A.

Discontinued operations occur when a firm sells or discontinues a clearly distinguishable portion of its business. The results of continuing operations are shown separately from the operating results of the discontinued portion of the business. Any gain or loss on the disposal is also disclosed separately.

Extraordinary gains and losses are items that meet two criteria: unusual in nature and not expected to recur in the foreseeable future, considering the firm's operating environment. In an interesting decision in 2001, the FASB declared that the terrorist attack on September 11 was not an extraordinary event. Although the FASB agreed that in layman's terminology the event was extraordinary, it concluded that recording revenues or expenses related to September 11 as extraordinary would not improve the financial reporting system. The FASB's task force realized the dilemma as it tried to apply extraordinary treatment to the airline industry. Separating losses caused by the attack from losses already incurred by the economic downturn was an impossible task.[4]

Net Earnings

Net earnings, or "the bottom line," represents the firm's profit after consideration of all revenue and expense reported during the accounting period. The *net profit margin* shows the percentage of profit earned on every sales dollar.

	2013	2012	2011
$\frac{\text{Net earnings}}{\text{Net sales}}$	$\frac{9{,}394}{215{,}600} = 4.4\%$	$\frac{5{,}910}{153{,}000} = 3.9\%$	$\frac{5{,}896}{140{,}700} = 4.2\%$

Earnings per Common Share

Earnings per common share is the net earnings available to common stockholders for the period divided by the average number of common stock shares outstanding. This figure shows the return to the common stock shareholder for every share owned. Sage Inc. earned $2.16 per share in 2013, compared with $1.36 per share in 2012 and 2011.

Companies with complex capital structures—which means existence of convertible securities (such as bonds convertible into common stock), stock options, and warrants—must calculate two amounts for earnings per share: *basic* and *diluted.* If convertible securities were converted into common stock and/or the options and warrants were exercised, there would be more shares outstanding for every dollar earned, and the potential for dilution is accounted for by the dual presentation. Sage Inc. has a complex capital structure and therefore presents both basic and diluted earnings per share. The diluted earnings per share number is slightly lower each year compared to the basic earnings per share because of the dilutive effect of stock options that employees could exercise in the future.

---

[4]Steve Liesman, "Accountants, in a Reversal, Say Costs from the Attack Aren't 'Extraordinary,'" *Wall Street Journal,* October 1, 2001.

Another issue that an analyst should consider in assessing earnings quality is any material changes in the number of common stock shares outstanding that will cause a change in the computation of earnings per share. Changes in the number of shares outstanding result from such transactions as treasury stock purchases, the purchase and retirement of a firm's own common stock, stock splits, and reverse stock splits. (Stock splits and reverse stock splits are explained in a later section of this chapter.)

Comprehensive Income

As discussed in Chapter 2 and earlier in this chapter, companies must now report total comprehensive income either on the face of the income statement, in the statement of stockholders' equity, or in a separate financial statement. For example, even though Applied Materials Inc. chooses to report total comprehensive income in the statement of shareholders' equity, if a separate statement had been used, it would appear as illustrated in Exhibit 3.4.

Currently, there are four items that may comprise a company's other comprehensive income: *foreign currency translation effects, unrealized gains and losses, additional pension liabilities,* and *cash flow hedges.* These items are outlined below; however, a detailed discussion of these topics is beyond the scope of this text. A more complete discussion of these four areas can be found in most intermediate or advanced accounting textbooks.

Foreign currency translation effects arise from changes in the equity of foreign subsidiaries (as measured in U.S. dollars) that occur as a result of changes in foreign currency exchange rates. When U.S. firms operate abroad, the foreign financial statements must be translated into U.S. dollars at the end of the accounting period. Because the value of the dollar changes in relation to foreign currencies, gains and losses can result from the translation process. These exchange gains and losses, which fluctuate from period to period, are "accumulated" in the stockholders' equity section in most cases.[5]

EXHIBIT 3.4 Applied Materials Inc. Statements of Comprehensive Income for the Years Ended October 30, 2008, October 29, 2009, and October 28, 2010 (in thousands)

	2008	2009	2010
Net income	$960,746	$(305,327)	$937,866
Components of comprehensive income (expense)			
Change in unrealized net gain (loss) on investments	(41,739)	44,956	4,410
Change in unrealized net gain on derivative investments	9,448	(7,729)	4,000
Change in defined benefit plan	(7,440)	(12,492)	(6,698)
Change in medical retiree benefit	1,866	(719)	(284)
Translation adjustments	(58)	874	1,918
Total comprehensive income (loss)	$922,823	$(280,437)	$941,212

[5]Exceptions are when the U.S. company designates the U.S. dollar as the "functional" currency for the foreign entity—such is the case, for example, when the foreign operations are simply an extension of the parent company's operations. Under this circumstance, the foreign translation gains and losses are included in the calculation of net income on the income statement.

Unrealized gains and losses on investments in debt and equity securities classified as available-for-sale are reported in comprehensive income. Cumulative net unrealized gains and losses are reported in the accumulated other comprehensive income section of stockholders' equity on the balance sheet.

Additional pension liabilities are reported as other comprehensive income when the accumulated benefit obligation is greater than the fair market value of plan assets less the balance in the accrued pension liability account or plus the balance in the deferred pension asset account.

Companies using *cash flow hedges* (derivatives designated as hedging the exposure to variable cash flows of a forecasted transaction) are required to initially report any gain or loss from a change in the fair market value of the cash flow hedge in other comprehensive income and subsequently reclassify the amount into earnings when the forecasted transaction affects earnings.[6]

The Statement of Stockholders' Equity

The statement of stockholders' equity details the transactions that affect the balance sheet equity accounts during an accounting period. Exhibit 3.5 shows the changes that have occurred in the equity accounts of Sage Inc. Changes to the common stock and additional paid-in capital accounts are due to employees exercising their stock options. The retained earnings account has been increased each year by the net earnings and reduced by the cash dividends that Sage Inc. has paid to their common stockholders. (Sage Inc.'s dividend payment policy is discussed in Chapter 5.)

In 2013, Sage Inc. paid cash dividends of $0.36 per share for a total of $1,582 thousand. The amount of the dividend payment was reduced from $0.43 and $0.42 per share in 2012 and 2011.

Some companies have *stock dividends, stock splits,* or *reverse stock splits* during an accounting period. With stock dividends, the company issues to existing shareholders additional shares of stock in proportion to current ownership. Stock dividends reduce the retained earnings account. Unlike a cash dividend, which results in the receipt of cash, a stock dividend represents nothing of value to the stockholder. The stockholder has more shares, but the proportion of ownership is exactly the same, and the company's net assets (assets minus liabilities) are exactly the same. The market value of the stock should drop in proportion to the additional shares issued.

Stock splits also result in the issuance of additional shares in proportion to current ownership and represent nothing of value to the stockholder; they are generally used to lower the market price of a firm's shares to make the common stock more affordable for the average investor. For example, if a company declares a 2–1 stock split, a stockholder with 100 shares ends up with 200 shares and the market price of

[6]FASB Statement of Financial Accounting Standards No. 133, "Accounting for Derivative Instruments and Hedging Activities," 1998.

EXHIBIT 3.5 Sage Inc. Consolidated Statements of Stockholders' Equity For the Years Ended December 31, 2013, 2012, and 2011 (in thousands)

	Common Stock and Additional Paid-in Capital			
	Shares	Amount	Retained Earnings	Total
Balance at December 31, 2010	4,340	$5,197	$24,260	$29,457
Net earnings			5,896	5,896
Proceeds from sale of shares from exercise of stock options, net of tax benefit	5	115		115
Stock-based compensation		9		9
Cash dividends			(1,841)	(1,841)
Balance at December 31, 2011	4,345	$5,321	$28,315	$33,636
Net earnings			5,910	5,910
Proceeds from sale of shares from exercise of stock options, net of tax benefit	10	176		176
Stock-based compensation		7		7
Cash dividends			(1,862)	(1,862)
Balance at December 31, 2012	4,355	$5,504	$32,363	$37,867
Net earnings			9,394	9,394
Proceeds from sale of shares from exercise of stock options, net of tax benefit	8	244		244
Stock-based compensation		12		12
Cash dividends			(1,582)	(1,582)
Balance at December 31, 2013	4,363	$5,760	$40,175	$45,935

the stock should fall by 50%. The company makes no accounting entry but does have a memorandum item noting the change in par value of the stock and the change in the number of shares outstanding. A reverse stock split is the opposite of a stock split and occurs when a company decreases, rather than increases, its outstanding shares. A 1–10 reverse stock split would have the effect of reducing 100 shares to 10 shares and the market price should increase 10 times. A reverse stock split usually occurs when a company is struggling financially.

Transactions other than the recognition of net profit/loss and the payment of dividends can cause changes in the retained earnings balance. These include prior period adjustments and certain changes in accounting principles. Prior period adjustments result primarily from the correction of errors made in previous accounting periods; the beginning retained earnings balance is adjusted for the year in which the error is discovered. Some changes in accounting principles, such as a change from LIFO to any other inventory method, also cause an adjustment to retained earnings for the cumulative effect of the change. Retained earnings can also be affected by transactions in a firm's own shares.

Earnings Quality, Cash Flow, and Segmental Accounting

Additional topics that are directly related to the income statement are covered in other sections of the book. The assessment of the quality of reported earnings is an essential element of income statement analysis. Many firms now report more than just the generally accepted accounting principles (GAAP) earnings numbers in their annual reports and quarterly press releases. These additional numbers are referred to as pro forma earnings, earnings before interest, taxes, depreciation, and amortization (EBITDA), core earnings, or adjusted earnings and have added not only to the confusion of investors, but have in many cases affected the quality of financial reporting. This important topic is discussed in Appendix 3A.

The earnings figure reported on the income statement is rarely the same as the cash generated during an accounting period. Because it is cash that a firm needs to service debt, pay suppliers, invest in new capital assets, and pay cash dividends, cash flow from operations is a key ingredient in analyzing operating performance. The calculation of cash flow from operations, how it differs from reported earnings, and the interpretation of cash flow as a performance measure are discussed in Chapter 4.

Appendix 5A deals with the supplementary information reported by companies that operate in several different business segments. Segmental data include revenue, operating profit or loss, assets, depreciation and amortization, and capital expenditures by industry components. These disclosures facilitate the analysis of operating performance and contribution by each segment of a diversified company.

"Another successful year, gentlemen. We broke even on operations and pulled a net profit on accounting procedures."

Cartoon Features Syndicate

Appendix 3A: A Guide to Earnings Quality

Qual-i-ty (n). Synonyms: excellence, superiority, class, eminence, value.

This appendix considers the *quality* of reported earnings, which is a critical element in evaluating financial statement data. The earnings statement encompasses a number of areas that provide management with opportunities for influencing the outcome of reported earnings in ways that may not best represent economic reality or the future operating potential of a firm. These include:

- Accounting choices, estimates, and judgments.
- Changes in accounting methods and assumptions.
- Discretionary expenditures.
- Nonrecurring transactions.
- Nonoperating gains and losses.
- Revenue and expense recognitions that do not match cash flow.

In evaluating a business firm, it is essential that the financial statement analyst consider the qualitative as well as the quantitative components of earnings for an accounting period. The higher the quality of financial reporting, the more useful is the information for business decision making. The analyst should develop an earnings figure that reflects the future ongoing potential of the firm. This process requires a consideration of qualitative factors and necessitates, in some cases, an actual adjustment of the reported earnings figure.

In addition to earnings quality, the quality of the information on the balance sheet (discussed in Chapter 2) and statement of cash flows (discussed in Chapter 4) is equally important. Because these financial statements are interrelated, quality of financial reporting issues often affects more than one financial statement.

The primary focus of this Appendix is to provide the financial statement user with a step-by-step guide that links the items on an earnings statement with the key areas in the financial statement data that affect earnings quality. Exhibit 3A.1 is a checklist for earnings quality.

The list does not, by any means, include every item that affects earnings quality. Rather, the examples illustrate some of the qualitative issues that are most commonly encountered in financial statement data. Another purpose of the Appendix is to provide the financial statement user with an approach to use in analyzing and interpreting the qualitative factors. The checklist represents an attempt to provide a framework for the analysis of earnings quality rather than a complete list of its components.

Although the examples in this book deal primarily with the financial reporting of wholesale, retail, and manufacturing firms, the concepts and techniques presented can also apply to other types of industries. For instance, there is a discussion in this

EXHIBIT 3A.1 A Checklist for Earnings Quality

I. Sales
   1. Premature revenue recognition
   2. Allowance for doubtful accounts
   3. Price versus volume changes
   4. Real versus nominal growth

II. Cost of Goods Sold
   5. Cost flow assumption for inventory
   6. Base LIFO layer liquidations
   7. Loss recognitions on write-downs of inventories (also see item 11)

III. Operating Expenses
   8. Discretionary expenses
   9. Depreciation
   10. Asset impairment
   11. Reserves
   12. In-process research and development

IV. Nonoperating Revenue and Expense
   13. Gains (losses) from sales of assets
   14. Interest income
   15. Equity income
   16. Income taxes
   17. Discontinued operations
   18. Extraordinary items

V. Other Issues
   19. Material changes in number of shares outstanding
   20. Operating earnings, a.k.a. core earnings, pro forma earnings, or EBITDA

Appendix of the provision for doubtful accounts as it affects earnings quality. The same principles, on a larger scale, would apply to the provision for loan loss reserves for financial institutions. Almost all of the items on the checklist—other than those directly related to cost of goods sold—would apply to most types of business firms, including service-oriented companies.

Using the Checklist

Each item on the checklist in Exhibit 3A.1 will be discussed and illustrated with examples from publicly held corporations.

I. Sales or Revenues

1. Premature Revenue Recognition

According to generally accepted accounting principles (GAAP), revenue should not be recognized until there is evidence that a true sale has taken place; that is, delivery of products has occurred or title to those products has passed to the buyer, or services have been rendered, the price has been determined, and collection is expected. Unfortunately, many firms have violated this accounting principle by recording revenue before these conditions have been met. While financial statement users cannot readily determine premature revenue recognition policy, they can look for certain clues in the financial statement information. An important place to start is the firm's revenue recognition policy, which is discussed in financial statement notes, to determine whether any changes have been made to the policy and if so, to evaluate the reason for the change and its impact. Analyzing the relationship among sales, accounts receivable, and inventory can signal red flags if these accounts are not moving in comparable patterns. Fourth-quarter spikes in revenue may also indicate premature revenue recognition for companies that do not typically experience high seasonal fourth-quarter sales.

Diebold Inc., manufacturer of automated teller machines, bank security systems, and voting machines, was charged on June 2, 2010, by the SEC for manipulating its earnings from at least 2002 through 2007 to meet financial forecasts. The SEC alleged that Diebold's financial management received reports, sometimes daily, that compared the company's actual earnings to the forecasts of analysts. The financial management of the firm created lists of ways to close any gaps between actual results and forecasts to include fraudulent accounting transactions to improperly recognize revenue. Diebold Inc. routinely used a technique referred to as "bill and hold" to recognize revenue prematurely. A "bill-and-hold" transaction allows a firm to record revenue on a sale before delivery of the product to a customer if the following criteria are met: (1) the buyer, not the seller, requests that the transaction be on a bill-and-hold basis; (2) the buyer has a substantial business purpose for ordering on a bill-and-hold basis; (3) there is a fixed delivery schedule that is reasonable and consistent with the buyer's business purpose; (4) the seller does not retain any specific performance obligations such that the earnings process is incomplete; and (5) the products are ready for shipment. Many bill-and-hold transactions recorded by Diebold Inc. did not meet these criteria. It was estimated that the reported pretax earnings were overstated by at least $127 million between 2002 and 2007.

In addition, Diebold Inc. also manipulated reserves and accruals, improperly delayed and capitalized expenses, and wrote up the value of inventory. Without admitting or denying the charges, Diebold Inc. agreed to pay $25 million to settle the SEC charges.[1]

Dell Inc., in 2007, admitted to financial statement manipulations that included premature revenue recognition. As a result, financial statements for the years 2003 through 2006 were restated. Senior executives and other employees overstated revenues to meet quarterly performance goals. As a reseller of other companies' software products, Dell should have deferred revenue recognition but chose instead to record the revenue prematurely. The restatement in fiscal 2005 caused a reduction in revenue for software sales in the amount of $105 million.[2]

Another scheme used to inflate revenues is to keep the accounting books open longer than the end of the quarter. Computer Associates used such a strategy prior to 2001, referred to as the "35-day month practice," to prematurely record $2.2 billion of revenue. Former chief executive Sanjay Kumar pleaded guilty to securities fraud

[1]U.S. Securities and Exchange Commission, Litigation Release No. 21543, June 2, 2010.

[2]Christopher Lawton, "Dell Details Accounting Woes; Methods for Recognizing Revenue From Software, Warranties Led to Errors," *Wall Street Journal,* October 31, 2007.

charges and obstruction of justice and received a 12-year prison sentence and $8 million in fines as a result of this scheme.[3]

2. Allowance for Doubtful Accounts

Most companies sell products on credit. Revenue is recognized on the income statement when the sales are made, and accounts receivable are carried on the balance sheet until the cash is collected. Because some customer accounts are never satisfied, the balance sheet includes an allowance for doubtful accounts. A discussion of sales, accounts receivable, and the allowance for doubtful accounts is provided in Chapters 2 and 3.

The allowance account, which is deducted from the balance sheet accounts receivable account, should reflect the volume of credit sales, the firm's past experience with customers, the customer base, the firm's credit policies, the firm's collection practices, economic conditions, and changes in any of these factors. There should be a consistent relationship, all other things being equal, between the rate of change in sales, accounts receivable, and the allowance for doubtful accounts. If the amounts are changing at different rates or in different directions—for example, if sales and accounts receivable are increasing, but the allowance account is decreasing or is increasing at a much smaller rate—the analyst should be alert to the potential for manipulation through the allowance account. Of course, there could also be a plausible reason for such a change.

As discussed in Chapter 2, the allowance for doubtful accounts is a type of reserve account and can be manipulated by under- or overestimating bad debt expenses. Underestimating bad debt expense will boost net income. On the other hand, by overestimating the allowance account, firms can set themselves up for a later correction that will ultimately boost net income. By analyzing the allowance for doubtful accounts as illustrated in Chapter 2, an astute analyst can make an assessment about the likelihood of manipulation.[4]

Companies should offer clear explanations of their accounts receivable and allowance for doubtful accounts in their notes if there are significant and abnormal changes to the accounts. Seagate Technology, in notes to its 2007 Form 10-K, explains why the firm's allowance account increased, despite a decreasing accounts receivable balance.

Accounts Receivable

(In Millions)	June 29, 2007	June 30, 2006
Accounts receivable	$1,433	$1,482
Allowance for doubtful accounts	(50)	(37)
	$1,383	$1,445

The Company terminated its distributor relationships with eSys and the Company ceased shipments of its products to eSys. eSys was the largest distributor of Seagate

[3] William M. Bulkeley, "CA Ex-CEO Kumar Receives 12-year Prison Term," *Wall Street Journal,* November 3, 2006.

[4] The underlying liquidity of accounts receivable is also extremely important in assessing earnings quality. This topic is covered in Chapters 4 and 5.

products (including Maxtor products) for the fiscal year ended June 30, 2006, representing approximately 5% of the Company's revenues.

The Company recorded $40 million of allowance for doubtful accounts in the three months ended September 29, 2006, due to the inherent uncertainties following the termination of the distribution relationships, eSys' continuing delinquency in payments and failure to pay amounts when promised, and eSys' failure to comply with the terms of its commercial agreements with the Company. The Company is pursuing collection of all amounts owed by eSys as promptly as possible. Any amounts recovered on these receivables will be recorded in the period received.

While the Company terminated its distributor relationships with eSys, the Company has and will continue to aggressively pursue any claims that may be assertable against eSys as a result of material breaches of the distribution agreements and any intentionally wrongful conduct that may have occurred. Specifically, the Company has commenced legal proceedings against eSys under a distribution agreement and a corporate guarantee, against its chief executive officer on a personal guarantee, and the Company may initiate further legal proceedings under various distribution agreements to recover all amounts owed for purchased product.

Many times, however, companies offer no explanation of questionable changes. Logitech International S.A. offers no explanation for the volatility in charges to bad debt expense or write-offs of accounts receivable that can be observed in the valuation schedule in the company's 2010 Form 10-K.

Schedule II
LOGITECH INTERNATIONAL S.A.VALUATION AND QUALIFYING ACCOUNTS
For the Fiscal Years Ending March 31, 2010, 2009, and 2008 (in thousands)

Fiscal Year	Description	Balance at Beginning of Period	Charged to Income Statement	Write-offs Charged to Allowance	Balance at End of Period
2010	Allowance for doubtful accounts	$6,705	($72)	($763)	$5,870
2009	Allowance for doubtful accounts	$2,497	$ 5,102	($894)	$6,705
2008	Allowance for doubtful accounts	$3,322	$603	$(1,428)	$2,497

In a few cases, no information about the allowance account can be found at all in the Form 10-K. Procter & Gamble Company no longer includes information on the balance sheet, in the notes, or in a valuation schedule to indicate the company even has an allowance for doubtful accounts. With over $5.3 billion in 2010 of accounts receivable it seems unlikely that the firm has no bad debt. In a conversation one of the authors had with an SEC employee, it was discovered that the SEC could not explain the lack of disclosure either. The quality of reported earnings is affected negatively by the lack of disclosure.

3. Price Versus Volume Changes

If a company's sales are increasing (or decreasing), it is important to determine whether the change is a result of price, volume, or a combination of both factors. Are sales growing because the firm is increasing prices or because more units are being sold, or both? It would seem that, in general, higher-quality earnings would be the product of both volume and price increases (during inflation). The firm would want to sell more units and keep prices increasing at least in line with the growth rate of general inflation.

Information regarding the reasons for sales growth (or decline) is one of the areas covered in a firm's management discussion and analysis section of the annual or 10-K report, discussed in Chapter 1. To relate sales growth to reasons for sales growth, use sales data from the income statement and the volume/price discussion from the management discussion and analysis section.

Micron Technology Inc.'s Consolidated Statements of Operations include the following:

	2010	2009
Net sales (in millions)	$8,482	$4,803

The following is an excerpt from the Micron Technology Management Discussion and Analysis of Financial Condition and Results of Operations:

> Total net sales for 2010 increased 77% as compared to 2009 primarily due to a 73% increase in Memory sales and the addition of $635 million of sales from Numonyx as a result of its acquisition in May 2010. The increase in Memory sales for 2010 as compared to 2009 primarily reflects significant increases in gigabits sold and improved average selling prices for certain products. Total net sales for 2009 decreased 18% as compared to 2008 primarily due to a 17% decrease in Memory sales and a 21% decrease in all Other sales.

A determination can be made from this information that the sales growth in 2010 was primarily the result of memory sales volume increases with some improvement of selling prices.

4. Real Versus Nominal Growth

A related issue is whether sales are growing in "real" (inflation-adjusted) as well as "nominal" (as reported) terms. The change in sales in nominal terms can be readily calculated from the figures reported on the income statement. An adjustment of the reported sales figure with the Consumer Price Index (CPI) (or some other measure of general inflation) will enable the analyst to make a comparison of the changes in real and nominal terms. To make the calculation to compare real with nominal sales, begin with the sales figures reported in the income statement, and adjust years prior to the current year with the CPI or some other price index. An example using information from the 2007 Annual Report of General Motors Corporation Automotive Division is shown on the next page:

Sales (in millions)	2007	2006	Percentage Change
As reported (nominal)	$178,199	$171,179	4.10
Adjusted (real)	$178,199	$176,019	1.24
Using base period CPI (1982 − 1984 = 100)			
(2007 CPI/2006 CPI) × 2006 Sales = Adjusted sales			
(207.3/201.6) × $171,179 = $176,019			

Sales, when adjusted for general inflation, grew at a rate of 1.24% which means that nominal sales growth has kept pace with the general rate of inflation. Another way to see this is to note that nominal sales increased 4.10% while the CPI increased from 201.6 to 207.3 or only 2.83%.

II. Cost of Goods Sold

5. Cost Flow Assumption for Inventory

During periods of inflation, the last-in, first-out (LIFO) cost flow assumption for inventory accounting, described in Chapter 2, produces lower earnings than first-in, first-out (FIFO) or average cost. Just the reverse occurs if the firm operates in an industry with volatile or falling prices. But LIFO results in the matching of current costs with current revenues and therefore produces higher-quality earnings than either FIFO or average cost. The inventory accounting system used by the company is described in the note to the financial statements that details accounting policies or the note discussing inventory. The following excerpt from the 2009 Form 10-K report of Silgan Holdings Inc. illustrates an interesting example of inventory method choices:

> Historically, the inventory value for our U.S. plastic container business was determined using the LIFO method of accounting. During the fourth quarter of 2009, we determined that the FIFO method of accounting was preferable for our plastic container business because FIFO provides a better matching of revenues to expenses due to a lag in the pass through of changes in resin costs to our customers and enhances the comparability of results to our peers. As a result, we changed the accounting method to value inventory of our U.S. plastic container business to the FIFO method. We have retrospectively adjusted all prior amounts as of the beginning of the earliest period presented. As a result of this retrospective adjustment, retained earnings at January 1, 2007 increased $3.1 million.

The value of inventory on the statement of financial position will better reflect the current cost of inventory; however, the firm is incorrect that the method does a better job matching revenues and expenses because the first goods in do not necessarily reflect the current costs.

6. Base LIFO Layer Liquidations

A base LIFO layer liquidation occurs with the use of LIFO in a situation in which the firm sells more goods than purchased during an accounting period. During inflation, this situation results in the lowest cost of goods sold expense from using LIFO because the older, less expensive items were sold. Usually, companies maintain a base layer of LIFO inventory that remains fairly constant. Goods are bought during the year and sales are made from the more recent purchases (for purposes of cost allocation). It is only when stocks of inventory are substantially reduced that the base layer is affected and LIFO earnings are higher. Base LIFO layer liquidations occur when companies are shrinking rather than increasing inventories. There is an actual reduction of inventory levels, but the earnings boost stems from the cost flow assumption: that the older and lower-priced products are those being sold. The effects of LIFO reductions, which are disclosed in notes to the financial statements, can be substantial. A base LIFO layer liquidation reduces the quality of earnings in the sense that there is an improvement in operating profit from what would generally be considered a negative occurrence: inventory reductions. In considering the future, ongoing potential of the company, it would be appropriate to exclude from earnings the effect of LIFO liquidations because a firm would not want to continue benefiting from inventory shrinkages. An example of a base LIFO layer liquidation occurred at Supervalo, Inc. in 2011.

> During fiscal 2011, 2010, and 2009, inventory quantities in certain LIFO layers were reduced. These reductions resulted in a liquidation of LIFO inventory quantities carried at lower costs prevailing in prior years as compared with the cost of fiscal 2011, 2010, and 2009 purchases. As a result, Cost of sales decreased by $11, $22, and $10 in fiscal 2011, 2010, and 2009, respectively.

7. Loss Recognitions on Write-Downs of Inventories

The principle of conservatism in accounting requires that firms carry inventory in the accounting records at the lower of cost (as determined by the cost flow assumption such as LIFO, FIFO, or average cost) or market. If the value of inventory falls below its original cost, the inventory is written down to market value. Market generally is determined by the cost to replace or reproduce the inventory but should not exceed the net realizable amount (selling price less completion and disposal costs) the company could generate from selling the item. The amount of the write-down will affect comparability, thus quality, of the profit margins from period to period.

When the write-down of inventory is included in cost of goods sold, the gross profit margin is affected in the year of the write-down. Significant write-downs of inventory are relatively infrequent; however, an example of an inventory write-down was announced by Ford Motor Company in January 2002. Due to the large drop in value of the metal palladium, used in auto manufacturing, the company announced they would record a $1 billion write-off. Ford had purchased this metal, once priced at less than $100 per ounce, for amounts over $1,000 per ounce. When prices fell, Ford revalued their palladium inventory to $440 per ounce.[5] In comparing the gross profit margin between periods, the analyst should be aware of the impact on the margin that occurs from such write-downs.

---

[5]Gregory L. White, "How Ford's Big Batch of Rare Metal Led to $1 Billion Write-Off," *Wall Street Journal*, February 6, 2002.

Sometimes, companies may write down the value of inventories every year in the three-year reporting period; one example is LaBarge Inc., a designer and manufacturer of specialized, custom electronic systems. The notes on inventory in LaBarge Inc.'s 2010 Form 10-K reveal the following information:

> For the fiscal years ended June 27, 2010, June 28, 2009, and June 29, 2008, expense for writing inventory down to lower cost or market charged to income before income taxes was $1.7 million, $1.5 million, and $1.9 million (excluding the impact of the charges related to Eclipse as described in Note 5 of the Notes to the Consolidated Financial Statements), respectively.

In this case, the analyst may view these write-downs as a recurring part of the firm's business operations.

III. Operating Expenses

8. Discretionary Expenses

A company can increase earnings by reducing variable operating expenses in a number of areas such as the repair and maintenance of capital assets, research and development, and advertising and marketing. If such discretionary expenses are reduced primarily to benefit the current year's reported earnings, the long-run impact on the firm's operating profit may be detrimental and thus the quality lowered. The analyst should review the trends of these discretionary expenses and compare them with the firm's volume of activity and level of capital investment. Amounts of discretionary expenditures are disclosed in the financial statements and notes. Advertising expenses are usually detailed in the summary of significant accounting policies note, such as the following for Cognex Corporation:

> Advertising costs are expensed as incurred and totaled $1,402,000 in 2010, $856,000 in 2009, and $1,354,000 in 2008.

Product revenue declined from $223,243,000 in 2008 to $158,379,000 in 2009 and then increased to $263,463,000 in 2010. In the Management's Discussion and Analysis, it is explained that marketing costs were reduced as a result of lower revenue expectations in 2009 and increased in 2010 to grow factory automation revenue as the firm returned to profitability.

9. Depreciation

The amount of annual depreciation expense recognized for an accounting period, as discussed in Chapter 2, depends on the choice of depreciation method and estimates regarding the useful life and salvage value of the asset being depreciated. Most companies use the straight-line method rather than an accelerated method for reporting purposes because it produces a smoother earnings stream and higher earnings in the early years of the depreciation period. The straight-line method, however, is lower in quality in most cases because it does not reflect the economic reality of product usefulness in that most machinery and equipment do not wear evenly over the depreciation period.

There are additional issues that affect earnings quality with regard to the depreciation expense figure. Companies that misclassify operating expenses as capital expenditures have created poor quality of financial reporting not only on the income statement, but on all financial statements. Recording an amount that should be deducted in its entirety in one year as a capital expenditure results in the expense being depreciated over several years. This is exactly what WorldCom did in 2001 and 2002. The firm was able to increase profits by $11 billion. The cash flow effects of this are discussed later in Chapter 4. While it is nearly impossible to determine that a company has misclassified expenses by reading the annual report or Form 10-K, a thorough financial statement analysis would most likely raise red flags that something was amiss.[6]

Another issue affecting the area of depreciation is that comparing companies is difficult when each firm chooses not only different depreciation methods, but also different lives for their long-lived assets. Depreciation policy is explained in the notes to the financial statements, such as the two following excerpts from 2010 Form 10-K annual reports from competitors Mattel Inc. and Hasbro Inc.:

> Mattel Inc.—Depreciation is computed using the straight-line method over estimated useful lives of 10 to 40 years for buildings, 3 to 10 years for machinery and equipment, and 10 to 20 years, not to exceed the lease term, for leasehold improvements. Tools, dies and molds are amortized using the straight-line method over 3 years.

> Hasbro Inc.—Depreciation is computed using accelerated and straight-line methods to depreciate the cost of property, plant and equipment over their estimated useful lives. The principal lives, in years, used in determining depreciation rates of various assets are: land improvements 15 to 19, buildings and improvements 15 to 25, and machinery and equipment 3 to 12. Tools, dies and molds are depreciated over a three-year period or their useful lives, whichever is less, using an accelerated method.

10. Asset Impairment

As was discussed in item 7, the write-down of asset values, following the principle of carrying assets at the lower of cost or market value, affects the comparability and thus the quality of financial data. The reasons for the write-downs would also be important in assessing the quality of the financial data. Information on asset write-downs is presented in notes to the financial statements. Firms also write down the carrying cost of property, plant, and equipment and intangible assets when there is a permanent impairment in value and when certain investments in marketable equity securities are carried at market value. Best Buy Inc. reported the following asset impairment charges in its 2011 Form 10-K related to goodwill:

> In fiscal 2009, we recorded a goodwill impairment charge of $62 relating to our former Speakeasy business. The decline in the fair value of Speakeasy was primarily the result of revenue forecasts that were lower than what we originally anticipated, which was partly due to lower-than-expected synergies with our other businesses. There were no goodwill impairments for any of our other reporting units in fiscal 2009.

---

[6]For additional reading about this issue, see Lyn Fraser and Aileen Ormiston, *Understanding the Corporate Annual Report: Nuts, Bolts and a Few Loose Screws,* Upper Saddle River, NJ: Prentice Hall, 2003.

In fiscal 2010, we identified no goodwill impairments. We determined that the fair value of the Speakeasy business, which had a remaining goodwill carrying value of $12, approximated its carrying value. For all of our other reporting units, we determined that the excess of fair value over carrying value was substantial.

In fiscal 2011, we identified no goodwill impairments. For all of our reporting units, we determined that the excess of fair value over carrying value was substantial. As a result of the sale of our Speakeasy business in the second quarter of fiscal 2011, we wrote off the carrying value of the goodwill associated with such business as of the date of sale. See Note 14, *Sale of Business*, for additional information regarding the sale.

The FASB has to a certain extent eliminated an earnings management opportunity resulting from asset impairment charges. If it is later deemed that too much was written off, a firm may not write up the value of the asset.

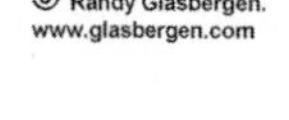

"Our company lost 900 million dollars last quarter. Your job is to make this look like the best thing that ever happened to us."

11. Reserves

Accrual accounting requires companies to estimate and accrue obligations for items that may be paid in future periods but should be accrued in the current period. The creation and use of these reserve accounts is required to properly match revenues and expenses; however, the abuse of reserve accounts has been an ongoing issue. Cookie-jar accounting, as the abuse is referred to, occurs when companies create or use reserve accounts for the purpose of setting aside funds in good years by overreserving (i.e., reducing net income) and then reducing charges or even reversing charges to the reserve accounts (i.e., increasing net income) in poor years. The net effect is to smooth out earnings from year to year. Examples of reserve accounts include the allowance for doubtful accounts (discussed in Chapter 2 and item 2 of this Appendix), and reserve accounts for items such as product warranties, restructuring, sales returns, and environmental obligations. In 2007, Dell Inc. admitted not only to recording revenue prematurely to manipulate financial statement information, but also to abusing its product warranty account by using it as a cookie jar.[7]

Companies will often take enormous write-offs in one period, referred to as "big bath" charges, to clean up their balance sheets. Generally, profits will improve in the subsequent period after the big bath has been taken. In 2007, Freeport-McMoRan Copper & Gold Inc. (Freeport) acquired Phelps-Dodge and recorded $6.2 billion of goodwill as a result of the purchase. For the fiscal year ended December 31, 2008, Freeport wrote down inventory to lower of cost or market, a $782 million charge, and also recorded goodwill and long-lived asset impairment charges totaling $16,965 million, including the write-off of the goodwill related to the Phelps-Dodge purchase. The firm ended the year with a net loss of $11,341 million. Many of the charges, according to the notes to the financial statements, were the result of steep declines in copper and molybdenum prices. Copper prices, $3.23 per pound in 2007, had declined to $1.32 per pound by December 31, 2008, and molybdenum declined from $30 per pound to $9.50 per pound in the same time frame. Net profit reported in 2009 and 2010 for Freeport was $2,527 and $4,273 million, respectively. Copper and molybdenum prices on April 29, 2011 were $4.23 and $16.87 per pound, respectively.[8] In 2007, many banks took the big bath in order to write off losses in the values of securities held by banks. If banks have overestimated losses, they could report higher profits in the future if the securities' values later rebound.[9]

12. In-Process Research and Development

In-process research and development charges are one-time charges taken at the time of an acquisition. The charged amounts are part of the acquisition price that the acquiring company determines are not yet viable research and development because they are still in process. These charges can be written off immediately under current accounting rules. Any revenue gains from the research in the future will cause higher earnings that have not been matched to the expenses that created them.

Estimating the value of the research and development that is to be written off is difficult, and, as a result, users of financial statements are unlikely to be able to determine whether these charges are appropriate. From a user's perspective, this is a problematic area because companies can write off significant amounts of research and development the year of an acquisition in order to boost earnings in later years. Eli Lilly and Company purchased ImClone, a biotechnology company, in 2008, for a purchase price of $6.5 billion and immediately wrote off $4.69 billion of in-process research and development. According to the notes to the financial statements in the 2008 Form 10-K, Eli Lilly believed this acquisition would "...offer both targeted therapies and

[7]Christopher Lawton, "Dell Details Accounting Woes; Methods for Recognizing Revenue From Software, Warranties Led to Errors," *Wall Street Journal,* October 31, 2007.

[8]Electrical Wholesaling, Penton Business Media, ewweb.com/current_copper_prices/, April 29, 2011, and Commodity Mine, InfoMine Inc., infomine.com, April 29, 2011.

[9]Cecilie Rohwedder, "Worries Shift To Overstating Summer Losses," *Wall Street Journal,* October 4, 2007.

oncolytic agents with a pipeline spanning all phases of clinical development." Further, the write-off was explained as follows:

> All of the estimated fair value of the acquired IPR&D is attributable to oncology-related products in development, including $1.33 billion to line extensions for Erbitux. A significant portion (81 percent) of the remaining value of acquired IPR&D is attributable to two compounds in Phase III clinical testing and one compound in Phase II clinical testing, all targeted to treat various forms of cancers.

Though these amounts may be accurate, investors and creditors have no way to know for sure.

IV. Nonoperating Revenue and Expense

13. Gains (Losses) from Sales of Assets

When a company sells a capital asset, such as property or equipment, the gain or loss is included in net income for the period. The sale of a major asset is sometimes made to increase earnings and/or to generate needed cash during a period when the firm is performing poorly. Such transactions are not part of the normal operations of the firm and should be excluded from net income when considering the future operating potential of the company.

The following table found in the Goodyear Tire & Rubber Company's 2010 Form 10-K illustrates nonoperating revenues and expenses:

Note 3. Other Expense

(In millions) Expense (income)	**2010**	**2009**	**2008**
Net foreign currency exchange losses	$159	$ 7	$ 57
Financing fees and financial instruments	95	39	97
Net (gains) losses on asset sales	(73)	30	(53)
Royalty income	(30)	(28)	(32)
Interest income	(11)	(17)	(68)
General and product liability—discontinued products	11	9	30
Subsidiary liquidation loss	—	18	16
Miscellaneous	35	(18)	12
	$186	$ 40	$ 59

The subsidiary liquidation loss would most likely be excluded when projecting future earnings. Typically the gains and losses from asset sales would also be excluded even if they are recurring items because it would be impossible to predict the amounts of future gains and losses.

14. Interest Income

Interest income is also nonoperating in nature except for certain types of firms such as financial institutions. Interest income results primarily from short-term temporary investments in marketable securities to earn a return on cash not immediately needed in the business. These security investments were explained in Chapter 2. In the assessment of earnings quality, the analyst should be alert to the materiality and variability in the amount of interest income because it is not part of operating income. Interest income is disclosed on the face of the income statement or in notes to the financial statements.

Hasbro Inc. reports a decreasing amount of interest income from 2008 to 2009, but then an increase in 2010. The reasons for the changes are explained in the Management's Discussion and Analysis in the 2010 Form 10-K:

> Interest income was $5,649 in 2010 compared to $2,858 in 2009. The increase primarily reflects higher invested cash balances in 2010. Interest income was $2,858 in 2009 compared to $17,654 in 2008. The decrease in interest income was primarily the result of lower returns on invested cash as well as lower average invested cash balances.

15. Equity Income

Use of the equity method to account for investments in unconsolidated subsidiaries, discussed and illustrated in Chapter 3, permits the investor to recognize as investment income the investor's percentage ownership share of the investee's reported income rather than recognizing income only to the extent of cash dividends actually received. Amazon.com Inc. has the following line item on its 2010 Statement of Operations:

> Equity-method investment activity, net of tax 7 (6) (9)

Further investigation reveals that the increase in 2010 is primarily due to recognition of a noncash gain on a previously held equity position in a company that was acquired in 2010. The equity investments have not performed well; however, this does not negatively affect Amazon.com's cash value because no cash has been paid by Amazon.com. It would be appropriate to eliminate this noncash item of earnings for comparative purposes by adding back equity losses or deducting equity earnings.

16. Income Taxes

The provision for income tax expense on the income statement differs from the tax actually paid, as was discussed in Chapters 2 and 3. When assessing the net earnings number, it is important to differentiate between increases and decreases to net earnings caused by tax events. A significant change in the effective tax rate may be a onetime nonrecurring item. Included in the income tax notes to the financial statements is a reconciliation of the U.S. federal statutory tax rate to the company's effective tax rate, such as the following excerpt from the 2010 General Electric Form 10-K:

Consolidated			
	2010	**2009**	**2008**
U.S. federal statutory income tax rate	35.0%	35.0%	35.0%
Tax on global activities including exports	(19.7)	(39.6)	(25.8)
U.S. business credits	(4.4)	(4.5)	(1.4)
All other—net	(3.5)	(2.4)	(2.2)
	(27.6)	(46.5)	(29.4)
Actual income tax rate	7.4%	(11.5%)	5.6%

Despite significant profits before taxes that range from over $19 billion in 2008, nearly $10 billion in 2009, and over $14 billion in 2010, General Electric Company has one of the lowest effective tax rates in the United States. As can be seen above, the key reason is that international tax rates are far less than the 35% U.S. statutory rate. By reinvesting overseas earnings abroad, U.S. tax law allows firms to avoid paying at the higher U.S. tax rates. Should the firm repatriate the earnings back to the United States, the dollars would be taxed at U.S. rates. When projecting future earnings, the analyst must consider whether the firm will need to repatriate funds in the future, causing higher taxes in that year. In addition, it is important to stay abreast of changes in tax law that would eliminate the current benefits of leaving earnings overseas. General Electric explains this in the notes to the financial statements in the 2010 Form 10-K:

> A significant portion of this reduction depends upon a provision of U.S. tax law that defers the imposition of U.S. tax on certain active financial services income until that income is repatriated to the United States as a dividend. This provision is consistent with international tax norms and permits U.S. financial services companies to compete more effectively with foreign banks and other foreign financial institutions in global markets. This provision, which expires at the end of 2011, has been scheduled to expire and has been extended by Congress on six previous occasions, including in December of 2010, but there can be no assurance that it will continue to be extended. In the event the provision is not extended after 2011, the current U.S. tax imposed on active financial services income earned outside the United States would increase, making it more difficult for U.S. financial services companies to compete in global markets. If this provision is not extended, we expect our effective tax rate to increase significantly after 2012.

17. Discontinued Operations

Discontinued operations should be excluded in considering future earnings. Two items are recorded if the discontinued operations have been sold: the gain or loss from operations of the division up to the time of sale, and the gain or loss as a result of the sale, both net of tax. The income statement disclosure for Bristol–Myers Squibb Inc., from its 2010 Form 10-K is as follows:

	Year Ended December 31, (dollars in millions)		
	2010	**2009**	**2008**
Net earnings from continuing operations	4,513	4,420	3,686
Discontinued operations:			
Earnings, net of taxes	—	285	578
Gain on disposal, net of taxes	—	7,157	1,979
Net earnings from discontinued operations	—	7,442	2,557
Net earnings	4,513	11,862	6,243
Net earnings attributable to noncontrolling interest	1,411	1,250	996
Net earnings attributable to Bristol-Myers Squibb Company	$ 3,102	$ 10,612	$ 5,247

It would be appropriate to deduct the net earnings on discontinued operations in 2008 and 2009 from net earnings for comparative purposes.

18. Extraordinary Items

Extraordinary items are gains and losses that are both unusual and infrequent in nature. They are shown separately, net of tax, on the income statement. Because very few transactions meet the definition of extraordinary, it is rare to see such items on an earnings statement. The following excerpt from the 2010 Form 10-K of Century Link Inc. explains the extraordinary item recorded in 2009:

> On July 1, 2009, we discontinued the accounting requirements of regulatory accounting upon the conversion of substantially all of our rate-of-return study areas to federal price cap regulation (based on the FCC's approval of our petition to convert our study areas to price cap regulation).
>
> Upon the discontinuance of regulatory accounting, we reversed previously established regulatory assets and liabilities. Depreciation rates of certain assets established by regulatory authorities for our telephone operations subject to regulatory accounting have historically included a component for removal costs in excess of the related salvage value. Notwithstanding the adoption of accounting guidance related to the accounting for asset retirement obligations, regulatory accounting required us to continue to reflect this accumulated liability for removal costs in excess of salvage value even though there was no legal obligation to remove the assets. Therefore, we did not adopt the asset retirement obligation provisions for our telephone operations that were subject to regulatory accounting. Upon the discontinuance of regulatory accounting, such accumulated liability for removal costs included in accumulated depreciation was removed and an asset retirement obligation was established. Upon the discontinuance of regulatory accounting, we were required to adjust the carrying amounts of property, plant, and equipment only to the extent the assets are impaired, as judged in the same manner applicable to nonregulated enterprises. We did not record an impairment charge related to the carrying value of the property, plant, and equipment of our regulated telephone operations as a result of the discontinuance of regulatory accounting.
>
> In the third quarter of 2009, upon the discontinuance of regulatory accounting, we recorded a noncash extraordinary gain in our consolidated statements of income comprised of the following components (dollars, except per share amounts, in thousands):

	Gain (loss)
Elimination of removal costs embedded in accumulated depreciation	$ 222,703
Establishment of asset retirement obligation	(1,556)
Elimination of other regulatory assets and liabilities	(2,585)
Net extraordinary gain before income tax expense and noncontrolling interests	218,562
Income tax expense associated with extraordinary gain	(81,060)
Net extraordinary gain before noncontrolling interests	137,502
Less: extraordinary gain attributable to noncontrolling interests	(1,545)
Extraordinary gain attributable to CenturyLink, Inc.	$ 135,957

The gain or loss should be eliminated from earnings when evaluating a firm's future earnings potential.

V. Other Issues

19. Material Changes in Number of Shares Outstanding

The number of common stock shares outstanding and thus the computation of earnings per share can change materially from one accounting period to the next. These changes result from such transactions as treasury stock purchases and the purchase and retirement of a firm's own common stock. The reasons for the repurchase of common stock should be determined if possible. Some firms use repurchase programs to obtain shares of stock to be used in employee stock option programs. Other firms offer no reason for their repurchase program. It is important to consider whether a firm is spending scarce resources to merely increase earnings per share (EPS). The effects of reducing outstanding shares of common stock result in an increase to EPS. In its Form 10-K for the fiscal year ended February 26, 2011, Best Buy Co. Inc. explains its repurchase program as follows:

> From time to time, we repurchase our common stock in the open market pursuant to programs approved by our Board. We may repurchase our common stock for a variety of reasons, such as acquiring shares to offset dilution related to equity-based incentives, including stock options and our employee stock purchase plan, and optimizing our capital structure.
>
> In June 2007, our Board authorized up to $5.5 billion in share repurchases. The program, which became effective on June 26, 2007, terminated and replaced a $1.5 billion share repurchase program authorized by our Board in June 2006. There is no expiration date governing the period over which we can repurchase shares under the June 2007 program.
>
> We repurchased and retired 32.6 million shares at a cost of $1.2 billion in fiscal 2011. We made no share repurchases in fiscal 2010 or 2009. At the end of fiscal 2011, $1.3 billion of the $5.5 billion share repurchase program authorized by our Board in June 2007 was available for future share repurchases.
>
> We consider several factors in determining when to make share repurchases including, among other things, our cash needs, the availability of funding and the market price of our stock. We expect that cash provided by future operating activities, as well as available cash and cash equivalents and short-term investments, will be the sources of funding for our share repurchase program. Based on the anticipated amounts to be generated from those sources of funds in relation to the remaining authorization approved by our Board under the June 2007 share repurchase program, we do not expect that future share repurchases will have a material impact on our short-term or long-term liquidity.

Based on the information in Best Buy's Statement of Stockholders' Equity, the firm paid approximately $37.28 per share to repurchase the stock and the stock price subsequently declined to $31.22 by the end of April 2011. In addition, while over 32 million shares of stock were repurchased, only 6 million shares of stock were issued as a result of stock options, vesting of restricted stock, and issuance of stock under employee stock purchase plans. This would imply that the primary reason for Best Buy to repurchase its stock was to increase the earnings per share to build investor confidence.

20. Operating Earnings, a.k.a. Core Earnings, Pro Forma Earnings, or EBITDA

Operating earnings or profit (discussed in Chapter 3) is an important figure for assessing the ongoing potential of a firm. Some companies have created their own operating profit numbers and tried to convince users that these figures are the ones to focus on instead of the GAAP-based amounts. These "company created" numbers go by a variety of names such as core earnings, pro forma earnings, or EBITDA. EBITDA, for example, refers to operating earnings before interest, tax, depreciation, and amortization expenses are deducted. Those who support focusing on EBITDA argue that depreciation and amortization charges are not cash items and should be ignored. In essence, they are asking that users ignore the fact that companies make long-term investments. Depreciation and amortization expenses are the allocation of an original cash amount spent for items such as equipment. In January 2003, the SEC adopted a new rule requiring companies that report pro forma financial information to present this information in a manner that is not misleading and also to reconcile the pro forma financial information with GAAP.

What Are the Real Earnings?

Each individual user of financial statements should adjust the earnings figure to reflect what that particular user believes is relevant to the decision at hand. Based on the checklist, Exhibit 3A.2 shows the items that should be considered as adjustments to earnings.

EXHIBIT 3A.2 Adjustments to Earnings

Start with net income, then consider the following adjustments:

(a) add or deduct amounts for questionable items charged to bad debt expense (item 2)
(b) deduct base LIFO layer liquidations (item 6)
(c) add back loss recognized on write-downs of assets (items 7 and 10)
(d) deduct amounts for discretionary expenses that the firm may have delayed (item 8)
(e) add or deduct amounts recorded as charges or credits to reserve accounts that are nonrecurring such as restructuring costs (item 11)
(f) add back charges for in-process research and development (item 12)
(g) add or deduct losses and gains from sales of assets (item 13)
(h) deduct nonrecurring amounts of interest income (item 14)
(i) add or deduct equity losses or income (item 15)
(j) add or deduct nonrecurring amounts of income tax expense (item 16)
(k) add or deduct losses or gains attributable to discontinued operations and extraordinary items (items 17 and 18)

SELF-TEST

Solutions are provided in Appendix B.

______ **1.** What does the income statement measure for a firm?
(a) The changes in assets and liabilities that occurred during the period.
(b) The financing and investment activities for a period.
(c) The results of operations for a period.
(d) The financial position of a firm for a period.

______ **2.** How many years' income statements and stockholders' equity information are included in the annual reports?
(a) Two.
(b) Three.
(c) Four.
(d) Five.

______ **3.** Which of the following items needs to be disclosed separately in the income statement?
(a) Discontinued operations.
(b) Salary expense.
(c) Warranty expense.
(d) Bad debt expense.

______ **4.** Which of the following statements is true with regard to common-size income statements?
(a) It expresses each income statement item as a percentage of total cost.
(b) It shows the relative magnitude of various expenses relative to sales and the profit margins.
(c) It is a useful analytical tool to compare firms with different levels of sales or total assets.
(d) It facilitates internal or structural analysis of a firm, evaluate trends, and make industry comparisons.

______ **5.** Which section of the annual or 10-K report covers the reasons for sales growth or decline?
(a) Earnings statement.
(b) Management Discussion and Analysis section.
(c) Annual report.
(d) None of the above.

______ **6.** The gross profit margin and ______________ are complements of each other.
(a) Net profit.
(b) Operating profit.
(c) Cost of goods sold percentage.
(d) None of the above.

______ **7.** Which method is used to allocate the cost of acquiring and developing natural resources, such as oil and gas, other minerals, and standing timber?
(a) Amortization.
(b) Depreciation.
(c) Impairment.
(d) Depletion.

______ **8.** How are costs of assets that benefit a firm for more than one year allocated?
(a) Depreciation.
(b) Depletion and amortization.
(c) Costs are divided by service lives of assets and allocated to repairs and maintenance.
(d) Both (a) and (b).

______ **9.** Why should the expenditures for repairs and maintenance correspond to the level of investment in capital equipment and to the age and condition of that equipment?
(a) Repairs and maintenance expense is calculated in the same manner as depreciation expense.
(b) Repairs and maintenance are depreciated over the remaining life of the assets involved.
(c) It is a generally accepted accounting principle that repairs and maintenance expense is generally between 5% and 10% of fixed assets.
(d) Inadequate repairs of equipment can impair the operating success of a business enterprise.

______ **10.** Why is the figure for operating profit important?
(a) This is the figure used for calculating federal income tax expense.
(b) The figure for operating profit provides a basis for assessing the success of a company apart from its financing and investment activities and separate from its tax status.
(c) The operating profit figure includes all operating revenues and expenses as well as interest and taxes related to operations.
(d) The figure for operating profit provides a basis for assessing the wealth of a firm.

______ **11.** Why can the equity method of accounting for investments in the voting stock of other companies cause distortions in net earnings?
(a) Significant influence may exist even if the ownership of voting stock is less than 20%.
(b) Income is recognized where no cash may ever be received.
(c) Income should be recognized in accordance with the accrual method of accounting.
(d) Income is recognized only to the extent of cash dividends received.

______ **12.** Why should the effective tax rate be evaluated when assessing earnings?
(a) It is important to understand whether earnings have increased because of tax techniques rather than from positive changes in core operations.
(b) Effective tax rates are irrelevant because they are mandated by law.
(c) Effective tax rates do not include the effects of foreign taxes.
(d) Net operating losses allow a firm to change its effective tax rates for each of the five years prior to the loss.

______ **13.** Which of the following items should be recorded as other comprehensive income?
(a) Foreign currency translation effects.
(b) Extraordinary gains and losses.
(c) Realized gains and losses.
(d) All of the above.

______ **14.** What are three profit measures calculated from the income statement?
(a) Operating profit margin, net profit margin, repairs and maintenance to fixed assets.
(b) Gross profit margin, cost of goods sold percentage, EBIT.
(c) Gross profit margin, operating profit margin, net profit margin.
(d) None of the above.

______ **15.** When is a dual presentation of basic and diluted earnings per share required?
(a) When a company has pension liabilities.
(b) When convertible securities are in fact converted.
(c) When a company has a simple capital structure.
(d) When a company has a complex capital structure.

______ **16.** What is a statement of stockholders' equity?
(a) It is the same as a retained earnings statement.
(b) It is a statement that reconciles only the treasury stock account.
(c) It is a statement that summarizes changes in the entire stockholders' equity section of the balance sheet.
(d) It is a statement reconciling the difference between stock issued at par value and stock issued at market value.

______ **17.** What results in the issuance of additional shares in proportion to current ownership and represent nothing of value to the stockholder?
(a) Reverse stock splits.
(b) Stock dividends.
(c) Stock splits.
(d) None of the above.

______ **18.** Which of the following cause(s) a change in the retained earnings account balance?
(a) Prior period adjustment.
(b) Payment of dividends.
(c) Net profit or loss.
(d) All of the above.

19. Match the following terms with the correct definitions:

______	(a) Depreciation.	______	(h) Cost method.
______	(b) Depletion.	______	(i) Single-step format.
______	(c) Amortization.	______	(j) Multiple-step format.
______	(d) Gross profit.	______	(k) Basic earnings per share.
______	(e) Operating profit.	______	(l) Diluted earnings per share.
______	(f) Net profit.	______	(m) Extraordinary events.
______	(g) Equity method.	______	(n) Discontinued operations.

Definitions

(1) Proportionate recognition of investee's net income for investments in voting stock of other companies.
(2) Presentation of income statement that provides several intermediate profit measures.
(3) Unusual events not expected to recur in the foreseeable future.
(4) Allocation of costs of tangible fixed assets.
(5) Difference between sales revenue and expenses associated with generating sales.
(6) Recognition of income from investments in voting stock of other companies to the extent of cash dividend received.
(7) Operations that will not continue in the future because the firm sold a major portion of its business.
(8) Difference between net sales and cost of goods sold.
(9) Allocation of costs of acquiring and developing natural resources.
(10) Earnings per share figure calculated by dividing the average number of common stock shares outstanding into the net earnings available to common stockholders.
(11) Presentation of income statement that groups all revenue items, then deducts all expenses, to arrive at net income.
(12) Earnings per share figure based on the assumption that all potentially dilutive securities have been converted to common stock.
(13) Allocation of costs of intangible assets.
(14) Difference between all revenues and expenses.

20. The following categories appear on the income statement of Joshua Jeans Company:

(a) Net sales.
(b) Cost of sales.
(c) Operating expenses.
(d) Other revenue/expense.
(e) Income tax expense.

Classify the following items according to income statement category:

______ (1) Depreciation expense.
______ (2) Interest revenue.
______ (3) Sales revenue.
______ (4) Advertising expense.
______ (5) Interest expense.
______ (6) Sales returns and allowances.
______ (7) Federal income taxes.
______ (8) Repairs and maintenance.
______ (9) Selling and administrative expenses.
______ (10) Cost of products sold.
______ (11) Dividend income.
______ (12) Lease payments.

Study Questions and Problems

3.1. What is the difference between a multiple-step and a single-step format of the earnings statement? Which format is the most useful for analysis?

3.2. What is the statement of stockholders' equity? How is it reported by companies?

3.3. What are the different ways of reporting the total comprehensive income by companies?

3.4. Discuss all reasons that could explain an increase or decrease in gross profit margin.

3.5. What are the different factors on which the amount of depreciation expense recognized in any accounting period will depend?

3.6. What are the different methods employed to account for investments in the voting stock of other companies?

3.7. Alpha Company purchased 40% of the voting common stock of Beta Company on January 1 and paid $500,000 for the investment. Beta Company reported $160,000 of earnings for the year and paid $50,000 in cash dividends. Calculate investment income and the balance sheet investment account for Alpha Company under the cost method and under the equity method.

3.8. What are special items with regard to the income statement?

3.9. What are the two criteria that gains and losses must meet in order to be classified as extraordinary gains and losses?

3.10. Mention four items that comprise a company's other comprehensive income.

3.11. An excerpt from the Sun Company's annual report is presented below. Calculating any profit measures deemed necessary, discuss the implications of the profitability of the company.

Sun Company Income Statements for the Years
Ended December 31, 2013, 2012, and 2011

	2013	2012	2011
Net sales	$236,000	$195,000	$120,000
Cost of goods sold	186,000	150,000	85,000
Gross profit	$ 50,000	$ 45,000	$ 35,000
Operating expenses	22,000	18,000	11,000
Operating profit	$ 28,000	$ 27,000	$ 24,000
Income taxes	12,000	11,500	10,500
Net income	$ 16,000	$ 15,500	$ 13,500

3.12. Prepare a multiple-step income statement for Jackrabbit Inc. from the following single-step statement.

Net sales	$1,480,000
Gain on sale of equipment	25,000
Interest income	13,000
	1,518,000
Costs and expenses:	
Cost of goods sold	864,000
Selling expenses	132,000
General and admin. expenses	178,000
Depreciation	28,000
Equity losses	11,000
Interest expense	16,000
Income tax expense	96,000
Net income	$ 193,000

3.13. Income statements for Yarrick Company for the years ending December 31, 2013, 2012, and 2011 are shown below. Prepare a common-size income statement and analyze the profitability of the company.

Yarrick Company Income Statements for the Years Ending December 31, 2013, 2012, and 2011

(in millions)	2013	2012	2011
Net sales	$237	$155	$134
Cost of goods sold	138	84	72
Gross profit	$ 99	$ 71	$ 62
Sales, general, and administrative expenses	42	31	39
Research and development	38	33	54
Operating profit	$ 19	$ 7	($ 31)
Income tax expense (benefit)	7	2	(11)
Net profit	$ 12	$ 5	($ 20)

3.14. LA Theatres Inc. has two distinct revenue sources, ticket and concession revenues. The following information from LA Theatres Inc. income statements for the past three years is available:

(in millions)	2013	2012	2011
Ticket revenue	$1,731	$1,642	$1,120
Concessions revenue	792	687	411
Total revenue	$2,523	$2,329	$1,531
Cost of goods sold—tickets	$ 951	$ 854	$ 549
Cost of goods sold—concessions	70	69	48
Total cost of goods sold	$1,021	$ 923	$ 597
Gross profit	$1,502	$1,406	$ 934

(a) Calculate gross profit margins for tickets and concessions for all three years. Calculate an overall gross profit margin for LA Theatres Inc. for all three years.
(b) Analyze the changes in gross profit margin for all three years.

3.15. Writing Skills Problem
Income statements are presented for the Elf Corporation for the years ending December 31, 2013, 2012, and 2011.

Elf Corporation Income Statements for the Years Ending December 31, 2013, 2012, and 2011

(in millions)	**2013**	**2012**	**2011**
Sales	$700	$650	$550
Cost of goods sold	350	325	275
Gross profit	$350	$325	$275
Operating expenses:			
Administrative	100	100	100
Advertising and marketing	50	75	75
Operating profit	$200	$150	$100
Interest expense	70	50	30
Earnings before tax	$130	$100	$ 70
Tax expense (50%)	65	50	35
Net income	$ 65	$ 50	$ 35

Required: Write a one-paragraph analysis of Elf Corporation's profit performance for the period.
To the Student: The focus of this exercise is on analyzing financial data rather than simply describing the numbers and trends. Analysis involves breaking the information into parts for study, relating the pieces, making comparisons, drawing conclusions, and evaluating cause and effect.

3.16. Research Problem
Locate the income statement of a company in each of the following industries: pharmaceutical, technology, retailer—groceries, and automobile manufacturer. (See Chapter 1 for help in locating a company's financial statements.) Calculate the gross profit margin, operating profit margin, and net profit margin for all companies. Write a short essay explaining the differences you find between the profit margins calculated and why you think the profit margins differ.

3.17. Internet Problem
Look up the FASB home page on the Internet at the following address: www.fasb.org/. Find the list of technical projects that are currently on the board's agenda. Choose one of the projects that will affect the income statement. Describe the potential change and how the income statement may be affected.

CASES

Case 3.1 Intel Case

The 2010 Intel Annual Report can be found at the following Web site: www.pearsoninternationaleditions.com/fraser.

(a) Using the consolidated statements of operations, analyze the profitability of Intel by preparing a common-size income statement and by calculating any other ratios deemed necessary for the past three years. Be sure to calculate sales growth and operating expense growth for each two-year period presented.

(b) Using the consolidated statements of stockholders' equity for Intel, explain the key reasons for the changes in the common stock, accumulated other comprehensive income, and retained earnings accounts. Evaluate these changes.

Case 3.2 Avnet Comprehensive Analysis Case Using the Financial Statement Analysis Template

Each chapter in the textbook contains a continuation of this problem. The objective is to learn how to do a comprehensive financial statement analysis in steps as the content of each chapter is learned. Using the 2010 Avnet Form 10-K, which can be found at www.pearsoninternationaleditions.com/fraser, complete the following requirements:

(a) Open the financial statement analysis template that you saved from the Chapter 1 Avnet problem and input the data from the Avnet income statement. When you have finished inputting the data, review the income statement to make sure there are no red blocks indicating that your numbers do not match the cover sheet information you input from the Chapter 1 problem. Make any necessary corrections before printing out both your input and the common-size income statement that the template automatically creates for you.

(b) Analyze the income statement of Avnet. Write a summary that includes important points that an analyst would use in assessing the profitability of Avnet.

Case 3.3 Taser International Inc.

The following are excerpts from the Taser International Inc. Form 10-K.

TASER INTERNATIONAL INC.
CONSOLIDATED STATEMENTS OF OPERATIONS
For the Years Ended December 31,

	2010	2009	2008
Net sales	$ 86,930,019	$ 104,251,560	$ 92,845,490
Cost of products sold	41,563,144	40,849,151	35,841,263
Gross margin	45,366,875	63,402,409	57,004,227
Sales, general, and administrative expenses	39,094,625	43,479,232	38,860,729
Research and development expenses	11,411,889	20,002,351	12,918,161
Income (loss) from operations	(5,139,639)	(79,174)	5,225,337
Interest and other income, net	25,819	170,547	1,717,967
Income (loss) before provision for income taxes	(5,113,820)	91,373	6,943,304
Provision (benefit) for income taxes	(729,385)	92,479	3,306,263
Net income (loss)	$ (4,384,435)	$ (1,106)	$ 3,637,041
Income (loss) per common and common equivalent shares			
Basic	$ (0.07)	$ (0.00)	$ 0.06
Diluted	$ (0.07)	$ (0.00)	$ 0.06
Weighted average number of common and common equivalent shares outstanding			
Basic	62,524,446	61,920,094	62,371,004
Diluted	62,524,446	61,920,094	64,070,869

The accompanying notes are an integral part of these consolidated financial statements.

Item 1. Business Overview

TASER International Inc.'s (the Company or TASER or we or our) core mission is to protect life, prevent conflict and resolve disputes through technologies that make communities safer. We are a market leader in the development, manufacture and sale of advanced Electronic Control Devices (ECDs) designed for use in the law enforcement, military, corrections, private security, and personal defense markets. Since our inception in 1993, we have remained committed to providing solutions to violent confrontation by developing devices with proprietary technology to incapacitate dangerous, combative, or high-risk subjects who pose a risk to law enforcement officers, innocent citizens, or themselves in a manner that is generally recognized as a safer alternative to other uses of force.

TASER solutions deliver significant results to our customers and to communities in which they are deployed. With more than 275 independent studies confirming the safety of TASER ECDs relative to other force options, TASER ECDs have proven a safer alternative to other responses to resistance in situations of conflict. Further, most reporting agencies demonstrate overall decreases in use of force, and decreases in suspect and officer injuries resulting from conflict. Reducing uses of force and gaining compliance by use of a TASER ECD has provided significant reductions in worker's compensation expenses and claims for excessive use of force for agencies, cities, and taxpayers.

Results of Operations

Net sales for the year ended December 31, 2010, were $86.9 million, a decrease of $17.3 million, or 17%, compared to $104.3 million in 2009. The decrease in 2010 was primarily volume driven with fewer individually significant international and Federal orders in 2010 as sales in 2009 included follow-on orders to larger customers in these market segments. Domestic law enforcement sales also declined over the prior year as agencies continue to operate with budget constraints in prevailing adverse economic conditions and did not have the level of stimulus funds that were available in 2009.

Sales, General and Administrative Expenses

For the years ended December 31, 2010, 2009, and 2008, sales, general and administrative expenses were comprised as follows (dollars in thousands):

	Year Ended December 31,		
	2010	2009	2008
Salaries, benefits and bonus	$ 10,586	$ 11,335	$ 9,349
Stock based compensation	2,728	3,219	1,552
Legal, professional and accounting	5,187	6,081	5,899
Sales and marketing	4,152	5,356	5,071
Consulting and lobbying services	2,872	3,863	3,478
Travel and meals	2,956	3,308	3,739
Depreciation and amortization	2,023	1,896	1,635
D&O and liability insurance	1,613	1,812	2,191
Other	6,978	6,609	5,947
Total	$ 39,095	$ 43,479	$ 38,861

Research and Development Expenses

Research and development expenses decreased $8.6 million, or 43%, to $11.4 million in 2010 compared to $20.0 in 2009. The net decrease is a combination of a $4.9 million reduction in indirect supplies and tooling attributable to the intensive hardware development for X3 and AXON conducted in 2009, which were needed in order to expedite development for product demonstrations at the TASER Conference and the International Association of Chiefs of Police ("IACP") trade shows. Approximately $3.2 million of EVIDENCE.COM data center and software maintenance related costs, including salary related costs, consulting, equipment leasing, rent and other overheads, were included in cost of products sold in 2010 following the commercial availability of the platform. These costs were included in research and development in the prior year while the platform was in the development phase.

Required:

Using the Consolidated Statements of Operations and the excerpts from the Taser International Inc. Form 10-K, analyze the profitability of Taser. Your analysis should include the following calculations for all three years:

(a) Common-size income statements.
(b) Growth rates of sales and total operating costs (include cost of products sold).
(c) Effective tax rates.

Your written analysis and interpretation should include explanations for why trends have occurred.

Case 3.4 Zebra Technologies Corporation

The following are excerpts from the Zebra Technologies Corporation Form 10-K.

Item 1. Business

The Company

Zebra delivers products and solutions that improve our customers' ability to put their critical assets to work smarter by identifying, tracking, and managing assets, transactions, and people.

We design, manufacture, and sell specialty printing devices that print variable information on demand at the point of issuance. These devices are used worldwide by manufacturers, service and retail organizations, and governments for automatic identification, data collection, and personal identification in applications that improve productivity, deliver better customer service, and provide more effective security. Our product range consists of direct thermal and thermal transfer label and receipt printers, passive radio frequency identification (RFID) printer/encoders, and dye sublimation card printers. We also sell a comprehensive range of specialty supplies consisting of self-adhesive labels, thermal transfer ribbons, thermal printheads, batteries, and other accessories, including software for label design and printer network management.

Note 7 Goodwill and Other Intangible Asset Data

During the fourth quarter of 2008, we determined that certain impairment indicators existed related to identified intangible assets and conducted an additional impairment test of intangibles. Due to the deterioration of the economy and a significant reduction in the price of our stock, we determined that our goodwill and other intangible assets were impaired, requiring total estimated impairment charges of $157,600,000 at December 31, 2008.

Note 17 Income Taxes

The provision for income taxes differs from the amount computed by applying the U.S. statutory Federal income tax rate of 35% to income before income taxes. The reconciliation of statutory and effective income taxes is presented below (in thousands):

	Year Ended December 31,		
	2010	**2009**	**2008**
Provision computed at statutory rate	$ 50,727	$ 24,683	$ (4,170)
State income tax, net of Federal tax benefit	1,666	566	1,127
Tax-exempt interest income	(554)	(1,047)	(1,997)
Acquisition related items	(315)	—	(2,450)
Asset impairment charges	—	—	35,360
Domestic manufacturing deduction	(70)	(700)	(1,715)
Research and experimental credit	(950)	(600)	(400)
Foreign rate differential	(7,799)	(1,263)	1,094
Other	452	1,780	(341)
Provision for income taxes	$ 43,157	$ 23,419	$ 26,508

ZEBRA TECHNOLOGIES CORPORATION
CONSOLIDATED STATEMENTS OF EARNINGS (LOSS)
(Amounts in thousands, except per share data)

	Year Ended December 31,		
	2010	**2009**	**2008**
Net sales			
Net sales of tangible products	$855,269	$701,044	$871,587
Revenue from services and software	101,579	102,541	105,113
Total net sales	956,848	803,585	976,700
Cost of sales			
Cost of sales of tangible products	455,007	401,727	452,208
Cost of services and software	40,972	41,137	45,187
Total cost of sales	495,979	442,864	497,395
Gross profit	460,869	360,721	479,305
Operating expenses:			
Selling and marketing	122,689	102,535	126,325
Research and development	101,930	86,390	95,800
General and administrative	79,710	81,395	81,644
Amortization of intangible assets	9,573	10,466	18,575
Litigation settlement	(1,082)	—	(5,302)
Exit, restructuring and integration costs	4,197	12,191	20,009
Asset impairment charges	—	(1,058)	157,600
Total operating expenses	317,017	291,919	494,651
Operating income (loss)	143,852	68,802	(15,346)
Other income (expense):			
Investment income	2,681	2,933	1,281
Foreign exchange gain (loss)	(213)	(45)	3,518
Other, net	(1,385)	(1,167)	(1,366)
Total other income	1,083	1,721	3,433
Income (loss) before income taxes	144,935	70,523	(11,913)
Income taxes	43,157	23,419	26,508
Net income (loss)	$101,778	$47,104	$(38,421)
Basic earnings (loss) per share	$1.78	$0.79	$(0.60)
Diluted earnings (loss) per share	$1.77	$0.79	$(0.60)
Basic weighted average shares outstanding	57,143	59,306	64,524
Diluted weighted average and equivalent shares outstanding	57,428	59,425	64,524

See accompanying notes to consolidated financial statements.

Required:

Using the Consolidated Statements of Operations and the excerpts from the Zebra Technologies Corporation Form 10-K, analyze the profitability of Zebra. Your analysis should include the following calculations for all three years:

(a) Common-size income statements.
(b) Gross profit margins for tangible products and services and software.
(c) Growth rates of total net sales and total operating expenses.
(d) Effective tax rates.

Your written analysis and interpretation should include explanations for why trends have occurred.

CHAPTER 4

Statement of Cash Flows

"Joan and Joe: A Tale of Woe"
Joe added up profits and went to see Joan,
Assured of obtaining a much-needed loan.
When Joe arrived, he announced with good cheer:
"My firm has had an outstanding year,
And now I need a loan from your bank."
Eyeing the statements, Joan's heart sank.
"Your profits are fine," Joan said to Joe.
"But where, oh where, is your company's cash flow?
I'm sorry to say: the answer is 'no'."

—L. FRASER

The authors of this book are aware, based on feedback from readers over many years, that the statement of cash flows is the most challenging of the required corporate financial statements to read and interpret. As we have emphasized throughout the book, however, this statement is also critically important in assessing a firm's financial performance. Cash flow from operating activities—one of the key figures on the statement of cash flows—has been a major element in bankruptcies all the way back to W.T. Grant and up to and including Lehman Brothers, the largest bankruptcy in U.S. history. No single reported figure on any set of financial statements can be relied on as a predictor of future performance or as a measure of historical performance. But there are certainly important items that should always be assessed, and cash flow from operations, as well as related components of a cash flow statement, are among those key elements.

What we want to do in this chapter is to help readers understand the statement of cash flows as an essential analytical tool. When a company sells its products or services on credit, for instance, the sales revenue for that transaction is recognized in the accounting period when the sale is made, and an accounts receivable is created to reflect what the customer owes. In other words, the company has income posted on its income statement for which no cash has been received: net income but no cash flowing in from that particular operation. If the reverse occurs and the company receives payment on the account in a later accounting period, no income is recorded because the income has already been recognized: cash flowing in but no income from that transaction. In essence, that is what the statement of cash flow measures: the actual cash flowing in and flowing out during an accounting period from all the firm's operations as well as from its other activities, such as borrowings and investing.

Why Cash Flow Is Important: An Example

The statement of cash flows shows how cash has been generated during a year or a quarter, and how it has been used. For example, in the case of companies such as W.T. Grant, Lehman Brothers, and countless others, the firms were reporting impressive amounts of net income, but they were not collecting the associated cash from the transactions that produced the income. Cash flow from operations was negative. In such situations, to continue to operate, the companies needed cash from a source other than their primary business operations, and they borrowed heavily. This entire picture is presented in living color on a statement of cash flows.

Consider the three years before Lehman Brothers' bankruptcy:

From the Statement of Cash Flows.
Lehman Brothers Holding Inc. Millions of U.S. Dollars
for period ending Nov. 30,

	2007	2006	2005
Net Income	4,192	4,007	3,260
Cash from operations	(45,595)	(36,376)	(12,205)
Cash from investing	(1,698)	(792)	(447)
Cash from financing	48,592	38,255	12,112
New debt	89,683	52,934	23,789

The company reported rising amounts of net income while failing to generate any cash from its operations; these deficits were offset by borrowings, with new debt topping almost $90 billion in 2007, the year before its bankruptcy in 2008.

Would every company in financial difficulties have positive net income and negative cash flow from operations? Absolutely not. Some have the reverse, reported losses on the income statement and positive cash flow from operations. Or erratic patterns over several years. The cash flow statement is just one important piece of the analytical tool set, and within the statement, cash flow from operations can be a critical measure of operating success. The items just presented for Lehman Brothers are only a beginning. In addition to reporting net income and cash flow from operations, the statement of cash flows also shows the adjustments made to net income in order to calculate cash flow from operations; those should be examined to determine why cash flow from operations is negative or positive. Further, the analyst should consider cash flows over a period of time, looking at patterns of performance and exploring underlying causes of strength and weakness.

Ample evidence has been provided over the years—by firms of every conceivable size, structure, and type of business operation—that it is possible for a company to post a healthy net income but still not have the cash needed to pay its employees, suppliers, and bankers. The statement of cash flows provides the relevant and necessary information to assess a company's cash inflows and outflows during an accounting period and over time. As shown above, cash flows—on a statement of cash flows—are segregated by *operating activities, investing activities,* and *financing activities.*[1] A positive net income figure on the income statement is ultimately insignificant unless a company can translate its earnings into cash, and the only source in financial statements for learning about cash generation is the statement of cash flows.

Statement of Cash Flows: Basic Principle

Throughout this chapter, examples are used to underline the importance of the statement of cash flows in financial analysis and to show readers how to use this key information. Fundamental to this process of interpreting the information presented in a statement of cash flows is an explanation of how the statement is prepared as well as further discussion of cash flow from operations as an analytical tool in evaluating financial performance. Based on the many comments received from students, instructors, and other readers of this book, the authors believe that understanding how the statement is prepared greatly enhances the usefulness of the statement for analytical purposes. As with the other chapters, Sage Inc. will serve as a background for preparing a statement of cash flows and discussing its usefulness for financial analysis.

But before looking at Sage Inc. we want to begin with an even more basic principle. The statement of cash flows is, in reality, another way of presenting the balance sheet of a company; except in the case of a balance sheet, which shows amounts at the *end* of the accounting period, the statement of cash flows shows the *changes* in the balance sheet accounts between periods. That's fundamentally all a statement of cash flows is: a way of showing changes in the balance sheet accounts (not really that complicated in its basic approach).

The change in cash between periods is explained by the changes in all the other balance sheet accounts, and each balance sheet account is related either to an operating activity (e.g., accounts receivable, inventory, accounts payable, net income in the retained earnings account), an investing activity (e.g., purchase or sale of property, plant, and equipment), or a financing activity (e.g., borrowing and repaying debt). Cash flow from operating activities requires adjusting net income to a cash basis by using the changes in balance sheet accounts that relate to operations, such as accounts receivable. Remember that revenue from credit sales is recognized as income before the accounts receivable is collected. So, if accounts receivable show an increase between the two accounting periods, more revenue has been recognized than has been actually collected in cash. Cash flow from operations includes all such adjustments so that the figure represents, in essence, the amount of "cash" income from the company's business operations.

Understanding this basic principle that a statement of cash flows is based on changes in the balance sheet accounts is a major step forward both in preparing and in

[1]Financing and investing activities not involving cash receipts and payments—such as the exchange of debt for stock or the exchange of property—are reported in a separate schedule on the statement of cash flows.

analyzing the statement. Because the balance sheet balances, the statement of cash flows balances. The change in cash between accounting periods is equal to cash flow from operating activities (net inflow or outflow) and cash flow from investing activities (net inflow or outflow) and cash flow from financing activities (net inflow or outflow). Using the example from Lehman Brothers, shown above, the statement of cash flows for 2007 balances to the change in cash between November 30, 2006, and November 30, 2007:

Lehman Brothers Statement of Cash Flows at
November 30, 2007, Millions of U.S. Dollars

Cash flow from operating activities	(45,595)
Cash flow from investing activities	(1,698)
Cash flow from financing activities	48,592
Change in cash	1,299

Lehman Brothers' cash account increased by $1,299 million between November 30, 2006 and 2007. This change is explained by the following: operations used cash (net outflow) of $45,945 million; investing activities, such as capital expenditures, used cash (net outflow) of $1,698 million; and the company borrowed (net inflow), on a net basis, $48,592 million. In other words, the company borrowed (change in long-term debt account) in order to cover the cash deficit in operations (net income adjusted to cash by changes in short-term asset and liability accounts) and its capital expenditures (change in long-term asset accounts).

Now, using this basic principle, let's look at how to prepare the statement of cash flows for Sage Inc.

Shutterstock

Preparing a Statement of Cash Flows

Preparing the statement of cash flows begins with a return to the balance sheet, covered in Chapter 2. The statement of cash flows requires a reordering of the information presented on a balance sheet. The balance sheet shows account balances at the end of an accounting period, and the statement of cash flows shows changes in those same account balances between accounting periods (see Figure 4.1). The statement is called a statement of *flows* because it shows *changes over time rather than the absolute dollar amount of the accounts at a point in time.* Because a balance sheet balances, the changes in all of the balance sheet accounts balance, and the changes that reflect cash inflows less the changes that result from cash outflows will equal the changes in the cash account.

FIGURE 4.1 How Cash Flows During an Accounting Period

Operating Activities

Inflows	*Outflows*
Cash from sales of goods or services	Payments for purchase of inventory
Returns on equity securities (dividends)	Payments for operating expenses (salaries, rent, etc.)
Returns on interest-earning assets (interest)	Payments for purchases from suppliers other than inventory
	Payments to lenders (interest)
	Payments for taxes

Investing Activities

Inflows	*Outflows*
Cash from sales of property, plant, and equipment	Purchases of property, plant, and equipment
Cash collections from loans (principal) to others	Loans (principal) to others
Cash from sales of debt or equity securities of other entities (except securities traded as cash equivalents)*	Purchases of debt or equity securities of other entities*
Cash from sale of a business segment	

Financing Activities

Inflows	*Outflows*
Proceeds from borrowing	Repayments of debt principal
Proceeds from issuing the firm's own equity securities	Repurchase of a firm's own shares
	Payment of dividends

Total Inflows less Total Outflows = Change in cash for the accounting period

*Cash flows from purchases, sales, and maturities of trading securities shall be classified based on the nature and purpose for which the securities were acquired.

EXHIBIT 4.1 Sage Inc. Consolidated Statements of Cash Flows for the Years Ended December 31, 2013, 2012, and 2011 (in Thousands)

	2013	2012	2011
Cash Flows from Operating Activities—Indirect Method			
Net income	$ 9,394	$ 5,910	$ 5,896
Adjustments to reconcile net income to cash provided (used) by operating activities			
Depreciation and amortization	3,998	2,984	2,501
Deferred income taxes	208	136	118
Cash provided (used) by current assets and liabilities			
Accounts receivable	(610)	(3,339)	(448)
Inventories	(10,272)	(7,006)	(2,331)
Prepaid expenses	247	295	(82)
Accounts payable	6,703	(1,051)	902
Accrued liabilities	(229)	(1,215)	(1,130)
Income taxes payable	585	(481)	203
Net cash provided (used) by operating activities	$ 10,024	($ 3,767)	$ 5,629
Cash Flows from Investing Activities			
Additions to property, plant, and equipment	(14,100)	(4,773)	(3,982)
Other investing activities	295	0	0
Net cash provided (used) by investing activities	($ 13,805)	($ 4,773)	($ 3,982)
Cash Flows from Financing Activities			
Sales of common stock	256	183	124
Increase (decrease) in short-term borrowings (includes current maturities of long-term debt)	(30)	1,854	1,326
Additions to long-term borrowings	5,600	7,882	629
Reductions of long-term borrowings	(1,516)	(1,593)	(127)
Dividends paid	(1,582)	(1,862)	(1,841)
Net cash provided (used) by financing activities	$ 2,728	$ 6,464	$ 111
Increase (decrease) in cash and cash equivalents	($ 1,053)	($ 2,076)	$ 1,758
Cash and cash equivalents, beginning of year	10,386	12,462	10,704
Cash and cash equivalents, end of year	9,333	10,386	12,462
Supplemental cash flow information:			
Cash paid for interest	$ 2,585	$ 2,277	$ 1,274
Cash paid for taxes	7,478	4,321	4,706

The accompanying notes are an integral part of these statements.

The statement of cash flows is prepared in exactly that way: by calculating the changes in all of the balance sheet accounts, including *cash;* then listing the changes in all of the accounts except cash as *inflows* or *outflows;* and categorizing the flows by *operating, financing,* or *investing* activities. The *inflows less the outflows balance to and explain the change in cash.*

To classify the account changes on the balance sheet, first review the definitions of the four parts of a statement of cash flows:

- Cash
- Operating activities
- Investing activities
- Financing activities

Cash includes cash and highly liquid short-term marketable securities, also called *cash equivalents.* Cash equivalents are included as cash for Sage Inc. because they represent, as explained in Chapter 2, short-term highly liquid investments that can be readily converted into cash. They include U.S. Treasury bills, certificates, notes, and bonds; negotiable certificates of deposit at financial institutions; and commercial paper. Some companies will separate marketable securities into two accounts: (1) cash and cash equivalents and (2) short-term investments. When this occurs, the short-term investments are classified as investing activities.

Operating activities include delivering or producing goods for sale and providing services and the cash effects of transactions and other events that enter into the determination of income.

Investing activities include (1) acquiring and selling or otherwise disposing of (a) securities that are not cash equivalents and (b) productive assets that are expected to benefit the firm for long periods of time and (2) lending money and collecting on loans.

Financing activities include borrowing from creditors and repaying the principal and obtaining resources from owners and providing them with a return on the investment.

With these definitions in mind, consider Exhibit 4.2, a worksheet for preparing the statement of cash flows that shows comparative 2013 and 2012 balance sheet accounts for Sage Inc. Included in this exhibit is a column with the account balance changes and the category (or categories) that applies to each account. Explanations of how each account change is used in a statement of cash flow will be provided in subsequent sections of this chapter.

The next step is to transfer the account changes to the appropriate area of a statement of cash flows.[2] In doing so, a determination must also be made of what constitutes an inflow and what constitutes an outflow when analyzing the change in an account balance. The following table should help:

Inflow	**Outflow**
− Asset account	+ Asset account
+ Liability account	− Liability account
+ Equity account	− Equity account

[2]Several alternative formats can be used for presenting the statement of cash flows, provided that the statement is reconciled to the change in cash and shows cash inflows and outflows from operating, financing, and investing activities.

EXHIBIT 4.2 Sage Inc. Worksheet for Preparing Statement of Cash Flows (in Thousands)

	2013	2012	Change (2013–2012)	Category
Assets				
(1) Cash	$ 9,333	$ 10,386	$ (1,053)	Cash
(2) Accounts receivable (net)	8,960	8,350	610	Operating
(3) Inventories	47,041	36,769	10,272	Operating
(4) Prepaid expenses	512	759	(247)	Operating
(5) Property, plant, and equipment	40,607	26,507	14,100	Investing
(6) Accumulated depreciation and amortization	(11,528)	(7,530)	(3,998)	Operating
(7) Goodwill	270	270	0	Investing
(8) Other assets	103	398	(295)	Investing
Liabilities and Stockholders' Equity				
Liabilities				
(9) Accounts payable	14,294	7,591	6,703	Operating
(10) Accrued liabilities	4,137	4,366	(229)	Operating
(11) Income taxes payable	1,532	947	585	Operating
(12) Short-term debt	5,614	6,012	(398)	Financing
(13) Current maturities of long-term debt	1,884	1,516	368	Financing
(14) Deferred income taxes	843	635	208	Operating
(15) Long-term borrowings				
Additions to long-term borrowings			5,600	
Reductions of long-term borrowings			(1,516)	
Net change in long-term debt	21,059	16,975	$ 4,084	Financing
Stockholders' Equity				
(16) Common stock and additional paid-in capital	5,760	5,504	256	Financing
(17) Retained earnings				
(a) Net income			9,394	Operating
(b) Dividends paid			(1,582)	Financing
Net change in retained earnings	$40,175	$32,363	$ 7,812	

The table indicates that a decrease in an asset balance and an increase in liability and equity accounts are inflows.[3] Examples from Exhibit 4.2 are the decrease in other assets (cash inflow from the sale of property not used in the business), the increase in long-term debt (cash inflow from borrowing), and the increase in common stock and additional paid-in capital (cash inflow from sales of equity securities). Outflows are represented by the increase in inventories (cash outflow to purchase inventory) and the decrease in notes payable (cash outflow to repay borrowings).

[3]In accounting terminology, an inflow results from the decrease in a debit balance account or an increase in a credit balance account; an outflow results from the increase in a debit balance account or the decrease in a credit balance account.

Note that accumulated depreciation appears in the asset section but actually is a contra-asset or credit balance account because it reduces the amount of total assets. Accumulated depreciation is shown in parentheses on the balance sheet and has the same effect as a liability account.

Another complication occurs from the impact of *two transactions in one account.* For example, the net increase in retained earnings has resulted from the combination of net income for the period, which increases the account, and the payment of dividends, which reduces the account. Multiple transactions can also affect other accounts, such as property, plant, and equipment, if a firm both acquires and sells capital assets during the period, and debt accounts if the firm both borrows and repays principal.

(1) Cash and cash equivalents are cash. The change in this account—a net decrease of $1,053 thousand—will be explained by the changes in all of the other accounts. This means that for the year ending 2013, the cash outflows have exceeded the cash inflows by $1,053 thousand.

(2)(3)(4) Accounts receivable, inventories, and prepaid expenses are all operating accounts relating to sales of goods, purchases of inventories, and payments for operating expenses.

(5) The net increase in property, plant, and equipment is an investing activity reflecting purchases of long-lived assets.

(6) The change in accumulated depreciation and amortization is classified as operating because it will be used as an adjustment to operating expenses or net income to determine cash flow from operating activities.

(7) Goodwill is an investing activity reflecting the amount paid for an acquisition in excess of the fair market value of the assets acquired.

(8) Other assets are holdings of land held for resale, representing an investing activity.

(9) Accounts payable is an operating account because it arises from purchases of inventory.

(10) Accrued liabilities are operating because they result from the accrual of operating expenses such as wages, rent, salaries, and insurance.

(11) Income taxes payable is an operating activity because it arises from taxes owed.

(12)(13) Short-term debt and current maturities of long-term debt result from borrowing (debt principal), a financing activity.

(14) The change in deferred income taxes is categorized as operating because it is part of the adjustment of tax expense to calculate cash flow from operating activities.

(15) The change in long-term debt, principal on borrowings, is a financing activity.

(16) Common stock and paid-in capital are also financing activities because the changes result from sales of the firm's own equity shares.

(17) The change in retained earnings, as explained in Chapter 3, is the product of two activities: (a) net income for the period, which is operating, and (b) the payment of cash dividends, which is a financing activity.

Calculating Cash Flow from Operating Activities

The Sage Inc. Consolidated Statements of Cash Flows begins with cash flow from operating activities. This represents the cash generated *internally*. In contrast, investing and financing activities provide cash from *external* sources. Firms may use one of two methods prescribed by the Financial Accounting Standards Board (FASB) for calculating and presenting cash flow from operating activities: the direct method and the indirect method. The *direct method* shows cash collections from customers, interest and dividends collected, other operating cash receipts, cash paid to suppliers and employees, interest paid, taxes paid, and other operating cash payments. The *indirect method* starts with net income and adjusts for deferrals; accruals; noncash items, such as depreciation and amortization; and nonoperating items, such as gains and losses on asset sales. The direct and indirect methods yield identical figures for net cash flow from operating activities because the underlying accounting concepts are the same. According to *Accounting Trends and Techniques*, 495 firms out of 500 used the indirect method in 2010.[4] The *indirect method* is illustrated and explained for Sage Inc. in the chapter and the *direct method* is illustrated in Appendix 4A.

Indirect Method

Exhibit 4.3 illustrates the steps necessary to convert net income to cash flow from operating activities. The steps shown in Exhibit 4.3 will be used to explain the calculation of cash flow from operating activities for Sage Inc. using the indirect method. Exhibit 4.3 includes some adjustments not present for Sage Inc.

Sage Inc. Indirect Method

Net income	$ 9,394
Adjustments to reconcile net income to cash provided by operating activities:	
+ Depreciation and amortization expense	3,998
+ Increase in deferred tax liability	208
Cash provided (used) by current assets and liabilities	
− Increase in accounts receivables	(610)
− Increase in inventory	(10,272)
+ Decrease in prepaid expenses	247
+ Increase in accounts payable	6,703
− Decrease in accrued liabilities	(229)
+ Increase in income taxes payable	585
Net cash flow from operating activities	$10,024

Depreciation and amortization are added back to net income because they reflect the recognition of a noncash expense. Remember that depreciation represents a cost allocation, not an outflow of cash. The acquisition of the capital asset was recognized as

[4] American Institute of Certified Public Accountants, *Accounting Trends and Techniques*, 2010.

EXHIBIT 4.3 Net Cash Flow from Operating Activities—Indirect Method

Net income*

Noncash/nonoperating revenue and expense included in income:

+ Depreciation, amortization, depletion expense for period

+ Increase in deferred tax liability
– Decrease in deferred tax liability

+ Decrease in deferred tax asset
– Increase in deferred tax asset

– Increase in investment account from equity income**
+ Decrease in investment account from equity income***

– Gain on sale of assets
+ Loss on sale of assets

Cash provided (used) by current assets and liabilities

+ Decrease in accounts receivable
– Increase in accounts receivable

+ Decrease in inventory
– Increase in inventory

+ Decrease in prepaid expenses
– Increase in prepaid expenses

+ Decrease in interest receivable
– Increase in interest receivable

+ Increase in accounts payable
– Decrease in accounts payable

+ Increase in accrued liabilities
– Decrease in accrued liabilities

+ Increase in income taxes payable
– Decrease in income taxes payable

+ Increase in deferred revenue
– Decrease in deferred revenue

Net cash flow from operating activities

*Before extraordinary items, accounting changes, discontinued operations.
**Amount by which equity income exceeds cash dividends received.
***Amount by which cash dividends received exceed equity income recognized.

an investing cash outflow (unless it was exchanged for debt or stock) in the statement of cash flows for the period in which the asset was acquired. So depreciation itself does not require any outflow of cash in the year it is recognized. Deducting depreciation expense in the current year's statement of cash flows would be double counting. Amortization is similar to depreciation—an expense that enters into the determination of net income but that does not require an outflow of cash. Depletion would be handled in the same manner as depreciation and amortization. The depreciation and amortization expense for Sage Inc. in 2013 is equal to the change in the balance sheet accumulated depreciation and amortization account. If the firm had dispositions of capital assets during the accounting period, however, the balance sheet change would not equal the expense recognition for the period because some of the account change would have resulted from the elimination of accumulated depreciation for the asset that was removed. The appropriate figure to subtract would be depreciation and amortization expense from the earnings statement.

The *deferred tax liability* account, as discussed in Chapter 2, reconciles the difference between tax expense recognized in the calculation of net income and the tax expense actually paid. The increase in the liability account for Sage Inc. is added back to net income because more tax expense was recognized in the calculation of net income than was actually paid for taxes.

The increase in *accounts receivable* is deducted because more sales revenue has been included in net income than has been collected in cash from customers.

The increase in *inventory* is subtracted because Sage Inc. has purchased more inventory than has been included in cost of goods sold. Cost of goods sold used in calculating net income includes only the inventory actually sold.

The decrease in *prepaid expenses* is added back because the firm has recognized an expense in the current period for which cash was paid in an earlier period, on a net basis.

The increase in *accounts payable* is added because less has been paid to suppliers for purchases of inventory than was included in cost of goods sold.

The decrease in *accrued liabilities* is subtracted from net income because it reflects the payment of cash for expenses recorded in a prior period.

The increase in *income taxes payable* is added because less has been paid for taxes than was recorded as income tax expense.

There are other potential adjustments, not required for Sage Inc., that enter into the net income adjustment for noncash expense and revenues. One such item is the recognition of investment income from unconsolidated subsidiaries by the equity method of accounting, discussed in Chapter 3. When a company uses the equity method, earnings can be recognized in the income statement in excess of cash actually received from dividends, or the reverse can occur, for example, in the case of a loss recorded by an investee. For a firm using the equity method, there would be a deduction from net income for the amount by which investment income recognized exceeded cash received. Other potential adjustment items include changes relating to deferred income, deferred expense, the amortization of bond discounts and premiums, extraordinary items, and gains or losses on sales of long-lived assets.

Although *gains and losses from asset sales* are included in the calculation of net income, they are not considered an operating activity. A gain should be deducted from net income, and a loss should be added to net income to determine cash flow from operating activities. The entire proceeds from sales of long-lived assets are included as cash inflows from investing.

Cash Flow from Investing Activities

Additions to *property, plant, and equipment* represent a net addition to Sage Inc.'s buildings, leasehold improvements, and equipment, a cash outflow of $14.1 million. Other investing activities for Sage Inc. result from a decrease in the *other assets* account on the balance sheet, which represent holdings of investment properties. The sale of these assets has provided a cash inflow of $295 thousand.

Cash Flow from Financing Activities

As a result of the exercise of stock options, Sage Inc. issued new shares of stock during 2013. The total cash generated from stock sales amounted to $256 thousand.

The two accounts—short-term debt and current maturities of long-term debt (carried as a current liability because the principal is payable within a year)—jointly explain Sage Inc.'s net reduction in short-term borrowings in 2013 of $30 thousand:

Short-term debt	($398)	Outflow
Current maturities of long-term debt	368	Inflow
	($ 30)	Net outflow

In preparing the statement of cash flows, long-term borrowings should be segregated into two components: additions to long-term borrowings and reductions of long-term borrowings. This information is provided in Note 2, Debt, to the Sage Inc. financial statements, where detail on the various long-term notes is provided. The two figures—additions to long-term debt and reductions of long-term debt—on the Sage Inc. statement of cash flows reconcile the change in the *long-term debt* account on the Sage Inc. balance sheet:

Additions to long-term borrowings	$5,600	Inflow
Reductions of long-term borrowings	(1,516)	Outflow
Increase in long-term debt	$4,084	

The payment of cash dividends by Sage Inc. in 2013 of $1,582 million is the final item in the financing activities section. The change in *retained earnings* results from the combination of net income recognition and the payment of cash dividends; this information is provided in the Sage Inc. Statement of Stockholders' Equity:

Net income	$9,394	Inflow
Dividends paid	(1,582)	Outflow
Change in retained earnings	$7,812	

It should be noted that the *payment* of cash dividends is the financing outflow; the *declaration* of a cash dividend would not affect cash.

Change in Cash

To summarize the cash inflows and outflows for 2013 for Sage Inc., the net cash provided by operating activities, less the net cash used by investing activities, plus the net cash provided by financing activities produced a net decrease in *cash* and *cash equivalents* for the period:

Net cash provided by operating activities	$10,024
Net cash used by investing activities	(13,805)
Net cash provided by financing activities	2,728
Decrease in cash and cash equivalents	(1,053)

FIGURE 4.2 Comparison of Cash Flows

	Walmart	Active Power Inc.
For the Year Ended:	January 31, 2010 (in millions)	December 31, 2010 (in thousands)
Net cash provided (used) by:		
Operating activities	$26,249	$ 68
Investing activities	(11,620)	(1,243)
Financing activities	(14,191)	9,084
Net increase in cash and cash equivalents	$ 632*	$7,927*

Walmart, a consumer goods retailer, generated enough cash from operations to easily cover the company's investing and financing activities, while also increasing the cash account. Active Power Inc., an energy company that provides products for the majority of power disturbances, also increased its cash account overall, but the majority of cash was not from operating activities. Instead, Active Power Inc. generated cash from financing activities to increase the cash balance.

*Net increase in cash and cash equivalents was also affected by cash flows from the effect of exchange rate changes of $194 for Walmart and $18 for Active Power Inc.

The statement for 2012 and 2011 would be prepared using the same process that was illustrated for 2013. The cash flows provided (used) by operating, investing, and financing activities vary considerably depending on the company, its performance for the year, its ability to generate cash, its financing and investment strategies, and its success in implementing these strategies. Figure 4.2 illustrates this for two companies in different industries.

Analyzing the Statement of Cash Flows

The statement of cash flows is an important analytical tool for creditors, investors, and other users of financial statement data that helps determine the following about a business firm:

- Its ability to generate cash flows in the future
- Its capacity to meet obligations for cash
- Its future external financing needs
- Its success in productively managing investing activities
- Its effectiveness in implementing financing and investing strategies

To begin the analysis of a statement of cash flows, it is essential to understand the importance of cash flow from operations, the first category on the statement.

Cash Flow from Operations

It is possible for a firm to be highly profitable and not be able to pay dividends or invest in new equipment. It is possible for a firm to be highly profitable and not be

Shutterstock/Natalilia Natykach

able to service debt. It is also possible for a firm to be highly profitable and go bankrupt. W. T. Grant is one of the classic examples.[5] How? The problem is cash. Consider the following questions:

1. You are a banker evaluating a loan request from a prospective customer. What is your primary concern when making a decision regarding approval or denial of the loan request?
2. You are a wholesaler of goods and have been asked to sell your products on credit to a potential buyer. What is the major determining factor regarding approval or denial of the credit sale?
3. You are an investor in a firm and rely on the receipt of regular cash dividends as part of your return on investment. What must the firm generate in order to pay dividends?

In each case, the answer is *cash*. The banker must decide whether the prospective borrower will have the cash to meet interest and principal payments on the debt. The wholesaler will sell goods on credit only to those customers who can satisfy their accounts. A company can pay cash dividends only by producing cash.

The ongoing operation of any business depends on its success in generating cash from operations. It is cash that a firm needs to satisfy creditors and investors. Temporary shortfalls of cash can be satisfied by borrowing or other means, such as selling long-lived assets, but ultimately a company must generate cash.

Cash flow from operations has become increasingly important as an analytical tool to determine the financial health of a business enterprise. Periods of high interest rates and inflation contributed to the enhanced attention paid to cash flow by investors and creditors. When interest rates are high, the cost of borrowing to cover short-term cash can be out of reach for many firms seeking to cover temporary cash shortages. Periods of inflation distort the meaningfulness of net income, through the understatement of depreciation and cost of goods sold expenses, making other measures of operating

[5] J. A. Largay and C. P. Stickney, "Cash Flows, Ratio Analysis, and the W. T. Grant Bankruptcy," *Financial Analysts Journal,* July–August 1980.

performance and financial success important. Even when interest rates and inflation are low, there are other factors that limit the usefulness of net income as a barometer of financial health. Consider the case of Nocash Corporation.

Nocash Corporation

The Nocash Corporation had sales of $100,000 in its second year of operations, up from $50,000 in the first year. Expenses, including taxes, amounted to $70,000 in year 2, compared with $40,000 in year 1. The comparative income statements for the two years indicate substantial growth, with year 2 earnings greatly improved over those reported in year 1.

Nocash Corporation Income Statement for Year 1 and Year 2

	Year 1	Year 2
Sales	$50,000	$100,000
Expenses	40,000	70,000
Net income	$10,000	$ 30,000

So far, so good—a tripling of profit for Nocash. There are some additional facts, however, that are relevant to Nocash's operations but that do not appear on the firm's income statement:

1. In order to improve sales in year 2, Nocash eased its credit policies and attracted customers of a substantially lower quality than in year 1.
2. Nocash purchased a new line of inventory near the end of year 1, and it became apparent during year 2 that the inventory could not be sold, except at substantial reductions below cost.
3. Rumors regarding Nocash's problems with regard to accounts receivable and inventory management prompted some suppliers to refuse the sale of goods on credit to Nocash.

The effect of these additional factors can be found on Nocash's balance sheet.

Nocash Corporation Balance Sheet at December 31

	Year 1	Year 2	$ Change
Cash	$ 2,000	$ 2,000	0
Accounts receivable	10,000	30,000	+20,000(1)
Inventories	10,000	25,000	+15,000(2)
Total assets	$22,000	$57,000	+35,000
Accounts payable	7,000	2,000	–5,000(3)
Notes payable—to banks	0	10,000	+10,000
Equity	15,000	45,000	+30,000
Total liabilities and equity	$22,000	$57,000	+35,000

(1)Accounts receivable increased at a faster pace than sales as a result of deterioration in customer quality.

(2)Ending inventory increased and included items that would ultimately be sold at a loss.

(3)Nocash's inability to purchase goods on credit caused a reduction in accounts payable.

If Nocash's net income is recalculated on a cash basis, the following adjustments would be made, using the account balance changes between year 1 and year 2:

Net income	$30,000
(1) Accounts receivable	(20,000)
(2) Inventories	(15,000)
(3) Accounts payable	(5,000)
Cash income	($10,000)

(1) The increase in accounts receivable is subtracted because more sales revenue was recognized in computing net income than was collected in cash.

Sales recognized in net income		$100,000
Sales collected		
Beginning accounts receivable	$ 10,000	
Plus: sales, year 2	100,000	
Less: ending accounts receivable	(30,000)	80,000
Difference between net income and cash flow		$ 20,000

(2) The increase in inventory is deducted, reflecting the cash outflow for inventory purchases in excess of the expense recognized through cost of goods sold.

Purchases for inventory*	$75,000
Less: cost of goods sold	(60,000)
Difference between net income and cash flow	$15,000

(3) The decrease in accounts payable is deducted because the cash payments to suppliers in year 2 were greater than the amount of expense recorded. (In essence, cash was paid for some year 1 accounts as well as year 2 accounts.)

Payments to suppliers**	$ 80,000
Less: purchases for inventory*	75,000
Difference between net income and cash flow	$ 5,000
*Ending inventory	$ 25,000
Plus: cost of goods sold	60,000
Less: beginning inventory	(10,000)
Purchases of inventory	$ 75,000
**Beginning accounts payable	$ 7,000
Plus: purchases	75,000
Less: ending accounts payable	(2,000)
Payments to suppliers	$ 80,000

How did Nocash cover its $10,000 cash shortfall? Note the appearance of a $10,000 note payable to banks on the year 2 balance sheet. The borrowing has enabled Nocash to continue to operate, but unless the company can begin to generate cash from operations, its problems will compound. Bankers sometimes refer to this problem as a company's "selling itself out of business." The higher the cost of borrowing, the more costly and difficult it will be for Nocash to continue to operate.

Sage Inc.: Analysis of the Statement of Cash Flows

An analysis of the statement of cash flows should, at a minimum, cover the following areas:

- Analysis of cash flow from operating activities
- Analysis of cash inflows
- Analysis of cash outflows

An example of an analysis of a statement of cash flows is presented for Sage Inc. in the following sections.

Sage Inc. Analysis: Cash Flow from Operating Activities

The statement of cash flows provides the figure "net cash flow from operating activities." An excerpt from the Statement of Cash Flows for Sage Inc. is shown in Exhibit 4.4. The analyst should be concerned with the following in reviewing this information:

- The success or failure of the firm in generating cash from operations
- The underlying causes of the positive or negative operating cash flow
- The magnitude of positive or negative operating cash flow
- Fluctuations in cash flow from operations over time

For Sage Inc. the first point of significance is the negative cash flow from operations in 2012 ($3,767 thousand). It should be noted that the negative cash flow occurred for a year in which the company reported positive net income of $5,910 thousand. The cash flow crunch was apparently caused primarily by a substantial growth in accounts receivable and inventories. Those increases were partly the result of the firm's expansion policies, and it would also be important to evaluate the quality of receivables and inventory—that is, are they collectable and salable? Sage Inc. was able to recover in 2013, returning to strongly positive cash generation of $10,024 thousand,

EXHIBIT 4.4 Sage Inc. Cash Flows from Operating Activities for the Years Ended December 31, 2013, 2012, and 2011 (in Thousands)

	2013	2012	2011
Cash Flows from Operating Activities—Indirect Method			
Net income	$ 9,394	$ 5,910	$ 5,896
Adjustments to reconcile net income to cash provided (used) by operating activities			
Depreciation and amortization	3,998	2,984	2,501
Deferred income taxes	208	136	118
Cash provided (used) by current assets and liabilities			
Accounts receivable	(610)	(3,339)	(448)
Inventories	(10,272)	(7,006)	(2,331)
Prepaid expenses	247	295	(82)
Accounts payable	6,703	(1,051)	902
Accrued liabilities	(229)	(1,215)	(1,130)
Income taxes payable	585	(481)	203
Net cash provided (used) by operating activities	$10,024	($3,767)	$5,629

in spite of the continuation of inventory growth to support the expansion. The company obtained good supplier credit in 2010 and controlled the growth in accounts receivable. It will be necessary to monitor Sage Inc.'s cash flow from operations closely and, in particular, the management of inventories. Inventory growth is desirable when supporting an expansion of sales but undesirable when, like Nocash Corporation, the inventory is not selling or is selling only at discounted prices.

The calculation of cash flow from operations illustrated for Sage Inc. can be made for any company from its balance sheet and income statement, using the procedures outlined in the examples. Cash flow from operations is especially important for those firms that are heavily invested in inventories and that use trade accounts receivables and payables as a major part of ordinary business operations. Such problems as sales growth that is too rapid, slow-moving or obsolete inventory, price discounting within the industry, a rise in accounts receivable of inferior quality, and the tightening of credit by suppliers can all impair the firm's ability to generate cash from operations and lead to serious financial problems, including bankruptcy.

Summary Analysis of the Statement of Cash Flows

Exhibit 4.5 is an excerpt from Sage Inc.'s Statement of Cash Flows and will be used with Exhibits 4.1 and 4.4 to illustrate how to prepare a summary analysis of the statement of cash flows. The summary analysis is one way to common size the cash flow statement. The purpose of the summary table is to provide an approach to analyzing a statement of cash flows that can be used for any firm that provides comparative cash flow data. The information in the summary table underlines the importance of internal cash generation—from operations—and the implications for investing and financing activities when this does and does not occur.

EXHIBIT 4.5 Sage Inc. Cash Flows from Investing and Financing Activities for the Years Ended December 31, 2013, 2012, and 2011 (in Thousands)

	2013	2012	2011
Cash Flows from Investing Activities			
Additions to property, plant, and equipment	(14,100)	(4,773)	(3,982)
Other investing activities	295	0	0
Net cash provided (used) by investing activities	($ 13,805)	($ 4,773)	($ 3,982)
Cash Flows from Financing Activities			
Sales of common stock	256	183	124
Increase (decrease) in short-term borrowings (includes current maturities of long-term debt)	(30)	1,854	1,326
Additions to long-term borrowings	5,600	7,882	629
Reductions of long-term borrowings	(1,516)	(1,593)	(127)
Dividends paid	(1,582)	(1,862)	(1,841)
Net cash provided (used) by financing activities	$ 2,728	$ 6,464	$ 111

EXHIBIT 4.6 Sage Inc. Summary Analysis Statement of Cash Flows

	2013	%	2012	%	2011	%
Inflows (dollars in thousands)						
Operations	$10,024	62.0	$ 0	0.0	$5,629	73.0
Other investing activities	295	1.8	0	0.0	0	0.0
Sales of common stock	256	1.6	183	1.8	124	1.6
Additions to short-term debt	0	0.0	1,854	18.7	1,326	17.2
Additions to long-term debt	5,600	34.6	7,882	79.5	629	8.2
Total	$16,175	100.0	$ 9,919	100.0	$7,708	100.0
Outflows (dollars in thousands)						
Operations	$ 0	0.0	$ 3,767	31.4	$ 0	0.0
Purchase of property, plant, and equipment	14,100	81.8	4,773	40.0	3,982	66.9
Reductions of short-term debt	30	0.2	0	0.0	0	0.0
Reductions of long-term debt	1,516	8.8	1,593	13.2	127	2.1
Dividends paid	$ 1,582	9.2	$ 1,862	15.4	$1,841	31.0
Total	$17,228	100.0	$11,995	100.0	$5,950	100.0
Change in cash and cash equivalents	($ 1,053)		($ 2,076)		$1,758	

Exhibit 4.6 presents the summary analysis table to facilitate the analysis of Sage Inc.'s statement of cash flows, including cash flow from operating activities. The columns of the exhibit with dollar amounts show the inflows and outflows over the three-year period from 2011 to 2013 for Sage Inc. The columns of Exhibit 4.6 with percentages show the cash inflows as a percentage of total inflows and the outflows as a percentage of total outflows.

First, consider the dollar amounts. It is apparent that the magnitude of Sage Inc.'s activity has increased sharply over the three-year period, with total cash inflows increasing from $7.7 million to $16.2 million and cash outflows from $6.0 million to $17.2 million. Using the summary analysis, an evaluation of the cash inflows and outflows for Sage Inc. is discussed next.

Analysis of Cash Inflows

In percentage terms, it is noteworthy that operations supplied 62% of needed cash in 2013 and 73% in 2011. As a result of negative cash from operations in 2012, the firm had to borrow heavily, with debt (short term and long term) accounting for 98% of 2012 inflows. Sage Inc. also borrowed in 2013 and 2011 to obtain needed cash not supplied by operations. Generating cash from operations is the preferred method for obtaining excess cash to finance capital expenditures and expansion, repay debt, and pay dividends; however, most firms at one time or another will use external sources to generate cash. Using external sources to generate the majority of cash year after year should be investigated further.

Analysis of Cash Outflows

The major increase in cash outflows is capital asset expansion. Although it appears that the purchases of property, plant, and equipment decreased in 2012 (40.0% of cash outflows) compared to 2011 (66.9% of cash outflows), realize that the common denominator in the summary analysis is one particular year's cash outflows. Capital expenditures actually increased in dollars from $3,982 thousand to $4,773 thousand, but the percentages are skewed in 2012 because of the negative cash flow from operations. Also notice that dividends paid increased from 2011 to 2012, decreasing in 2013 (in dollars), yet the percentages decline each year because each year's total cash outflows vary.

When analyzing the cash outflows, the analyst should consider the necessity of the outflow and how the outflow was financed. Sage Inc. was able to cover capital expenditures easily with excess cash generated by operations in 2011. Capital expenditures are usually a good investment for most firms as purchasing new equipment and expansion should result in future revenues and cash flows from operations. Because of the negative cash flow from operations in 2012, Sage Inc. had to borrow to finance capital expenditures, repayment of debt, and dividend payments. In 2013, the company's strong generation of cash from operations supported most of the capital expenditures (82%) with only 35% external financing. It is favorable that Sage Inc. has financed long-term assets (capital expenditures) with either internally generated cash or long-term debt. Generally, it is best for firms to finance short-term assets with short-term debt and long-term assets with long-term debt or issuance of stock. Financing acquisitions and capital expenditures with short-term debt is risky because the firm may not generate cash flow quickly enough to repay short-term debt.

Repayment of debt is a necessary outflow. If the firm has generated cash from debt in prior years, a cash outflow in a subsequent year to repay debt will be required. The notes to the financial statements reveal future debt repayments and are useful in assessing how much cash will be needed in upcoming years to repay outstanding debt.

Dividends are paid at the discretion of the board of directors. In theory, firms should only pay dividends if the company has excess cash, not needed for (a) expansion; (b) property, plant, or equipment; or (c) repayment of debt. It appears that Sage Inc. may have reduced the dividends in 2013 as a result of the lack of cash from operations in 2012.

Qualitative Issues Relating to the Statement of Cash Flows

Since the requirement of the statement of cash flows in the 1980s, analysts have focused more heavily on cash flow from operations (CFO) as a measure of operating performance, but users should be aware that the CFO figure, while useful, can also be affected by the same kind of qualitative issues that affect the balance sheet and earnings statement.

The demise of WorldCom in 2002 brought to the forefront one issue of manipulating CFO when WorldCom recorded as capital expenditures billions of dollars that should have been recorded as operating expenses. For the cash flow statement, these outflows appear as investing activities rather than as a direct reduction of cash flow from operations. (The expense portion of a capital expense is depreciation, which is added back to net income in determining cash flow from operating activities.) The effects of recording operating expenses as capital expenditures are illustrated by the following example:

> A company records $100 million in operating expenses as a capital expenditure to be depreciated over 10 years with no salvage value.
>
> - Net income is overstated by $90 million. (Only the $10 million in depreciation expense has been included as an expense.)
> - Cash flow from operations is overstated by $100 million. On the statement of cash flows, depreciation expense of $10 million is added back to net income in determining cash flow from operations.
> - Investing activity outflows are overstated by $100 million.

Other techniques exist for companies to inflate the CFO figure. Through the management of current asset and liability accounts, companies can cause increases to CFO. For example, by selling accounts receivable, a firm receives cash immediately, recorded as a decrease in accounts receivable and an increase to CFO. Delaying cash payment on accounts payable also has the effect of increasing CFO. Significant changes in current asset and current liability accounts should be scrutinized in the assessment of CFO.

The SEC's concerns about how companies accounted for vendor financing transactions in their cash flow statements led to restatements in 2004 of prior cash flow numbers at companies such as General Motors, Ford Motor Company, General Electric, and Caterpillar. The SEC has made it clear that vendor financing is a result of operating activities and, as such, should be included as part of CFO, not cash from investing activities as the above-mentioned companies were reporting these amounts. Caterpillar's CFO, positive before the restatement, declined $6.3 billion in 2002 and $7.7 billion in 2003 after the restatement, causing CFO to be negative both years.[6]

Nonfinancial companies that invest in trading securities (discussed in Chapter 2) record purchases and sales of these securities in the operating activities section of the cash flow statement. While this treatment is within GAAP guidelines, these items are investing, not operating, activities and should be eliminated if the financial statement user wants a more accurate operating figure for cash flow. CFO should also be adjusted for any other items that are deemed nonrecurring or nonoperating. In addition to the elimination of cash flows from investments in trading securities, cash flows from items such as discontinued operations or nonrecurring expenses or income should be removed for analytical purposes.

[6] Michael Rapoport, "'Cash Flow' Isn't What It Used to Be," *Wall Street Journal*, March 24, 2005.

Are We There Yet?

The journey through the maze of information has taken us through the financial statements as well as many other items in an annual report, including an assessment of the quality of financial reporting. The final step in the process of interpreting financial statements for intelligent business decision-making is an in-depth analysis of financial statement data, presented in Chapter 5.

Shutterstock

Appendix 4A: Statement of Cash Flows—Direct Method

Direct Method

Exhibit 4A.1 illustrates the statement of cash flows prepared using the direct method, and Exhibit 4A.2 illustrates the calculation of net cash flow from operating activities by the direct method. This method translates each item on the accrual-based income statement to a cash revenue or expense item. The calculation of cash flow from operating activities in Exhibit 4A.2 represents an approximation of the *actual* receipts and payments of cash required by the direct method.

The steps shown in Exhibit 4A.2 will be used to explain the calculation of net cash flow from operating activities on the Sage Inc. Statement of Cash Flows for 2013.

Sage Inc. Direct Method

Sales	$215,600	
Increase in accounts receivable	(610)	
Cash collections on sales		214,990
Cost of goods sold	129,364	
Increase in inventory	10,272	
Increase in accounts payable	(6,703)	
Cash payments for supplies		–132,933
Selling and administrative expenses		–45,722
Other operating expenses	21,271	
Depreciation and amortization	(3,998)	
Decrease in prepaid expense	(247)	
Increase in accrued liabilities	229	
Cash paid for other operating expense		–17,255
Interest revenue		+422
Interest expense		–2,585
Tax expense	7,686	
Increase in deferred tax liability	(208)	
Increase in income taxes payable	(585)	
Cash paid for taxes		–6,893
Net cash flow from operating activities		$ 10,024

The increase in accounts receivable is subtracted from sales revenue because more sales revenue was recognized in the income statement than was received in cash.

The increase in inventories is added to cost of goods sold because more cash was paid to purchase inventories than was included in cost of goods sold expense; that is, cash was used to purchase inventory that has not yet been sold.

The increase in accounts payable is subtracted from cost of goods sold because Sage Inc. was able to defer some payments to suppliers for purchases of inventory; more cost of goods sold expense was recognized than was actually paid in cash.

EXHIBIT 4A.1 Sage Inc. Consolidated Statements of Cash Flows for the Years Ended December 31, 2013, 2012, and 2011 (in Thousands)

	2013	2012	2011
Cash Flow from Operating Activities—Direct Method			
Cash received from customers	$214,990	$149,661	$140,252
Interest received	422	838	738
Cash paid to suppliers for inventory	(132,933)	(99,936)	(83,035)
Cash paid to employees (S&A Expenses)	(45,722)	(33,493)	(32,765)
Cash paid for other operating expenses	(17,255)	(13,758)	(13,784)
Interest paid	(2,585)	(2,277)	(1,274)
Taxes paid	(6,893)	(4,802)	(4,503)
Net cash provided (used) by operating activities	$ 10,024	($ 3,767)	$ 5,629
Cash Flow from Investing Activities			
Additions to property, plant, and equipment	(14,100)	(4,773)	(3,982)
Other investing activities	295	0	0
Net cash provided (used) by investing activities	($ 13,805)	($ 4,773)	($ 3,982)
Cash Flow from Financing Activities			
Sales of common stock	256	183	124
Increase (decrease) in short-term borrowings (includes current maturities of long-term debt)	(30)	1,854	1,326
Additions to long-term borrowings	5,600	7,882	629
Reductions of long-term borrowings	(1,516)	(1,593)	(127)
Dividends paid	(1,582)	(1,862)	(1,841)
Net cash provided (used) by financing activities	$ 2,728	$ 6,464	$ 111
Increase (decrease) in cash and marketable securities	($ 1,053)	($ 2,076)	$ 1,758
Supplementary Schedule			
Cash Flow from Operating Activities—Indirect Method			
Net income	$ 9,394	$ 5,910	$ 5,896
Noncash revenue and expense included in net income			
Depreciation and amortization	3,998	2,984	2,501
Deferred income taxes	208	136	118
Cash provided (used) by current assets and liabilities			
Accounts receivable	(610)	(3,339)	(448)
Inventories	(10,272)	(7,006)	(2,331)
Prepaid expenses	247	295	(82)
Accounts payable	6,703	(1,051)	902
Accrued liabilities	(229)	(1,215)	(1,130)
Income taxes payable	585	(481)	203
Net cash provided (used) by operations	$ 10,024	($ 3,767)	$ 5,629

Depreciation and amortization expense is subtracted from other operating expenses. Remember that depreciation represents a cost allocation, not an outflow of cash. The acquisition of the capital asset was recognized as an investing cash outflow (unless it was exchanged for debt or stock) in the statement of cash flows for the period in which the asset was acquired. So depreciation itself does not require any outflow of cash in the year it is recognized. Deducting depreciation expense in the current year's statement of cash flows would be double counting. Amortization is similar to depreciation—an expense that enters into the determination of net income but does not require an outflow of cash. Depletion would be handled in the same manner as depreciation and amortization. The depreciation and amortization expense for Sage Inc. in 2013 is equal to the change in the balance sheet accumulated depreciation and amortization account. If the firm had dispositions of capital assets during the accounting period, however, the balance sheet change would not equal the expense recognition for the period because some of the account change would have resulted from the elimination of accumulated depreciation for the asset that was removed. The appropriate figure to subtract would be depreciation and amortization expense from the earnings statement.

The decrease in prepaid expense is subtracted from other operating expenses because the firm is recognizing as expense in 2013 items for which cash was paid in the previous year; that is, the firm is utilizing on a net basis some of the prior years' prepayments.

The decrease in accrued liabilities is added to other operating expenses because Sage Inc. has paid more in cash than has been recognized on the income statement.

The increases in the deferred tax liability and income taxes payable accounts are subtracted from tax expense to obtain cash payments for taxes.

The deferred tax liability, explained in Chapter 2, was created as a reconciliation between the amount of tax expense reported on the income statement and the cash actually paid or payable to the IRS. If a deferred tax liability increases from one year to the next, tax expense deducted on the earnings statement to arrive at net income has exceeded cash actually paid for taxes. Thus, an increase in the deferred tax liability account is subtracted from tax expense to arrive at cash from operations. A decrease in deferred tax liabilities would be added. A change in deferred tax assets would be handled in the opposite way from the deferred tax liability. The increase in income taxes payable is also subtracted from tax expense because Sage Inc. has recognized more in expense on the income statement than has been paid in cash.

Exhibit 4A.2 includes other possible adjustments, not present for R.E.C. Inc., that would be made to calculate net cash flow from operating activities by the direct method.

EXHIBIT 4A.2 Sage Inc. Net Cash Flow from Operating Activities Direct Method

Sales	− Increase in accounts receivable + Decrease in accounts receivable + Increase in deferred revenue − Decrease in deferred revenue	= Cash collections from customers
Cost of Goods Sold	+ Increase in inventory − Decrease in inventory − Increase in accounts payable + Decrease in accounts payable	= Cash paid to suppliers
Salary Expense	− Increase in accrued salaries payable + Decrease in accrued salaries payable	= Cash paid to employees
Other Operating Expenses	− Depreciation, amortization, depletion expense for period + Increase in prepaid expenses − Decrease in prepaid expenses − Increase in accrued operating expenses + Decrease in accrued operating expenses	= Cash paid for other operating expenses
Interest Revenue	− Increase in interest receivable + Decrease in interest receivable	= Cash revenue from interest
Interest Expense	− Increase in accrued interest payable + Decrease in accrued interest payable	= Cash paid for interest
Investment Income	− Increase in investment account from equity income* + Decrease in investment account from equity income**	= Cash revenue from dividends
Tax Expense	− Increase in deferred tax liability + Decrease in deferred tax liability − Decrease in deferred tax asset + Increase in deferred tax asset − Increase in income taxes payable + Decrease in income taxes payable − Decrease in prepaid tax + Increase in prepaid tax	= Cash paid for taxes
Net cash flow from operating activities		

*Amount by which equity income recognized exceeds cash dividends received.

**Amount by which cash dividends received exceed equity income recognized.

SELF-TEST

Solutions are provided in Appendix B.

______ **1.** The statement of cash flows measures:
(a) The actual cash flowing out during an accounting period.
(b) The actual cash flowing in during an accounting period.
(c) The actual cash flowing in and flowing out during an accounting period.
(d) The estimated cash flowing in and flowing out during an accounting period.

______ **2.** The statement of cash flows is, in reality, another way of presenting the ____________ of a company.
(a) Income statement.
(b) Cash book.
(c) Balance sheet.
(d) Statement of changes in equity.

______ **3.** How would revenue from sales of common stock be classified?
(a) Operating outflow.
(b) Operating inflow.
(c) Investing inflow.
(d) Financing inflow.

______ **4.** How would payments for dividend be classified?
(a) Operating outflow.
(b) Operating inflow.
(c) Investing outflow.
(d) Financing outflow.

______ **5.** How would collection from customers be classified?
(a) Operating outflow.
(b) Operating inflow.
(c) Investing inflow.
(d) Financing inflow.

______ **6.** How would the cash from sales of debt or equity be classified?
(a) Operating outflow.
(b) Operating inflow.
(c) Investing inflow.
(d) Financing inflow.

______ **7.** What type of accounts are accounts receivable and inventory?
(a) Cash accounts.
(b) Operating accounts.
(c) Financing accounts.
(d) Investing accounts.

______ **8.** What type of accounts are marketable securities and buildings?
(a) Cash accounts.
(b) Operating accounts.
(c) Financing accounts.
(d) Investing accounts.

______ **9.** The change in retained earnings is affected by which of the following?
(a) Net income and common stock.
(b) Net income and paid-in capital.
(c) Net income and payment of dividends.
(d) Payment of dividends and common stock.

______ **10.** Which method of calculating cash flow from operations requires the adjustment of net income for deferrals, accruals, noncash, and nonoperating expenses?
(a) The direct method.
(b) The indirect method.
(c) The inflow method.
(d) The outflow method.

______ **11.** An inflow of cash would result from which of the following?
(a) The increase in an asset account other than cash.
(b) The decrease in an asset account other than cash.
(c) The decrease in an equity account.
(d) The decrease in a liability account.

______ **12.** An outflow of cash would result from which of the following?
(a) The decrease in an asset account other than cash.
(b) The increase in a liability account.
(c) The decrease in a liability account.
(d) The increase in an equity account.

______ **13.** What are internal sources of cash?
(a) Cash inflows from operating activities.
(b) Cash inflows from investing activities.
(c) Cash inflows from financing activities.
(d) All of the above.

______ **14.** What are external sources of cash?
(a) Cash inflows from operating activities.
(b) Cash inflows from investing activities.
(c) Cash inflows from financing activities.
(d) Both (b) and (c).

______ **15.** Which of the following items is included in the adjustment of net income to obtain cash flow from operating activities?
(a) Depreciation expense for the period.
(b) The change in deferred taxes.
(c) The amount by which equity income recognized exceeds cash received.
(d) All of the above.

______ **16.** Which statement is true for gains and losses from capital asset sales?
(a) They do not affect cash and are excluded from the statement of cash flows.
(b) They are included in cash flows from operating activities.
(c) They are included in cash flows from investing activities.
(d) They are included in cash flows from financing activities.

______ **17.** Which of the following current assets is included in the adjustment of net income to obtain cash flow from operating activities?
(a) Accounts receivable.
(b) Inventory.
(c) Prepaid expenses.
(d) All of the above.

______ **18.** Which of the following current liability accounts is included in the adjustment of expenses to obtain cash flow from operating activities?
(a) Accounts payable.
(b) Notes payable and current maturities of long-term debt.
(c) Accrued liabilities.
(d) Both (a) and (c).

______ **19.** How is it possible for a firm to be profitable and still go bankrupt?
(a) Earnings have increased more rapidly than sales.
(b) The firm has positive net income but has failed to generate cash from operations.
(c) Net income has been adjusted for inflation.
(d) Sales have not improved even though credit policies have been eased.

______ **20.** Why has cash flow from operations become increasingly important as an analytical tool?
(a) Inflation has distorted the meaningfulness of net income.
(b) High interest rates can put the cost of borrowing to cover short-term cash needs out of reach for many firms.
(c) Firms may have uncollected accounts receivable and unsalable inventory on the books.
(d) All of the above.

______ **21.** Which of the following statements is false?
(a) A negative cash flow can occur in a year in which net income is positive.
(b) An increase in accounts receivable represents accounts not yet collected in cash.
(c) An increase in accounts payable represents accounts not yet collected in cash.
(d) To obtain cash flow from operations, the reported net income must be adjusted.

______ **22.** Which of the following could lead to cash flow problems?
(a) Obsolete inventory, accounts receivable of inferior quality, easing of credit by suppliers.
(b) Slow-moving inventory, accounts receivable of inferior quality, tightening of credit by suppliers.
(c) Obsolete inventory, increasing notes payable, easing of credit by suppliers.
(d) Obsolete inventory, improved quality of accounts receivable, easing of credit by suppliers.

The following information is available for Jacqui's Jewelry and Gift Store:

Net income	$ 8,000
Depreciation expense	2,500
Increase in deferred tax liabilities	1,500
Decrease in accounts receivable	7,000
Increase in inventories	12,500
Decrease in accounts payable	3,500
Increase in accrued liabilities	2,000
Increase in property and equipment	21,000
Increase in short-term notes payable	5,500
Decrease in long-term bonds payable	20,500

Use the indirect method to answer questions 23–26.

______ **23.** What is net cash flow from operating activities?
(a) ($3,000)
(b) ($1,000)
(c) $5,000
(d) $13,000

______ **24.** What is net cash flow from investing activities?
(a) $14,000
(b) ($14,000)
(c) $21,000
(d) ($16,000)

______ **25.** What is net cash flow from financing activities?
(a) $15,000
(b) ($15,000)
(c) $17,000
(d) ($14,000)

______ **26.** What is the change in cash?
(a) ($13,000)
(b) $11,000
(c) $2,000
(d) ($2,000)

Study Questions and Problems

4.1. How are the cash inflows and outflows segregated in the statement of cash flows?

4.2. Define the following terms as they relate to the statement of cash flows: cash, operating activities, investing activities, and financing activities.

4.3. How are the balance sheet and the statement of cash flows related?

4.4. How are the financing and investing activities not involving cash receipts and payments reported in the cash flow statement?

4.5. Identify the following as financing activities (F) or investing activities (I):
(a) Purchase of equipment.
(b) Purchase of treasury stock.

(c) Reduction of long-term debt.
(d) Sale of building.
(e) Resale of treasury stock.
(f) Increase in short-term debt.
(g) Issuance of common stock.
(h) Purchase of land.
(i) Purchase of common stock of another firm.
(j) Payment of cash dividends.
(k) Gain on sale of land.
(l) Repayment of debt principal.

4.6. Indicate which of the following current assets and current liabilities are operating accounts (O) and thus included in the adjustment of net income to cash flow from operating activities and which are cash (C), investing (I), or financing (F) accounts.
(a) Accounts payable.
(b) Accounts receivable.
(c) Notes payable (to bank).
(d) Marketable securities.
(e) Accrued expenses.
(f) Inventory.
(g) Prepaid expenses.
(h) Current portion of long-term debt.
(i) Dividends payable.
(j) Income taxes payable.
(k) Interest payable.
(l) Certificates of deposit.

4.7. Indicate whether each of the following items would result in net cash flow from operating activities being higher (H) or lower (L) than net income.
(a) Decrease in accounts payable.
(b) Depreciation expense.
(c) Decrease in inventory.
(d) Gain on sale of assets.
(e) Increase in accounts receivable.
(f) Increase in deferred tax liabilities.
(g) Decrease in accrued liabilities.
(h) Increase in prepaid expenses.
(i) Increase in deferred revenue.
(j) Decrease in interest receivable.

4.8. Indicate whether each of the following events would cause an inflow or an outflow of cash and whether it would affect the investing (I) or financing (F) activities on the statement of cash flows.
(a) Sale of plant and equipments.
(b) Purchase of marketable securities.
(c) Buyback of company's common stock.
(d) Redemption of debentures.
(e) Purchase of equipment.
(f) Payment of dividends.
(g) Sales of marketable securities.
(h) Borrowing from bank.
(i) Repayments of long-term debt.
(j) Sale of a business segment.

4.9. Condensed financial statements for Dragoon Enterprises follow.
(a) Calculate the amount of dividends Dragoon paid using the information given.
(b) Prepare a statement of cash flows using the indirect method.

Dragoon Enterprises Comparative Balance Sheets
December 31, 2012 and 2011

	2012	2011
Cash	$ 1,200	$ 850
Accounts receivable	1,750	1,200
Inventory	1,250	1,360
Plant and equipment	4,600	3,900
Accumulated depreciation	(1,200)	(1,100)
Long-term investments	970	1,110
Total Assets	8,570	7,320
Accounts payable	1,100	800
Accrued wages payable	250	350
Interest payable	70	120
Income tax payable	200	50
Bonds payable	1,100	1,400
Capital stock	1,000	930
Paid-in capital	400	70
Retained earnings	4,450	3,600
Total Liabilities and Equity	$ 8,570	$ 7,320

Income Statement for Year Ended December 31, 2012

Sales	$ 9,500
Cost of goods sold	6,650
Gross profit	2,850
Other expenses	
Selling and administrative	1,200
Depreciation	100
Interest	150
Income tax	350
Net income	$ 1,050

4.10. The following income statement and balance sheet information are available for two firms, Firm A and Firm B.

(a) Calculate the amount of dividends Firm A and Firm B paid using the information given.

(b) Prepare a statement of cash flows for each firm using the indirect method.

(c) Analyze the difference in the two firms.

Income Statement for Year Ended December 31, 2012

	Firm A	Firm B
Sales	$1,000,000	$1,000,000
Cost of goods sold	700,000	700,000
Gross profit	300,000	300,000
Other expenses		
Selling and administrative	120,000	115,000
Depreciation	10,000	30,000
Interest expense	20,000	5,000
Earnings before taxes	150,000	150,000
Income tax expense	75,000	75,000
Net Income	$ 75,000	$ 75,000

Changes in Balance Sheet Accounts December 31, 2011, to December 31, 2012

	Firm A	Firm B
Cash and cash equivalents	$ 0	$ +10,000
Accounts receivable	+40,000	+5,000
Inventory	+40,000	−10,000
Property, plant, and equipment	+20,000	+70,000
Less accumulated depreciation	(+10,000)	(+30,000)
Total Assets	$ +90,000	$ +45,000
Accounts payable	$ −20,000	$ −5,000
Notes payable (current)	+17,000	+2,000
Long-term debt	+20,000	−10,000
Deferred taxes (noncurrent)	+3,000	+18,000
Capital, stock	—	—
Retained earnings	+70,000	+40,000
Total Liabilities and Equity	$ +90,000	$ +45,000

4.11. The following comparative balance sheets and income statement are available for Little Bit Inc. Prepare a statement of cash flows for 2012 using the indirect method and analyze the statement.

	December 31,	
	2012	2011
Cash	$ 40,000	$ 24,000
Accounts receivable (net)	48,000	41,500
Inventory	43,000	34,500
Prepaid expenses	19,000	15,000
Total Current Assets	$150,000	$115,000
Plant and equipment	$ 67,000	$ 61,000
Less accumulated depreciation	(41,000)	(23,000)
Plant and equipment (net)	$ 26,000	$ 38,000
Long-term investments	90,000	89,000
Total Assets	$266,000	$242,000
Accounts payable	$ 13,000	$ 11,000
Accrued liabilities	55,000	71,000
Total Current Liabilities	$ 68,000	$ 82,000
Long-term debt	25,000	8,000
Deferred taxes	4,000	3,500
Total Liabilities	$ 97,000	$ 93,500
Common stock ($1 par) and additional paid-in capital	112,000	97,000
Retained earnings	57,000	51,500
Total Liabilities and Equity	$266,000	$242,000

Income Statement for 2012		
Sales		$155,000
Cost of goods sold		83,000
Gross profit		$ 72,000
Selling and administrative	$ 45,700	
Depreciation	18,000	63,700
Operating profit		$ 8,300
Interest expense		2,000
Earnings before tax		$ 6,300
Tax expense		800
Net income		$ 5,500

4.12. The following cash flows were reported by Techno Inc. in 2012 and 2011.

(In thousands)	2012	2011
Net income	$316,354	$242,329
Noncash charges (credits) to income		
Depreciation and amortization	68,156	62,591
Deferred taxes	15,394	22,814
	$399,904	$327,734
Cash Provided (Used) by Operating Assets and Liabilities:		
Receivables	(288,174)	(49,704)
Inventories	(159,419)	(145,554)
Other current assets	(1,470)	3,832
Accounts payable, accrued liabilities	73,684	41,079
Total Cash Provided by Operations	$ 24,525	$177,387
Investment activities		
Additions to plant and equipment	(94,176)	(93,136)
Other investment activities	14,408	(34,771)
Net investment activities	($ 79,768)	($127,907)
Financing activities		
Purchases of treasury stock	(45,854)	(39,267)
Dividends paid	(49,290)	(22,523)
Net changes in short-term borrowings	125,248	45,067
Additions to long-term borrowings	135,249	4,610
Repayments of long-term borrowings		(250,564)
Net financing activities	$ 165,353	($262,677)
Increase (decrease) in cash	$ 110,110	($213,197)
Beginning cash balance	78,114	291,311
Ending cash balance	$ 188,224	$ 78,114

(a) Explain the difference between net income and cash flow from operating activities for Techno in 2012.
(b) Analyze Techno Inc.'s cash flows for 2012 and 2011.

4.13. Writing Skills Problem
Write a short article (250 words) for a local business publication in which you explain why cash flow from operations is important information for small business owners.

4.14. Research Problem
Choose five companies from different industries and locate their statements of cash flows for the most recent year.
(a) Create a table to compare the dollars provided or used by operating, investing, and financing activities, as well as the overall increase or decrease in cash.
(b) Create a second table for each company comparing this same information for each of the three years presented in that company's statement of cash flows. Include an additional column that looks at the combined cash flows for all three years.

(c) Write a short analysis of the information gathered. Your discussion should address, among other things, whether cash flow from operating activities is large enough to cover investing and financing activities, and if not, how the company is financing its activities. Discuss differences and similarities between the companies you have chosen.

4.15. Internet Problem

Prior to the financial recession in the late 2000s, some companies had built up significant cash balances. By 2010, discussions began about whether "cash hoarding" by firms was an appropriate activity or if it was hurting the economic recovery. Research this issue and answer the following questions:

(a) What are the advantages of having a large cash balance?
(b) What are the disadvantages of having a large cash balance?
(c) What companies currently have sizable amounts of cash and liquid investments on their balance sheets?

CASES

Case 4.1 Intel Case

The 2010 Intel Annual Report can be found at the following Web site: www.pearsoninternationaleditions.com/fraser.

(a) Prepare a summary analysis of the Statements of Cash Flows for all three years.

(b) Analyze the Consolidated Statements of Cash Flows for Intel for 2010, 2009, and 2008.

Case 4.2 Avnet Comprehensive Analysis Case Using the Financial Statement Analysis Template

Each chapter in the textbook contains a continuation of this problem. The objective is to learn how to do a comprehensive financial statement analysis in steps as the content of each chapter is learned. Using the 2010 Avnet Form 10-K, which can be found at www.pearsoninternationaleditions.com/fraser, complete the following requirements:

(a) Open the financial statement analysis template that you saved from the Chapter 1 Avnet problem and input the data from the Avnet cash flow statement. When you have finished inputting the data, review the cash flow statement to make sure there are no red blocks indicating that your numbers do not match the cover sheet information you input from the Chapter 1 problem. Make any necessary corrections before printing out both your input and the common-size cash flow statement that the template automatically creates for you.

(b) Analyze the Consolidated Statements of Cash Flows for Avnet for 2010, 2009, and 2008. Write a summary that includes important points that an analyst would use in assessing the ability of Avnet to generate cash flows and the appropriateness of the use of cash flows.

Case 4.3 Gerber Scientific Inc.

According to Gerber Scientific Inc.'s (Gerber) Form 10-K, the firm develops, manufactures, distributes, and services automated equipment and software in three industries worldwide. Of its total revenue of $458.4 million for fiscal 2010, Gerber generated $257.2 million in sales of printing equipment, software, and related supplies to customers in the sign making and specialty graphics industry; $155.1 million in sales of sophisticated design and cutting equipment and software to customers in the apparel and industrial markets; and $46.1 million in sales of processing equipment, software, and related supplies to customers in the ophthalmic lens processing industry. Gerber's statements of cash flows follow:

GERBER SCIENTIFIC, INC.
Consolidated Statements of Cash Flows

	For the Fiscal Years Ended April 30,		
In thousands of dollars	2010	2009	2008
Cash flows from operating activities:			
Net (loss) income	$ (1,458)	$ 2,236	$ 14,504
Adjustments to reconcile net (loss) income to cash provided by operating activities:			
Depreciation and amortization	9,452	9,991	9,518
Deferred income taxes	(3,210)	(5,953)	2,501
Other-than-temporary impairment charge	—	2,290	—
Stock-based compensation	3,787	3,241	1,805
Loss (gain) on sale of assets	2,464	(622)	(2,287)
Other noncash items	2,177	2,220	2,191
Changes in operating accounts, excluding effects of acquisitions:			
Accounts receivable	5,126	25,795	(5,719)
Inventories	5,996	5,820	(6,220)
Prepaid expenses and other assets	71	79	696
Accounts payable and other accrued liabilities	706	(27,424)	(7,095)
Accrued compensation and benefits	(15)	(7,899)	311
Net cash provided by operating activities	25,096	9,774	10,205
Cash flows from investing activities:			
Capital expenditures	(4,489)	(8,187)	(8,589)
Proceeds from sale of available for sale investments	464	705	751
Purchases of available for sale investments	(308)	(457)	(753)
Proceeds from sale of net assets	13,709	2,622	345
Business acquisitions	(3,473)	(34,273)	(4,650)
Investments in intangible assets	(1,368)	(828)	(868)
Net cash provided by (used for) investing activities	4,535	(40,418)	(13,764)

Cash flows from financing activities:			
Debt repayments	(117,176)	(80,271)	(314,256)
Debt proceeds	89,525	110,686	321,862
Debt issuance costs	(494)	(1,174)	(993)
Common stock activities	(486)	898	1,373
Other financing activities	(341)	—	—
Net cash (used for) provided by financing activities	(28,972)	30,139	7,986
Effect of exchange rate changes on cash	333	(3,074)	1,413
Increase (decrease) in cash and cash equivalents	992	(3,579)	5,840
Cash and cash equivalents at beginning of year	10,313	13,892	8,052
Cash and cash equivalents at end of year	$ 11,305	$ 10,313	$ 13,892
Supplemental Schedule of Cash Flow Information			
Cash paid during the year for:			
Interest	$ 3,475	$ 2,856	$ 3,655
Income taxes, net of refunds	$ 4,517	$ 4,456	$ 5,290

The accompanying notes are an integral part of these consolidated financial statements.

Required:

1. Using the Consolidated Statements of Cash Flows for Gerber, prepare a summary analysis for the years ended April 30, 2010, 2009, and 2008.
2. Write an analysis and interpretation of the cash flows for Gerber for all three years. Be sure to analyze the cash flows from operating activities, as well as the overall cash inflows and outflows for the firm.
3. Evaluate the creditworthiness of Gerber based on only the cash flow statements.
4. What information from the balance sheet would be useful to a creditor in determining whether to loan Gerber money?

Case 4.4 Agilysys Inc.

The following are excerpts from the 2010 Agilysys Inc. Form 10-K.

Item 1. Business

Reference herein to any particular year or quarter refers to periods within the Company's fiscal year ended March 31. For example, fiscal 2010 refers to the fiscal year ended March 31, 2010.

Overview

Agilysys Inc. ("Agilysys" or the "Company") is a leading provider of innovative information technology ("IT") solutions to corporate and public-sector customers, with special expertise in select markets, including retail and hospitality. The Company develops technology solutions—including hardware, software, and services—to help customers resolve their most complicated IT data center and point-of-sale needs. The Company possesses data center expertise in enterprise architecture and high availability, infrastructure optimization, storage and resource management, and business continuity. Agilysys' point-of-sale solutions include: proprietary property management, inventory and procurement, point-of-sale, and document management software, proprietary services including expertise in mobility and wireless solutions for retailers, and resold hardware, software, and services. A significant portion of the point-of-sale related revenue is recurring from software support and hardware maintenance agreements. Headquartered in Solon, Ohio, Agilysys operates extensively throughout North America, with additional sales and support offices in the United Kingdom and Asia. Agilysys has three reportable business segments: Hospitality Solutions Group ("HSG"), Retail Solutions Group ("RSG"), and Technology Solutions Group ("TSG").

Note 8. Financing Arrangements

The following is a summary of long-term obligations at March 31, 2010, and 2009:

	2010	2009
IBM floor plan agreement	$ –	$ 74,159
Capital lease obligations	695	395
	695	74,554
Less: current maturities	(311)	(74,397)
Long-term capital lease obligations	$ 384	$ 157

IBM Floor Plan Agreement

On February 22, 2008, the Company entered into the Fourth Amended and Restated Agreement for Inventory Financing (Unsecured) ("Inventory Financing Agreement") with IBM Credit LLC, a wholly-owned subsidiary of International Business Machines Corporation ("IBM"). In addition to providing the Inventory Financing Agreement, IBM has engaged and may engage as a primary supplier to the Company in the ordinary course of business. Under the Inventory Financing Agreement, the Company may finance the purchase of products from authorized suppliers up to an aggregate outstanding amount of $145 million. On February 2, 2009, IBM lowered the credit line from $150 million to $100 million due to the loss of a significant syndicate partner in the credit line. There were no changes, except for the lower credit line, and both parties continued to operate under the existing terms. The Company entered into the IBM flooring arrangement in February 2008 to realize the benefit of extended payment terms. This Inventory Financing Agreement provided the Company 75 days of interest-free financing, which was better than the trade accounts payable terms provided by the Company's vendors. Prior to February 2008, the Company solely utilized trade accounts payable to finance working capital.

The Company was in discussions with IBM regarding an increase or overline component to the inventory financing agreement, whether through establishing a new comprehensive financing agreement or due to the passage of time as credit market conditions improve. However, on May 4, 2009, the Company decided to terminate its Inventory Financing Agreement with IBM and primarily fund working capital through open accounts payable provided by its trade vendors, or the Credit Facility discussed above. At the time of the termination, there was $60.9 million outstanding under this Inventory Financing Agreement that the Company subsequently repaid using cash on hand.

AGILYSYS INC. AND SUBSIDIARIES
Consolidated Statements of Cash Flows

	Year Ended March 31		
(In thousands)	2010	2009	2008
Operating activities			
Net income (loss)	$ 3,547	$ (284,134)	$ 3,659
Add: Loss (income) from discontinued operations	29	1,947	(1,801)
Income (loss) from continuing operations	3,576	(282,187)	1,858
Adjustments to reconcile income (loss) from continuing operations to net cash provided by (used for) operating activities (net of effects from business acquisitions):			
Asset impairment charges	293	249,983	—
Impairment of investment in The Reserve Fund's Primary Fund	—	3,001	—
Impairment of investment in cost basis company	—	—	4,921
Gain on cost investment	—	(56)	(8,780)
Gain on redemption of cost investment	—	—	(1,330)
Gain on redemption of investment in The Reserve Fund's Primary Fund	(2,505)	—	—
Loss (gain) on sale of securities	91	—	(6)
Loss on disposal of property and equipment	—	494	12
Depreciation	3,914	4,032	3,261
Amortization	12,400	23,651	20,552
Deferred income taxes	6,596	(7,035)	(2,649)
Stock-based compensation	2,426	457	6,039
Excess tax benefit from exercise of stock options	(9)	—	(97)
Change in cash surrender value of corporate-owned life insurance policies	(802)	4,610	720

Changes in operating assets and liabilities:			
Accounts receivable	49,481	14,909	24,794
Inventories	12,839	(1,763)	(5,713)
Accounts payable	41,889	(68,809)	(53,144)
Accrued liabilities	(15,213)	(23,520)	(11,675)
Income taxes payable	(9,021)	14,483	(138,694)
Other changes, net	365	(1,808)	2,013
Other noncash adjustments, net	(2,396)	(10,849)	(1,322)
Total adjustments	100,348	201,780	(161,098)
Net cash provided by (used for) operating activities	103,924	(80,407)	(159,240)
Investing activities			
Proceeds from (claim on) The Reserve Fund's Primary Fund	4,772	(5,268)	—
Proceeds from borrowings against corporate-owned life insurance policies	12,500	—	844
Additional investments in corporate-owned life insurance policies	(1,712)	(5,996)	(7,623)
Proceeds from redemption of cost basis investment	—	9,513	4,770
Proceeds from sale of marketable securities	61	81	6,088
Additional investments in marketable securities	(45)	(4)	(52)
Acquisition of business, net of cash acquired	—	(2,381)	(236,210)
Purchase of property and equipment	(13,306)	(7,056)	(8,775)
Net cash provided by (used for) investing activities	2,270	(11,111)	(240,958)
Financing activities			
Floor plan financing agreement, net	(74,468)	59,607	14,552
Proceeds from borrowings under credit facility	5,077	—	—
Principal payments under credit facility	(5,077)	—	—
Debt financing costs	(1,578)	—	—
Purchase of treasury shares	—	—	(149,999)
Principal payment under long-term obligations	(216)	(67)	(197)
Issuance of common shares	89	—	1,447
Excess tax benefit from exercise of stock options	9	—	213
Dividends paid	(1,360)	(2,718)	(3,407)
Net cash (used for) provided by financing activities	(77,524)	56,822	(137,391)
Effect of exchange rate changes on cash	695	911	1,314
Cash flows provided by (used for) continuing operations	29,365	(33,785)	(536,275)
Cash flows of discontinued operations—operating	(74)	94	1,995
Net increase (decrease) in cash	29,291	(33,691)	(534,280)
Cash at beginning of year	36,244	69,935	604,215
Cash at end of year	$65,535	$ 36,244	$ 69,935
Supplemental disclosures of cash flow information:			
Cash payments for interest	$ 410	$ 74	$ 618
Cash (refunds) payments for income taxes, net	$ (2,715)	$ 339	$ 140,450
Change in value of available-for-sale securities, net of taxes	$ (16)	$ (17)	$ (169)

See accompanying notes to consolidated financial statements.

Required:

1. Using the Consolidated Statements of Cash Flows for Agilysys Inc., prepare a summary analysis for the years ended March 31, 2010, 2009, and 2008.
2. Write an analysis and interpretation of the cash flows for Agilysys Inc. for all three years. Be sure to analyze the cash flows from operating activities, as well as the overall cash inflows and outflows for the firm.
3. Explain what information you gain from the statement of cash flows that cannot be found directly from the balance sheet or income statement.

The Analysis of Financial Statements

Ratios are tools, and their value is limited when used alone. The more tools used, the better the analysis. For example, you can't use the same golf club for every shot and expect to be a good golfer. The more you practice with each club, however, the better able you will be to gauge which club to use on one shot. So too, we need to be skilled with the financial tools we use.

—DIANNE MORRISON
Chief Executive Officer, Sage Inc.

The preceding chapters have covered in detail the form and content of the four basic financial statements found in the annual reports of U.S. firms: the balance sheet, the income statement, the statement of stockholders' equity, and the statement of cash flows. Appendix 3A presented an in-depth approach to evaluating the quality of reported earnings. This chapter will develop tools and techniques for the interpretation of financial statement information.

Objectives of Analysis

Before beginning the analysis of any firm's financial statements, it is necessary to specify the objectives of the analysis. The objectives will vary depending on the perspective of the financial statement user and the specific questions that are addressed by the analysis of the financial statement data.

A *creditor* is ultimately concerned with the ability of an existing or prospective borrower to make interest and principal payments on borrowed funds. The questions raised in a credit analysis should include:

- What is the *borrowing cause*? What do the financial statements reveal about the reason a firm has requested a loan or the purchase of goods on credit?

- What is the firm's *capital structure*? How much debt is currently outstanding? How well has debt been serviced in the past?
- What will be the *source of debt repayment*? How well does the company manage working capital? Is the firm generating cash from operations?

The credit analyst will use the historical record of the company, as presented in the financial statements, to answer such questions and to predict the potential of the firm to satisfy future demands for cash, including debt service.

The *investor* attempts to arrive at an estimation of a company's future earnings stream in order to attach a value to the securities being considered for purchase or liquidation. The investment analyst poses such questions as:

Shutterstock

- What is the company's *performance record,* and what are the *future expectations*? What is its record with regard to growth and stability of earnings? Of cash flow from operations?
- How much *risk* is inherent in the firm's existing capital structure? What are the *expected returns,* given the firm's current condition and future outlook?
- How successfully does the firm compete in its industry, and how well positioned is the company to hold or improve its *competitive position*?

The investment analyst also uses historical financial statement data to forecast the future. In the case of the investor, the ultimate objective is to determine whether the investment is sound.

Financial statement analysis from the standpoint of management relates to all of the questions raised by creditors and investors because these user groups must be satisfied for the firm to obtain capital as needed. Management must also consider its employees, the general public, regulators, and the financial press. Management looks to financial statement data to determine:

- How *well* has the firm performed and *why*? What *operating areas* have contributed to success and which have not?

- What are the *strengths and weaknesses* of the company's financial position?
- What *changes* should be implemented to improve future performance?

Financial statements provide insight into the company's current status and lead to the development of policies and strategies for the future. It should be pointed out, however, that management also has responsibility for preparing the financial statements. The analyst should be alert to the potential for management to influence the outcome of financial statement reporting in order to appeal to creditors, investors, and other users. It is important that any analysis of financial statements includes a careful reading of the notes to the financial statements, and it may be helpful to supplement the analysis with other material in the annual report and with other sources of information apart from the annual report.

Sources of Information

The financial statement user has access to a wide range of data sources in the analysis of financial statements. The objective of the analysis will dictate to a considerable degree not only the approach taken in the analysis but also the particular resources that should be consulted in a given circumstance. The beginning point, however, should always be the financial statements themselves and the notes to the financial statements. In addition, the analyst will want to include the following resources.

Proxy Statement

The proxy statement, discussed in Chapter 1, contains useful information about the board of directors, director and executive compensation, option grants, audit-related matters, related party transactions, and proposals to be voted on by shareholders.

Auditor's Report

The report of the independent auditor contains the expression of opinion as to the fairness of the financial statement presentation. Most auditor's reports are *unqualified,* which means that in the opinion of the auditor the financial statements present fairly the financial position, the results of operations, and the cash flows for the periods covered by the financial statements. A *qualified* report, an adverse opinion, or a disclaimer of opinion, is rare and therefore suggests that a careful evaluation of the firm be made. An unqualified opinion with explanatory language should be reviewed carefully by the analyst. In addition, the analyst should read the report and certification regarding the effectiveness of the internal controls over financial reporting.

Management Discussion and Analysis

The Management Discussion and Analysis of the Financial Condition and Results of Operations, discussed in Chapter 1, is a section of the annual report that is required and monitored by the Securities and Exchange Commission (SEC). In this section, management presents a detailed coverage of the firm's liquidity, capital resources, and operations. The material can be especially helpful to the financial analyst because it includes facts and estimates not found elsewhere in the annual report. For example, this report is expected to cover forward-looking information such as projections of capital expenditures and how such investments will be financed. There is detail about the mix of price relative to volume increases for products sold. Management must disclose any favorable or unfavorable trends and any significant events or uncertainties that relate to the firm's historical or prospective financial condition and operations.

Supplementary Schedules

Certain supplementary schedules are required for inclusion in an annual report and are frequently helpful to the analysis. For example, companies that operate in several unrelated lines of business provide a breakdown of key financial figures by operating segment.

Form 10-K and Form 10-Q

Form 10-K is an annual document filed with the SEC by companies that sell securities to the public and contains much of the same information as the annual report issued to shareholders. It also shows additional detail that may be of interest to the financial analyst, such as schedules listing information about management, a description of material litigation and governmental actions, and elaborations of some financial statement disclosures. Form 10-Q, a less extensive document, provides quarterly financial information. Both reports, as well as other SEC forms filed by companies, are available through the SEC Electronic Data Gathering, Analysis, and Retrieval (EDGAR) database.

Other Sources

There is a considerable body of material outside the corporate annual report that can contribute to an analysis of financial statements. In addition to online resources, most academic libraries and many public libraries have available computerized search systems and computerized databases that can greatly facilitate financial analysis. Although not a replacement for the techniques that are discussed in this chapter, these research materials supplement and enhance the analytical process as well as provide time-saving features. Computerized financial statement analysis packages are also available that perform some of the ratio calculations and other analytical tools described in this chapter. (See the financial statement analysis template available at www.pearsoninternationaleditions.com/fraser.)

Other general resources useful as aids in the analysis of financial statements can be found in the general reference section of public and university libraries. The following sources provide comparative statistical ratios to help determine a company's relative position within its industry:

1. Dun & Bradstreet Information Services, *Industry Norms and Key Business Ratios.* Murray Hill, NJ.
2. The Risk Management Association, *Annual Statement Studies.* Philadelphia, PA.

When analyzing a company it is also important to review the annual reports of suppliers, customers, and competitors of that company. The bankruptcy of a supplier could affect the firm's supply of raw materials, whereas the bankruptcy of a customer could negatively impact the collection of accounts receivable and future sales. Knowing how one company compares financially to its competitors and understanding other factors such as innovation and customer service provided by the competition allows for a better analysis to predict the future prospects of the firm.

Additional resources for comparative and other information about companies can be found on the following free Internet sites:[1]

1. Yahoo!, http://finance.yahoo.com/
2. Market Watch, www.marketwatch.com
3. Reuters, www.investor.reuters.com

Many other Internet sites charge subscription fees to access information, but public and university libraries often subscribe, making this information free to the public. Libraries are currently in the process of converting information from hard copy format to online databases; the following useful references may be available at a local library:

1. Mergent Inc., *Mergent Manuals* and *Mergent Handbook.* New York, NY. (The online version is Mergentonline.)
2. Standard & Poor's Corporation, *Corporation Records, The Outlook, Stock Reports,* and *Stock Guide.* New York, NY. (The online version is *Standard and Poor's Net Advantage.*)
3. Value Line Inc., *The Value Line Investment Survey.* New York, NY (www.valueline .com).
4. Zack's Investment Research Inc., *Earnings Forecaster.* Chicago, IL (www.zacks.com).
5. Gale Research Inc., *Market Share Reporter.* Farmington Hills, MI (www.gale .cengage.com).
6. For mutual funds: Morningstar, *Morningstar Guide to Mutual Funds.* Chicago, IL (www.morningstar.com).

The following Web sites contain useful investment and financial information including company profile and stock prices; some sites charge fees for certain information:

1. SEC EDGAR Database, www.sec.gov/edgar.shtml
2. Hoover's Corporate Directory, www.hoovers.com
3. Dun & Bradstreet, www.dnb.com
4. Standard & Poor's, ycharts.com
5. CNN Financial Network, money.cnn.com

Articles from current periodicals such as *Bloomberg BusinessWeek, Forbes, Fortune,* and the *Wall Street Journal* can add insight into the management and operations of individual firms as well as provide perspective on general economic and industry trends. The financial analysis described in this chapter should be used in the context of the economic and political environment in which the company operates. Reading about the economy regularly in business publications allows the analyst to assess the impact of unemployment, inflation, interest rates, gross domestic product, productivity, and other economic indicators on the future potential of particular firms and industries.

Tools and Techniques

Various tools and techniques are used by the financial statement analyst to convert financial statement data into formats that facilitate the evaluation of a firm's financial condition and performance, both over time and in comparison with industry competitors.

[1] Internet sites are constantly changing; therefore, the content and Web addresses may change after publication of this book.

These include common-size financial statements, which express each account on the balance sheet as a percentage of total assets and each account on the income statement as a percentage of net sales; financial ratios, which standardize financial data in terms of mathematical relationships expressed in the form of percentages or times; trend analysis, which requires the evaluation of financial data over several accounting periods; structural analysis, which looks at the internal structure of a business enterprise; industry comparisons, which relate one firm with averages compiled for the industry in which it operates; and most important of all, common sense and judgment. These tools and techniques will be illustrated by walking through a financial statement analysis of Sage Inc. This first part will cover number crunching—the calculation of key financial ratios. The second part will provide the integration of these numbers with other information—such as the statement of cash flows from Chapter 4 and background on the economy and the environment in which the firm operates—to help analyze Sage Inc.'s performance over a five-year period and to assess the firm's strengths, weaknesses, and future prospects.

DK Images

Common-Size Financial Statements

Common-size financial statements were covered in Chapters 2 and 3. Exhibits 2.2 (p. 70) and 3.3 (p. 120) present the common-size balance sheet and common-size income statement, respectively, for Sage Inc. The information from these statements presented in prior chapters is summarized again and will be used in the comprehensive analysis illustrated in this chapter.

From the common-size balance sheet in Exhibit 2.2, it can be seen that inventories have become more dominant over the five-year period in the firm's total asset structure and in 2013 comprised almost half (49.4%) of total assets. Holdings of cash and cash equivalents have decreased from a 20% combined level in 2009 and 2010 to about 10% in 2013. The company has elected to make this shift to accommodate the inventory requirements of new store openings. The firm has opened 43 new stores in the past two years, and the effect of this market strategy is also reflected in the overall asset structure. Buildings, leasehold improvements, equipment, and accumulated depreciation and amortization have increased as a percentage of total assets. On the liability side, the proportion of debt required to finance investments in assets has risen, primarily from long-term borrowing.

The common-size income statement shown in Exhibit 3.3 reveals the trends of expenses and profit margins. Cost of goods sold has increased slightly in percentage terms, resulting in a small decline in the gross profit percentage. To improve this margin, the firm will either have to raise its own retail prices, change the product mix, or devise ways to reduce costs on goods purchased for resale. In the area of operating expenses, depreciation and amortization have increased relative to sales, again reflecting costs associated with new store openings. Selling and administrative expenses rose in 2011, but the company controlled these costs more effectively in 2012 and 2013 relative to overall sales. Operating and net profit percentages will be discussed more extensively in connection with the five-year trends of financial ratios later in the chapter. It can be seen from the common-size income statements that both profit percentages deteriorated through 2012 and rebounded in the most recent year as Sage Inc. enjoyed the benefits of an economic recovery and profits from expansion.

Key Financial Ratios

The Sage Inc. financial statements will be used to compute a set of key financial ratios for the years 2013 and 2012. Later in the chapter, these ratios will be evaluated in the context of Sage Inc.'s five-year historical record and in comparison with industry competitors. The five categories of ratios to be covered are (1) liquidity ratios, which measure a firm's ability to meet cash needs as they arise; (2) activity ratios, which measure the liquidity of specific assets and the efficiency of managing assets; (3) leverage ratios, which measure the extent of a firm's financing with debt relative to equity and its ability to cover interest and other fixed charges; (4) profitability ratios, which measure the overall performance of a firm and its efficiency in managing assets, liabilities, and equity; and (5) market ratios, which measure returns to stockholders and the value the marketplace puts on a company's stock.

Before delving into the Sage Inc. financial ratios, it is important to introduce a word of caution in the use of financial ratios generally. Although extremely valuable as analytical tools, financial ratios also have limitations. They can serve as screening devices, indicate areas of potential strength or weakness, and reveal matters that need further investigation. But financial ratios do not provide answers in and of themselves, and they are not predictive. Financial ratios should be used with caution and common sense, and they should be used in combination with other elements of financial analysis. It should also be noted that there is no one definitive set of key financial ratios, there is no uniform definition for all ratios, and there is no standard that should be met for each ratio. Finally, there are no "rules of thumb" that apply to the interpretation of financial ratios. Each situation should be evaluated within the context of the particular firm, industry, and economic environment.[2]

Figures from the Sage Inc. Consolidated Balance Sheets, Statements of Earnings, and Statements of Cash Flows, Exhibits 5.1 (pp. 220–221) and 4.1 (p. 173), are used to illustrate the calculation of financial ratios for 2013 and 2012, and these financial ratios will subsequently be incorporated into a five-year analysis of the firm.

[2]Analysts sometimes use an average number in the denominator of ratios that have a balance sheet account in the denominator. This is preferable when the company's balance sheet accounts vary significantly from one year to the next. The illustrations in this chapter do not use an average number in the denominator.

EXHIBIT 5.1 Sage Inc. Consolidated Balance Sheets December 31, 2013 and 2012 (in Thousands)

	2013	2012
Assets		
Current Assets		
Cash and cash equivalents	$9,333	$10,386
Accounts receivable, less allowance for doubtful accounts of $448 in 2013 and $417 in 2012	8,960	8,350
Inventories	47,041	36,769
Prepaid expenses and other assets	512	759
Total current assets	65,846	56,264
Property, Plant, and Equipment		
Land	811	811
Buildings and leasehold improvements	18,273	11,928
Equipment	21,523	13,768
	40,607	26,507
Less accumulated depreciation and amortization	11,528	7,530
Net property, plant, and equipment	29,079	18,977
Goodwill	270	270
Other Assets	103	398
Total Assets	$95,298	$75,909
Liabilities and Stockholders' Equity		
Current Liabilities		
Accounts payable	$14,294	$ 7,591
Accrued liabilities	4,137	4,366
Income taxes payable	1,532	947
Short-term debt	5,614	6,012
Current maturities of long-term debt	1,884	1,516
Total current liabilities	27,461	20,432
Deferred Federal Income Taxes	843	635
Long-Term Debt	21,059	16,975
Commitments and Contingencies (See Notes 3 and 5)		
Total liabilities	49,363	38,042
Stockholders' Equity		
Common stock, par value $0.01, authorized, 10,000,000 shares; issued, 4,363,000 shares in 2013 and 4355,000 shares in 2012, and additional paid-in capital	5,760	5,504
Retained Earnings	40,175	32,363
Total stockholders' equity	45,935	37,867
Total Liabilities and Stockholders' Equity	$95,298	$75,909

The accompanying notes are an integral part of these statements.

Sage Inc. Consolidated Statements of Earnings for the Years Ended December 31, 2013, 2012 and 2011 (in Thousands Except per Share Amounts)

	2013	2012	2011
Net sales	$215,600	$153,000	$140,700
Cost of goods sold	129,364	91,879	81,606
Gross profit	86,236	61,121	59,094
Selling and administrative expenses	45,722	33,493	32,765
Advertising	14,258	10,792	9,541
Depreciation and amortization	3,998	2,984	2,501
Impairment charges	3,015	2,046	3,031
Operating profit	19,243	11,806	11,256
Other income (expense)			
Interest income	422	838	738
Interest expense	(2,585)	(2,277)	(1,274)
Earnings before income taxes	17,080	10,367	10,720
Provision for income taxes	7,686	4,457	4,824
Net earnings	$ 9,394	$ 5,910	$ 5,896
Earnings per common share:			
Basic	$ 2.16	$ 1.36	$ 1.36
Diluted	$ 2.12	$ 1.33	$ 1.33
Weighted average common shares outstanding:			
Basic	4,359	4,350	4,342
Diluted	4,429	4,442	4,431

The accompanying notes are an integral part of these statements.

Liquidity Ratios: Short-Term Solvency

Current Ratio

	2013	2012
$\frac{\text{Current assets}}{\text{Current liabilities}}$	$\frac{65{,}846}{27{,}461} = 2.40\text{ times}$	$\frac{56{,}264}{20{,}432} = 2.75\text{ times}$

The current ratio is a commonly used measure of short-run solvency, the ability of a firm to meet its debt requirements as they come due. Current liabilities are used as the denominator of the ratio because they are considered to represent the most urgent debts, requiring retirement within one year or one operating cycle. The available cash resources to satisfy these obligations must come primarily from cash or the conversion to cash of other current assets. Some analysts eliminate prepaid expenses from the numerator because they are not a potential source of cash but, rather, represent future obligations that have already been satisfied. The current ratio for Sage Inc. indicates that, at year-end 2013, current assets covered current liabilities 2.4 times, down from 2012. To interpret the significance of this ratio, it will be necessary to evaluate the trend of liquidity over a longer period and to compare Sage Inc.'s coverage with industry competitors. It is also essential to assess the composition of the components that comprise the ratio.

As a barometer of short-term liquidity, the current ratio is limited by the nature of its components. Remember that the balance sheet is prepared as of a particular date, and the actual amount of liquid assets may vary considerably from the date on which the balance sheet is prepared. Further, accounts receivable and inventory may not be truly liquid. A firm could have a relatively high current ratio but not be able to meet demands for cash because the accounts receivable are of inferior quality or the inventory is salable only at discounted prices. It is necessary to use other measures of liquidity, including cash flow from operations and other financial ratios that rate the liquidity of specific assets, to supplement the current ratio.

Quick or Acid-Test Ratio

	2013		2012	
$\frac{\text{Current assets} - \text{Inventory}}{\text{Current liabilities}}$	$\frac{65{,}846 - 47{,}041}{27{,}461}$	= 0.68 times	$\frac{56{,}264 - 36{,}769}{20{,}432}$	= 0.95 times

The quick or acid-test ratio is a more rigorous test of short-run solvency than the current ratio because the numerator eliminates inventory, considered the least liquid current asset and the most likely source of losses. Like the current ratio and other ratios, there are alternative ways to calculate the quick ratio. Some analysts eliminate prepaid expenses and supplies (if carried as a separate item) from the numerator. The quick ratio for Sage Inc. indicates some deterioration between 2012 and 2013; this ratio must also be examined in relation to the firm's own trends and to other firms operating in the same industry.

Cash Flow Liquidity Ratio

	2013		2012	
$\frac{\text{Cash and cash equivalents + Marketable securities + CFO*}}{\text{Current liabilities}}$	$\frac{9{,}333 + 0 + 10{,}024}{27{,}461}$	= 0.70 times	$\frac{10{,}386 + 0 + (3{,}767)}{20{,}432}$	= 0.32 times

* Cash flow from operating activities.

Another approach to measuring short-term solvency is the cash flow liquidity ratio,[3] which considers cash flow from operating activities (from the statement of cash flows). The cash flow liquidity ratio uses in the numerator, as an approximation of cash resources, cash and marketable securities, which are truly liquid current assets, and

[3]For additional reading about this ratio and its applications, see Lyn Fraser, "Cash Flow from Operations and Liquidity Analysis, A New Financial Ratio for Commercial Lending Decisions," *Cash Flow,* Robert Morris Associates, Philadelphia, PA. For other cash flow ratios, see C. Carslaw and J. Mills, "Developing Ratios for Effective Cash Flow Statement Analysis," *Journal of Accountancy,* November 1991; D. E. Giacomino and D. E. Mielke, "Cash Flows: Another Approach to Ratio Analysis," *Journal of Accountancy,* March 1993; and John R. Mills and Jeanne H. Yamamura, "The Power of Cash Flow Ratios," *Journal of Accountancy*, October 1998.

cash flow from operating activities, which represents the amount of cash generated from the firm's operations, such as the ability to sell inventory and collect the cash.

Note that both the current ratio and the quick ratio decreased between 2012 and 2013, which could be interpreted as a deterioration of liquidity. But the cash flow ratio increased, indicating an improvement in short-run solvency. Which is the correct assessment? With any ratio, the analyst must explore the underlying components. One major reason for the decreases in the current and quick ratios was the 88% growth in accounts payable in 2013, which could actually be a plus if it means that Sage Inc. strengthened its ability to obtain supplier credit. Also, the firm turned around from negative to positive its generation of cash from operations in 2013, explaining the improvement in the cash flow liquidity ratio and indicating stronger short-term solvency.

Average Collection Period

	2013	2012
$\frac{\text{Net accounts receivable}}{\text{Average daily sales}}$	$\frac{8{,}960}{215{,}600/365} = 15\text{ days}$	$\frac{8{,}350}{153{,}000/365} = 20\text{ days}$

The average collection period of accounts receivable is the average number of days required to convert receivables into cash. The ratio is calculated as the relationship between net accounts receivable (net of the allowance for doubtful accounts) and average daily sales (sales/365 days). Where available, the figure for credit sales can be substituted for net sales because credit sales produce the receivables. The ratio for Sage Inc. indicates that during 2013 the firm collected its accounts in 15 days on average, which is an improvement over the 20-day collection period in 2012.

The average collection period helps gauge the liquidity of accounts receivable, the ability of the firm to collect from customers. It may also provide information about a company's credit policies. For example, if the average collection period is increasing over time or is higher than the industry average, the firm's credit policies could be too lenient and accounts receivables not sufficiently liquid. The loosening of credit could be necessary at times to boost sales, but at an increasing cost to the firm. On the other hand, if credit policies are too restrictive, as reflected in an average collection period that is shortening and less than industry competitors, the firm may be losing qualified customers.

The average collection period should be compared with the firm's stated credit policies. If the policy calls for collection within 30 days and the average collection period is 60 days, the implication is that the company is not stringent in collection efforts. There could be other explanations, however, such as temporary problems due to a depressed economy. The analyst should attempt to determine the cause of a ratio that is too long or too short.

Another factor for consideration is the strength of the firm within its industry. There are circumstances that would enable a company in a relatively strong financial position within its industry to extend credit for longer periods than weaker competitors.

Days Inventory Held

	2013	2012
$\frac{\text{Inventory}}{\text{Average daily cost of sales}}$	$\frac{47{,}041}{129{,}364/365} = 133\text{ days}$	$\frac{36{,}769}{91{,}879/365} = 146\text{ days}$

The days inventory held is the average number of days it takes to sell inventory to customers. This ratio measures the efficiency of the firm in managing its inventory. Generally, a low number of days inventory held is a sign of efficient management; the faster inventory sells, the fewer funds tied up in inventory. On the other hand, too low a number could indicate understocking and lost orders, a decrease in prices, a shortage of materials, or more sales than planned. A high number of days inventory held could be the result of carrying too much inventory or stocking inventory that is obsolete, slow-moving, or inferior; however, there may be legitimate reasons to stockpile inventory, such as increased demand, expansion and opening of new retail stores, or an expected strike. Sage Inc.'s days inventory held has decreased in 2013, an improvement over 2012.

The type of industry is important in assessing days inventory held. It is expected that florists and produce retailers would have a relatively low days inventory held because they deal in perishable products, whereas retailers of jewelry or farm equipment would have higher days inventory held, but higher profit margins. When making comparisons among firms, it is essential to check the cost flow assumption, discussed in Chapter 2, used to value inventory and cost of goods sold.

Days Payable Outstanding

	2013		2012	
$\frac{\text{Accounts payable}}{\text{Average daily cost of sales}}$	$\frac{14{,}294}{129{,}364/365}$	= 41 days	$\frac{7{,}591}{91{,}879/365}$	= 31 days

The days payable outstanding is the average number of days it takes to pay payables in cash. This ratio offers insight into a firm's pattern of payments to suppliers. Delaying payment of payables as long as possible is desirable because the firm can earn a return on cash held. Sage Inc. is taking longer to pay suppliers in 2013 compared to 2012.

Cash Conversion Cycle or Net Trade Cycle

The cash conversion cycle or net trade cycle is the normal operating cycle of a firm that consists of buying or manufacturing inventory, with some purchases on credit and the creation of accounts payable; selling inventory, with some sales on credit and the creation of accounts receivable; and collecting the cash. The cash conversion cycle measures this process in number of days and is calculated as follows for Sage Inc.:

	2013	2012
Average collection period	15 days	20 days
plus		
Days inventory held	133 days	146 days
minus		
Days payable outstanding	(41 days)	(33 days)
equals		
Cash conversion or net trade cycle	107 days	133 days

The cash conversion cycle helps the analyst understand why cash flow generation has improved or deteriorated by analyzing the key balance sheet accounts—accounts receivable, inventory, and accounts payable—that affect cash flow from operating activities. Sage Inc. has improved its cash conversion cycle by improving collection of accounts receivable, moving inventory faster, and taking longer to pay accounts payable. Despite this improvement, the firm has a mismatching of cash inflows and outflows since it takes 148 days to sell inventory and collect the cash, yet Sage Inc.'s suppliers are being paid in 41 days. As mentioned previously, the company opened 43 new stores, and that is most likely the cause of the high level of inventory. In the future, Sage Inc. should be able to improve further the days inventory held and the cash conversion cycle.

Activity Ratios: Asset Liquidity, Asset Management Efficiency

Accounts Reveivable Turnover

	2013	2012
$\frac{\text{Net sales}}{\text{Net accounts receivable}}$	$\frac{215{,}600}{8{,}960} = 24.06$ times	$\frac{153{,}000}{8{,}350} = 18.32$ times

Inventory Turnover

	2013	2012
$\frac{\text{Cost of goods sold}}{\text{Inventory}}$	$\frac{129{,}364}{47{,}041} = 2.75$ times	$\frac{91{,}879}{36{,}769} = 2.50$ times

Accounts Payable Turnover

	2013	2012
$\frac{\text{Cost of goods sold}}{\text{Accounts payable}}$	$\frac{129{,}364}{14{,}294} = 9.05$ times	$\frac{91{,}879}{7{,}591} = 12.10$ times

The accounts receivable, inventory, and payables turnover ratios measure how many times, on average, accounts receivable are collected in cash, inventory is sold, and payables are paid during the year. These three measures are mathematical complements to the ratios that make up the cash conversion cycle, and therefore measure exactly what the average collection period, days inventory held, and days payable outstanding measure for a firm; they are merely an alternative way to look at the same information.

Sage Inc. converted accounts receivable into cash 24 times in 2013, up from 18 times in 2012. Inventory turned over 2.75 times in 2013 compared to 2.5 times in 2012, meaning that inventory was selling slightly faster. The lower payables turnover indicates that the firm is taking longer to repay payables.

Fixed Asset Turnover

	2013	2012
$\frac{\text{Net sales}}{\text{Net property, plant, equipment}}$	$\frac{215{,}600}{29{,}079} = 7.41$ times	$\frac{153{,}000}{18{,}977} = 8.06$ times

Total Asset Turnover

	2013	2012
$\frac{\text{Net sales}}{\text{Total assets}}$	$\frac{215{,}600}{95{,}298} = 2.26\text{ times}$	$\frac{153{,}000}{75{,}909} = 2.02\text{ times}$

The fixed asset turnover and total asset turnover ratios are two approaches to assessing management's effectiveness in generating sales from investments in assets. The fixed asset turnover considers only the firm's investment in property, plant, and equipment and is extremely important for a capital-intensive firm, such as a manufacturer with heavy investments in long-lived assets. The total asset turnover measures the efficiency of managing all of a firm's assets. Generally, the higher these ratios, the smaller is the investment required to generate sales and thus the more profitable is the firm. When the asset turnover ratios are low relative to the industry or the firm's historical record, either the investment in assets is too heavy and/or sales are sluggish. There may, however, be plausible explanations; for example, the firm may have undertaken an extensive plant modernization or placed assets in service at year-end, which will generate positive results in the long-term. Large amounts of cash, cash equivalents, marketable securities, and long-term investments unrelated to the core operations of the firm will cause the total asset turnover to be lower as the return on these items is recorded in nonoperating revenue accounts, not sales.

For Sage Inc., the fixed asset turnover has slipped slightly, but the total asset turnover has improved. The firm's investment in fixed assets has grown at a faster rate (53%) than sales (41%), and this occurrence should be examined within the framework of the overall analysis of Sage Inc. The increase in total asset turnover is the result of improvements in inventory and accounts receivable turnover.

Leverage Ratios: Debt Financing and Coverage

Debt Ratio

	2013	2012
$\frac{\text{Total liabilities}}{\text{Total assets}}$	$\frac{49{,}363}{95{,}298} = 51.8\%$	$\frac{38{,}042}{75{,}909} = 50.1\%$

Long-Term Debt to Total Capitalization

	2013	2012
$\frac{\text{Long-term debt}}{\text{Long-term debt + Stockholders' equity}}$	$\frac{21{,}059}{21{,}059 + 45{,}935} = 31.4\%$	$\frac{16{,}975}{16{,}975 + 37{,}867} = 31.0\%$

Debt to Equity

	2013	2012
$\frac{\text{Total liabilities}}{\text{Stockholders' equity}}$	$\frac{49{,}363}{45{,}935} = 1.07\ \%$	$\frac{38{,}042}{37{,}867} = 1.00\ \%$

Each of the three debt ratios measures the extent of the firm's financing with debt. The amount and proportion of debt in a company's capital structure is extremely important to the financial analyst because of the trade-off between risk and return. Use of debt involves risk because debt carries a fixed commitment in the form of interest charges and principal repayment. Failure to satisfy the fixed charges associated with debt will ultimately result in bankruptcy. A lesser risk is that a firm with too much debt has difficulty obtaining additional debt financing when needed or finds that credit is available only at extremely high rates of interest. Although debt implies risk, it also introduces the potential for increased benefits to the firm's owners. When debt is used successfully—if operating earnings are more than sufficient to cover the fixed charges associated with debt—the returns to shareholders are magnified through financial leverage, a concept that is explained and illustrated later in this chapter.

The debt ratio considers the proportion of all assets that are financed with debt. The ratio of long-term debt to total capitalization reveals the extent to which long-term debt is used for the firm's permanent financing (both long-term debt and equity). The debt-to-equity ratio measures the riskiness of the firm's capital structure in terms of the relationship between the funds supplied by creditors (debt) and investors (equity). The higher the proportion of debt, the greater is the degree of risk because creditors must be satisfied before owners in the event of bankruptcy. The equity base provides, in effect, a cushion of protection for the suppliers of debt. Each of the three ratios has increased somewhat for Sage Inc. between 2012 and 2013, implying a slightly riskier capital structure.

The analyst should be aware that the debt ratios do not present the whole picture with regard to risk. There are fixed commitments, such as lease payments, that are similar to debt but are not included in debt. The fixed charge coverage ratio, illustrated later, considers such obligations. Off–balance-sheet financing arrangements, discussed in Chapter 2 also have the characteristics of debt and must be disclosed in notes to the financial statements. These arrangements should be included in an evaluation of a firm's overall capital structure.

Times Interest Earned

	2013	2012
$\frac{\text{Operating profit}}{\text{Interest expense}}$	$\frac{19{,}243}{2{,}585} = 7.4$ times	$\frac{11{,}806}{2{,}277} = 5.2$ times

Cash Interest Coverage

	2013	2012
$\frac{\text{CFO + Interest paid + Taxes paid}^4}{\text{Interest paid}}$	$\frac{10{,}024 + 2{,}585 + 7{,}478}{2{,}585} = 7.77$ times	$\frac{(3{,}767) + 2{,}277 + 4{,}321}{2{,}277} = 1.24$ times

[4]The amounts for interest and taxes paid are found in the supplemental disclosures on the statement of cash flows.

For a firm to benefit from debt financing, the fixed interest payments that accompany debt must be more than satisfied from operating earnings.[5] The higher the times interest earned ratio the better; however, if a company is generating high profits, but no cash flow from operations, this ratio is misleading. It takes cash to make interest payments! The cash interest coverage ratio measures how many times interest payments can be covered by cash flow from operations before interest and taxes. Although Sage Inc. increased its use of debt in 2013, the company also improved its ability to cover interest payments from operating profits and cash from operations. Note that in 2012, the firm could cover interest payments only 1.24 times due to the poor cash generated from operations before interest and taxes. The times interest earned ratio in 2012 is somewhat misleading in this instance.

Fixed Charge Coverage

	2013	2012
$\frac{\text{Operating profit + Rent expense*}}{\text{Interest expense + Rent expense*}}$	$\frac{19{,}243 + 13{,}058}{2{,}585 + 13{,}058} = 2.1$ times	$\frac{11{,}806 + 7{,}111}{2{,}277 + 7{,}111} = 2.0$ times

*Rent expense = operating lease payments (see Appendix 1A, Note 3 in Chapter 1).

The fixed charge coverage ratio is a broader measure of coverage capability than the times interest earned ratio because it includes the fixed payments associated with leasing. Operating lease payments, generally referred to as rent expense in annual reports, are added back in the numerator because they were deducted as an operating expense to calculate operating profit. Operating lease payments are similar in nature to interest expense in that they both represent obligations that must be met on an annual basis. The fixed charge coverage ratio is important for firms that operate extensively with operating leases. Sage Inc. experienced a significant increase in the amount of annual lease payments in 2013 but was still able to improve its fixed charge coverage slightly.

Cash Flow Adequacy

	2013	2012
$\frac{\text{Cash flow from operating activites}}{\text{Capital expenditures + Debt repayments + Dividends paid}}$	$\frac{10{,}024}{14{,}100 + 30 + 1{,}516 + 1{,}582} = 0.58$ times	$\frac{(3{,}767)}{4{,}773 + 1{,}593 + 1{,}862} = (0.46)$ times

Credit rating agencies often use cash flow adequacy ratios to evaluate how well a company can cover annual payments of items such as debt, capital expenditures, and dividends from operating cash flow. Cash flow adequacy is generally

[5] The operating return, operating profit divided by assets, must exceed the cost of debt and interest expense divided by liabilities.

defined differently by analysts; therefore, it is important to understand what is actually being measured. Cash flow adequacy is being used here to measure a firm's ability to cover capital expenditures, debt maturities, and dividend payments each year. Companies over the long run should generate enough cash flow from operations to cover investing and financing activities of the firm. If purchases of fixed assets are financed with debt, the company should be able to cover the principal payments with cash generated by the company. A larger ratio would be expected if the company pays dividends annually because cash used for dividends should be generated internally by the company, rather than by borrowing. As indicated in Chapter 4, companies must generate cash to be successful. Borrowing each year to pay dividends and repay debt is a questionable cycle for a company to be in over the long run.

In 2013, Sage Inc. had a cash flow adequacy ratio of 0.58 times, an improvement over 2012 when the firm failed to generate cash from operations.

Profitability Ratios: Overall Efficiency and Performance

Gross Profit Margin

	2013	2012
$\frac{\text{Gross profit}}{\text{Net sales}}$	$\frac{86{,}236}{215{,}600} = 40.0\%$	$\frac{61{,}121}{153{,}000} = 39.9\%$

Operating Profit Margin

	2013	2012
$\frac{\text{Operating profit}}{\text{Net sales}}$	$\frac{19{,}243}{215{,}600} = 8.9\%$	$\frac{11{,}806}{153{,}000} = 7.7\%$

Net Profit Margin

	2013	2012
$\frac{\text{Net earnings}}{\text{Net sales}}$	$\frac{9{,}394}{215{,}600} = 4.4\%$	$\frac{5{,}910}{153{,}000} = 3.9\%$

Gross profit margin, operating profit margin, and net profit margin represent the firm's ability to translate sales dollars into profits at different stages of measurement. The gross profit margin, which shows the relationship between sales and the cost of products sold, measures the ability of a company both to control costs of inventories or manufacturing of products and to pass along price increases through sales to customers. The operating profit margin, a measure of overall operating efficiency, incorporates all of the expenses associated with ordinary business activities. The net profit margin measures profitability after consideration of all revenue and expense, including interest, taxes, and nonoperating items.

There was little change in the Sage Inc. gross profit margin, but the company improved its operating margin. Apparently, the firm was able to control the growth of operating expenses while sharply increasing sales. There was also a slight increase in net profit margin, a flow-through from operating margin, but it will be necessary to look at these ratios over a longer term and in conjunction with other parts of the analysis to explain the changes.

Cash Flow Margin

	2013	2012
$\frac{\text{Cash flow from operating activities}}{\text{Net sales}}$	$\frac{10{,}024}{215{,}600} = 4.6\%$	$\frac{(3{,}767)}{153{,}000} = (2.5\%)$

Another important perspective on operating performance is the relationship between cash generated from operations and sales. As pointed out in Chapter 4, it is cash, not accrual-measured earnings, that a firm needs to service debt, pay dividends, and invest in new capital assets. The cash flow margin measures the ability of the firm to translate sales into cash.

In 2013, Sage Inc. had a cash flow margin that was greater than its net profit margin, the result of a strongly positive generation of cash. The performance in 2013 represents a solid improvement over 2012 when the firm failed to generate cash from operations and had a negative cash flow margin.

Return on Total Assets (ROA) or Return on Investment (ROI)

	2013	2012
$\frac{\text{Net earnings}}{\text{Total assets}}$	$\frac{9{,}394}{95{,}298} = 9.9\%$	$\frac{5{,}910}{75{,}909} = 7.8\%$

Return on Equity (ROE)

	2013	2012
$\frac{\text{Net earnings}}{\text{Stockholders' equity}}$	$\frac{9{,}394}{45{,}935} = 20.5\%$	$\frac{5{,}910}{37{,}867} = 15.6\%$

Return on investment and return on equity are two ratios that measure the overall efficiency of the firm in managing its total investment in assets and in generating return to shareholders. Return on investment or return on assets indicates the amount of profit earned relative to the level of investment in total assets. Return on equity measures the return to common shareholders; this ratio is also calculated as return on common equity if a firm has preferred stock outstanding. Sage Inc. registered a solid improvement in 2013 of both return ratios. It is noteworthy that the increase in return on equity is greater than the increase in return on assets. This is a result of the increased leverage or use of debt by Sage Inc. (see the example in Figure 5.3 in this chapter).

Cash Return on Assets

	2013	2012
Cash flow from operating activities / Total assets	10,024 / 95,298 = 10.5%	(3,767) / 75,909 = (5.0%)

The cash return on assets offers a useful comparison to return on investment. Again, the relationship between cash generated from operations and an accrual-based number allows the analyst to measure the firm's cash-generating ability of assets. Cash will be required for future investments.

Market Ratios

Four market ratios of particular interest to the investor are earnings per common share, the price-to-earnings ratio, the dividend payout ratio, and dividend yield. Despite the accounting and finance scandals, including Lehman Brothers, Enron, and WorldCom, which illustrated the flaws in the earnings numbers presented to the public, investors continue to accept and rely on the earnings per share and price-to-earnings ratios. A discussion of these ratios is included because the reporting of these numbers does, in fact, have a significant impact on stock price changes in the marketplace. The authors hope, however, that readers of this book understand that a thorough analysis of the company, its environment, and its financial information offers a much better gauge of the future prospects of the company than looking exclusively at earnings per share and price-to-earnings ratios. These two ratios are based on an earnings number that can be misleading at times given the many accounting choices and techniques used to calculate it.

Earnings per common share is net income for the period divided by the weighted average number of common shares outstanding. One million dollars in earnings will look different to the investor if there are 1 million shares of stock outstanding or 100,000 shares. The earnings per share ratio provides the investor with a common denominator to gauge investment returns.

The basic earnings per share computations for Sage Inc. are made as follows:

	2013	2012	2011
Net earnings / Average shares outstanding	9,394,000 / 4,359,041 = 2.16	5,910,000 / 4,350,088 = 1.36	5,896,000 / 4,342,012 = 1.36

Earnings per share figures must be disclosed on the face of the income statement for publicly held companies.

The price-to-earnings ratio (P/E ratio) relates earnings per common share to the market price at which the stock trades, expressing the "multiple" that the stock market places on a firm's earnings. For instance, if two competing firms had annual earnings of \$2.00 per share, and Company 1 shares sold for \$10.00 each and Company 2 shares were selling at \$20.00 each, the market is placing a different value on the same \$2.00 earnings: a multiple of 5 for Company 1 and 10 for Company 2. The P/E ratio is the function of a myriad of factors, which include the quality of earnings, future earnings potential, and the performance history of the company.[6]

The P/E ratio for Sage Inc. would be determined as follows:

	2013	2012	2011
$\frac{\text{Market price of common stock}}{\text{Earnings per share}}$	$\frac{30.00}{2.16} = 13.9$	$\frac{17.00}{1.36} = 12.5$	$\frac{25.00}{1.36} = 18.4$

The P/E ratio is higher in 2013 than 2012 but below the 2011 level. This could be due to developments in the market generally and/or because the market is reacting cautiously to the firm's good year. Another factor could be the reduction of cash dividend payments.

The dividend payout ratio is determined by the formula cash dividends per share divided by earnings per share:

	2013	2012	2011
$\frac{\text{Dividends per share}}{\text{Earnings per share}}$	$\frac{0.36}{2.16} = 16.7\%$	$\frac{0.43}{1.36} = 31.6\%$	$\frac{0.42}{1.36} = 30.9\%$

Sage Inc. reduced its cash dividend payment in 2013. It is unusual for a company to reduce cash dividends because this decision can be read as a negative signal regarding the future outlook. It is particularly uncommon for a firm to reduce dividends during a good year. The explanation provided by management is that the firm has adopted a new policy that will result in lower dividend payments in order to increase the availability of internal funds for expansion; management expects the overall long-term impact to be extremely favorable to shareholders and has committed to maintaining the $0.36 per share annual cash dividend.

The dividend yield shows the relationship between cash dividends and market price:

	2013	2012	2011
$\frac{\text{Dividends per share}}{\text{Market price of common stock}}$	$\frac{0.36}{30.00} = 1.2\%$	$\frac{0.43}{17.00} = 2.5\%$	$\frac{0.42}{25.00} = 1.7\%$

The Sage Inc. shares are yielding a 1.2% return based on the market price at year-end 2013; an investor would likely choose Sage Inc. as an investment more for its long-term capital appreciation than for its dividend yield.

Figure 5.1 shows in summary form the use of key financial ratios discussed in the chapter.

[6]Using diluted earnings per share in market ratios offers a worst-case scenario figure that analysts may find useful.

FIGURE 5.1 Summary of Financial Ratios

Summary of Financial Statement Analysis
How to Use Financial Ratios

Liquidity
- Short-Run Solvency: Current Ratio; Quick Ratio; Cash Flow Liquidity Ratio
- Liquidity of Current Assets: Average Collection Period; Days Inventory Held; Days Payable Outstanding; Cash Conversion Cycle

Leverage
- Amount of Debt: Debt/Assets; Debt/Equity; Long-Term Debt / Total Capitalization
- Coverage of Debt: Times Interest Earned; Cash Interest Coverage; Fixed Charge Coverage; Cash Flow Adequacy
- Financial Leverage Index

Operating Efficiency
- Asset Management: Accounts Receivable Turnover; Inventory Turnover; Accounts Payable Turnover; Fixed Asset Turnover; Total Asset Turnover; Return on Total Assets

Profitability
- Margins: Gross Profit Margin; Operating Profit Margin; Net Profit Margin; Cash Flow Margin
- Returns: Return on Total Assets; Return on Equity; Cash Return on Assets

Market Measures
- Earnings per Share; Price/Earnings; Dividend Payout; Dividend Yield

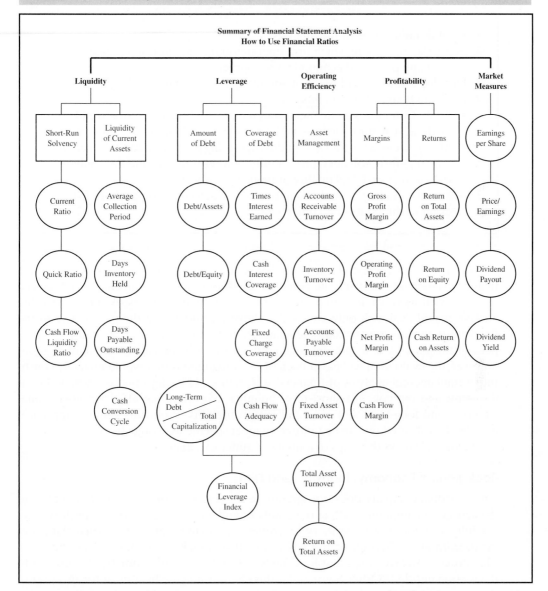

Analyzing the Data

Would you as a bank loan officer extend \$1.5 million in new credit to Sage Inc.? Would you as an investor purchase Sage Inc. common shares at the current market price of \$30 per share? Would you as a wholesaler of running shoes sell your products on credit to Sage Inc.? Would you as a recent college graduate accept a position as manager-trainee with Sage Inc.? Would you as the chief financial officer of Sage Inc. authorize the opening of 25 new retail stores during the next two years?

FIGURE 5.2 Steps of a Financial Statement Analysis

1. Establish objectives of the analysis.
2. Study the industry in which firm operates and relate industry climate to current and projected economic developments.
3. Develop knowledge of the firm and the quality of management.
4. Evaluate financial statements.
   - Tools: Common-size financial statements, key financial ratios, trend analysis, structural analysis, and comparison with industry competitors.
   - Major Areas: Short-term liquidity, operating efficiency, capital structure and long-term solvency, profitability, market ratios, segmental analysis (when relevant), and quality of financial reporting.
5. Summarize findings based on analysis and reach conclusions about firm relevant to the established objectives.

To answer such questions, it is necessary to complete the analysis of Sage Inc.'s financial statements, utilizing the common-size financial statements and key financial ratios as well as other information presented throughout the book. Ordinarily, the analysis would deal with only one of the above questions, and the perspective of the financial statement user would determine the focus of the analysis. Because the purpose of this chapter is to present a general approach to financial statement analysis, however, the evaluation will cover each of five broad areas that would typically constitute a fundamental analysis of financial statements: (1) background on firm, industry, economy, and outlook; (2) short-term liquidity; (3) operating efficiency; (4) capital structure and long-term solvency; and (5) profitability. From this general approach, each analytical situation can be tailored to meet specific user objectives.

Figure 5.2 shows the steps of a financial statement analysis.

Background: Economy, Industry, and Firm

An individual company does not operate in a vacuum. Economic developments and the actions of competitors affect the ability of any business enterprise to perform successfully. It is therefore necessary to preface the analysis of a firm's financial statements with an evaluation of the environment in which the firm conducts business. This process involves blending hard facts with guesses and estimates. Reference to the section entitled "Other Sources" in this chapter may be beneficial for this part of the analysis. A brief section discussing the business climate of Sage Inc. follows.[7]

Sage Inc. is the third largest retailer of recreational products in the United States. The firm offers a broad line of sporting goods and equipment and active sports apparel in medium to higher price ranges. Sage Inc. sells equipment used in running, aerobics, walking, basketball, golf, tennis, skiing, football, scuba diving, and other sports; merchandise for

[7]The background section of Sage Inc. is based on an unpublished paper by Kimberly Ann Davis, "A Financial Analysis of Oshman's Sporting Goods, Inc."

camping, hiking, fishing, and hunting; men's and women's sporting apparel; gift items; games; and consumer electronic products. The firm also sells sporting goods on a direct basis to institutional customers such as schools and athletic teams.

The general and executive offices of the company are located in Dime Box, Texas, and these facilities were expanded in 2013. Most of the retail stores occupy leased spaces and are located in major regional or suburban shopping districts throughout the southwestern United States. Eighteen new retail outlets were added in late 2012, and 25 new stores were opened in 2013. The firm owns distribution center warehouses located in Arizona, California, Colorado, Utah, and Texas.

The recreational products industry is affected by current trends in consumer preferences, a cyclical sales demand, and weather conditions. The running boom has shifted to walking and aerobics; golf, once on the downswing, is increasing in popularity. Recreational product retailers also rely heavily on sales of sportswear for their profits because the markup on sportswear is generally higher than on sports equipment, and these products are also affected by consumer preference shifts. With regard to seasonality, most retail sales occur in November, December, May, and June. Sales to institutions are highest in August and September. Weather conditions also influence sales volume, especially of winter sports equipment—come on, Rocky Mountain snow!

Competition within the recreational products industry is based on price, quality, and variety of goods offered as well as the location of outlets and the quality of services offered. Sage Inc.'s two major competitors are also full-line sporting goods companies. One operates in the northwest and the other primarily in the eastern and southeastern United States, reducing direct competition among the three firms.

The current outlook for the sporting goods industry is promising, following a recessionary year in 2012.[8] Americans have become increasingly aware of the importance of physical fitness and have become more actively involved in recreational activities. The 25-to-44 age group is the most athletically active and is projected to be the largest age group in the United States during the next decade. The southwestern United States is expected to provide a rapidly expanding market because of its population growth and excellent weather conditions for year-round recreational participation.

Short-Term Liquidity

Short-term liquidity analysis is especially important to creditors, suppliers, management, and others who are concerned with the ability of a firm to meet near-term demands for cash. The evaluation of Sage Inc.'s short-term liquidity position began with the preparation and interpretation of the firm's common-size balance sheet. From that assessment, it was evident that inventories have increased relative to cash and cash equivalents in the current asset section, and there has been an increase in the proportion of debt, both short and long term. These developments were traced primarily to policies and financing needs related to new store openings. Additional evidence useful to short-term liquidity analysis is provided by a five-year trend of selected financial ratios and a comparison with industry averages. Sources of comparative industry ratios include Dun & Bradstreet, *Industry Norms and Key Business Ratios,* New York, NY; The Risk Management Association, *Annual Statement Studies,* Philadelphia, PA; and

[8]The recession is assumed for purposes of writing this book and does not represent the authors' forecast.

Standard & Poor's Corporation, *Industry Surveys,* New York, NY. As a source of industry comparative ratios, the analyst may prefer to develop a set of financial ratios for one or more major competitors.

Sage Inc.	2013	2012	2011	2010	2009	Industry Average 2013
Current ratio	2.40	2.75	2.26	2.18	2.83	2.53
Quick ratio	0.68	0.95	0.87	1.22	1.20	0.97
Cash flow liquidity	0.70	0.32	0.85	0.78	0.68	*
Average collection period	15 days	20 days	13 days	11 days	10 days	17 days
Days inventory held	133 days	146 days	134 days	122 days	114 days	117 days
Days payable outstanding	41 days	33 days	37 days	34 days	35 days	32 days
Cash conversion cycle	107 days	133 days	110 days	99 days	89 days	102 days
Cash flow from operating activities ($ thousands)	10,024	(3,767)	5,629	4,925	3,430	*

*Not available

Liquidity analysis predicts the future ability of the firm to meet prospective needs for cash. This prediction is made from the historical record of the firm, and no one financial ratio or set of financial ratios or other financial data can serve as a proxy for future developments. For Sage Inc., the financial ratios are somewhat contradictory.

The current and quick ratios have trended downward over the five-year period, indicating a deterioration of short-term liquidity. On the other hand, the cash flow liquidity ratio improved strongly in 2013 after a year of negative cash generation in 2012. The average collection period for accounts receivable and the days inventory held ratio—after worsening between 2009 and 2012—also improved in 2013. These ratios measure the quality or liquidity of accounts receivable and inventory. The average collection period increased to a high of 20 days in 2012, which was a recessionary year in the economy, then decreased to a more acceptable 15-day level in 2013. Days payable outstanding has varied each year, but has increased overall from 2009 to 2013. As long as the company is not late paying bills, this should not be a significant problem. The cash conversion cycle worsened from 2009 to 2012 due to an increasing collection period and longer number of days inventory was held. In 2013, a significant improvement in management of current assets and liabilities has caused the cash conversion cycle to drop by 26 days from the high of 133 days in 2012. It is now much closer to the industry average.

The common-size balance sheet for Sage Inc. revealed that inventories now comprise about half of the firm's total assets. The growth in inventories has been necessary to satisfy the requirements associated with the opening of new retail outlets but has been accomplished by reducing holdings of cash and cash equivalents. This represents a trade-off of highly liquid assets for potentially less liquid assets. The efficient management of inventories is a critical ingredient for the firm's ongoing liquidity. In 2013, days inventory held improved in spite of the buildups necessary to stock new stores. Sales demand in 2013 was more than adequate to absorb the 28% increase in inventories recorded for the year.

The major question in the outlook for liquidity is the ability of the firm to produce cash from operations. Problems in 2012 resulted partly from the depressed state of the economy and poor ski conditions, which reduced sales growth. The easing of sales demand hit the company in a year that marked the beginning of a major market expansion. Inventories and receivables increased too fast for the limited sales growth of a recessionary year, and Sage also experienced some reduction of credit availability from suppliers that felt the economic pinch. The consequence was a cash crunch and negative cash flow from operations.

In 2013, Sage Inc. enjoyed considerable improvement, generating more than $10 million in cash from operations and progress in managing inventories and receivables. There appears to be no major problem with the firm's short-term liquidity position at the present time. Another poor year, however, might well cause problems similar to those experienced in 2012. The timing of further expansion of retail outlets will be of critical importance to the ongoing success of the firm.

Operating Efficiency

Sage Inc.	**2013**	**2012**	**2011**	**2010**	**2009**	**Industry Average 2013**
Accounts receivable turnover	24.06	18.32	28.08	33.18	36.50	21.47
Inventory turnover	2.75	2.50	2.74	2.99	3.20	3.12
Accounts payable turnover	9.05	12.10	9.90	10.74	10.43	11.40
Fixed asset turnover	7.41	8.06	8.19	10.01	10.11	8.72
Total asset turnover	2.26	2.02	2.13	2.87	2.95	2.43

The turnover ratios measure the operating efficiency of the firm. The efficiency in managing the company's accounts receivable, inventory, and accounts payable was discussed in the short-term liquidity analysis. Sage Inc.'s fixed asset turnover has decreased over the past five years and is now below the industry average. As noted earlier, Sage Inc. has increased its investment in fixed assets as a result of home office and store expansion. The asset turnover ratios reveal a downward trend in the efficiency with which the firm is generating sales from investments in fixed and total assets. The total asset turnover rose in 2013, progress traceable to improved management of inventories and receivables. The fixed asset turnover ratio is still declining, a result of expanding offices and retail outlets, but should improve if the expansion is successful.

Capital Structure and Long-Term Solvency

The analytical process includes an evaluation of the amount and proportion of debt in a firm's capital structure as well as the ability to service debt. Debt implies risk because debt involves the satisfaction of fixed financial obligations. The disadvantage of debt financing is that the fixed commitments must be met for the firm to continue operations. The major advantage of debt financing is that, when used successfully, shareholder returns are magnified through financial leverage. The concept of financial leverage can best be illustrated with an example (Figure 5.3).

Sage Inc.	**2013**	**2012**	**2011**	**2010**	**2009**	**Industry Average 2013**
Debt to total assets	51.8%	50.1%	49.2%	40.8%	39.7%	48.7%
Long-term debt to total capitalization	31.4%	31.0%	24.1%	19.6%	19.8%	30.4%
Debt to equity	1.07	1.00	0.96	0.68	0.66	0.98

The debt ratios for Sage Inc. reveal a steady increase in the use of borrowed funds. Total debt has risen relative to total assets, long-term debt has increased as a proportion of the firm's permanent financing, and external or debt financing has increased relative to internal financing. Given the greater degree of risk implied by borrowing, it is important to determine (1) why debt has increased, (2) whether the firm is employing debt successfully, and (3) how well the firm is covering its fixed charges.

Why has debt increased? The Summary Statement of Cash Flows, discussed in Chapter 4 and repeated here as Exhibit 5.2, provides an explanation of borrowing cause. Exhibit 5.2 shows the inflows and outflows of cash both in dollar amounts and percentages.

Exhibit 5.2 shows that Sage Inc. has substantially increased its investment in capital assets, particularly in 2013 when additions to property, plant, and equipment accounted for 82% of the total cash outflows. These investments have been financed largely by borrowing, especially in 2012 when the firm had a sluggish operating performance and no internal cash generation. Operations supplied 73% of Sage Inc.'s cash in 2011 and 62% in 2013, but the firm had to borrow heavily in 2012 (98% of cash inflows). The impact of this borrowing is seen in the firm's debt ratios.

EXHIBIT 5.2 Sage Inc. Summary Analysis Statement of Cash Flows (in Thousands)

	2013	**%**	**2012**	**%**	**2011**	**%**
Inflows (dollars in thousands)						
Operations	$10,024	62.0	$ 0	0.0	$5,629	73.0
Other investing activities	295	1.8	0	0.0	0	0.0
Sales of common stock	256	1.6	183	1.8	124	1.6
Additions to short-term debt	0	0.0	1,854	18.7	1,326	17.2
Additions to long-term debt	5,600	34.6	7,882	79.5	629	8.2
Total	$16,175	100.0	$ 9,919	100.0	$7,708	100.0
Outflows (dollars in thousands)						
Operations	$ 0	0.0	$ 3,767	31.4	$ 0	0.0
Purchase of property, plant, and equipment	14,100	81.8	4,773	40.0	3,982	66.9
Reductions of short-term debt	30	0.2	0	0.0	0	0.0
Reductions of long-term debt	1,516	8.8	1,593	13.2	127	2.1
Dividends paid	$ 1,582	9.2	$ 1,862	15.4	$1,841	31.0
Total	$17,228	100.0	$11,995	100.0	$5,950	100.0
Change in cash and cash equivalents	($ 1,053)		($ 2,076)		$1,758	

FIGURE 5.3 Example of Financial Leverage

Sockee Sock Company has $100,000 in total assets, and the firm's capital structure consists of 50% debt and 50% equity:

Debt	$ 50,000
Equity	50,000
Total assets	$100,000

Cost of debt = 10%
Average tax rate = 40%

If Sockee has $20,000 in operating earnings, the return to shareholders as measured by the return on equity ratio would be 18%:

Operating earnings	$20,000
Interest expense	5,000
Earnings before tax	15,000
Tax expense	6,000
Net earnings	$ 9,000

Return on equity: 9,000/50,000 = 18%

If Sockee is able to double operating earnings from $20,000 to $40,000, the return on equity will more than double, increasing from 18% to 42%:

Operating earnings	$40,000
Interest expense	5,000
Earnings before tax	35,000
Tax expense	14,000
Net earnings	$21,000

Return on equity: 21,000/50,000 = 42%

The magnified return on equity results from financial leverage. Unfortunately, leverage has a double edge. If operating earnings are cut in half from $20,000 to $10,000, the return on equity is more than halved, declining from 18% to 6%:

Operating earnings	$10,000
Interest expense	5,000
Earnings before tax	5,000
Tax expense	2,000
Net earnings	$ 3,000

Return on equity: 3,000/50,000 = 6%

The amount of interest expense is fixed, regardless of the level of operating earnings. When operating earnings rise or fall, financial leverage produces positive or negative effects on shareholder returns. In evaluating a firm's capital structure and solvency, the analyst must constantly weigh the potential benefits of debt against the risks inherent in its use.

How effectively is Sage Inc. using financial leverage? The answer is determined by calculating the financial leverage index (FLI), as follows:

$$\frac{\text{Return on equity}}{\text{Adjusted return on assets}} = \text{Financial leverage index}$$

The adjusted return on assets in the denominator of this ratio is calculated as follows:

$$\frac{\text{Net earnings} + \text{interest expense } (1 - \text{tax rate})^9}{\text{Total assets}}$$

When the FLI is greater than 1, which indicates that return on equity exceeds return on assets, the firm is employing debt beneficially. An FLI of less than 1 means the firm is not using debt successfully. For Sage Inc., the adjusted return on assets and FLI are calculated as follows:

	2013	2012	2011
$\frac{\text{Net earnings + interest expense(1 − tax rate)}}{\text{Total assets}}$	$\frac{9{,}394 + 2{,}585(1 - 0.45)}{95{,}298}$	$\frac{5{,}910 + 2{,}277(1 - 0.43)}{75{,}909}$	$\frac{5{,}896 + 1{,}274(1 - 0.45)}{66{,}146}$

	2013	2012	2011
$\frac{\text{Return on equity}}{\text{Adjusted return on assets}}$	$\frac{20.45}{11.35} = 1.8$	$\frac{15.61}{9.50} = 1.6$	$\frac{17.53}{9.97} = 1.8$

The FLI for Sage Inc. of 1.8 in 2013, 1.6 in 2012, and 1.8 in 2011 indicates a successful use of financial leverage for the three-year period when borrowing has increased. The firm has generated sufficient operating returns to more than cover the interest payments on borrowed funds.

How well is Sage Inc. covering fixed charges? The answer requires a review of the coverage ratios.

Sage Inc.	**2013**	**2012**	**2011**	**2010**	**2009**	**Industry Average 2013**
Times interest earned	7.44	5.18	8.84	13.34	12.60	7.2
Cash interest coverage	7.77	1.24	9.11	11.21	11.90	*
Fixed charge coverage	2.09	2.01	2.27	2.98	3.07	2.5
Cash flow adequacy	0.58	(0.46)	0.95	1.03	1.24	*

*Not available

[9] The effective tax rate to be used in this ratio was calculated in Chapter 3.

Given the increased level of borrowing, the times interest earned and cash interest coverage ratios have declined over the five-year period but times interest earned remains above the industry average. Cash interest coverage indicates that Sage Inc. is generating enough cash to actually make the cash payments. Sage Inc. leases the majority of its retail outlets so the fixed charge coverage ratio, which considers lease payments as well as interest expense, is a more relevant ratio than times interest earned. This ratio has also decreased, as a result of store expansion and higher payments for leases and interest. Although below the industry average, the firm is still covering all fixed charges by more than two times out of operating earnings, and coverage does not at this point appear to be a problem. The fixed charge coverage ratio is a ratio to be monitored closely in the future, however, particularly if Sage Inc. continues to expand. The cash flow adequacy ratio has dropped below 1.0 in 2011, 2012, and 2013, indicating the company does not generate enough cash from operations to cover capital expenditures, debt repayments, and cash dividends. To improve this ratio, the firm needs to begin reducing accounts receivables and inventories, thereby increasing cash from operations. Once the expansion is complete this should occur; however, if the expansion continues, cash flow adequacy will likely remain below 1.0.

Profitability

The analysis now turns to a consideration of how well the firm has performed in terms of profitability, beginning with the evaluation of several key ratios.

Sage Inc.	**2013**	**2012**	**2011**	**2010**	**2009**	**Industry Average 2013**
Gross profit margin	40.00%	39.95%	42.00%	41.80%	41.76%	37.25%
Operating profit margin	8.93%	7.72%	8.00%	10.98%	11.63%	7.07%
Net profit margin	4.36%	3.86%	4.19%	5.00%	5.20%	3.74%
Cash flow margin	4.65%	(2.46)%	4.00%	4.39%	3.92%	*

*Not available

Profitability—after a relatively poor year in 2012 due to economic recession, adverse ski conditions, and the costs of new store openings—now looks more promising. Management adopted a growth strategy reflected in aggressive marketing and the opening of 18 new stores in 2012 and 25 in 2013. With the exception of the cash flow margin, the profit margins are all below their 2009 and 2010 levels but have improved in 2013 and are above industry averages. The cash flow margin, as a result of strong cash generation from operations in 2013, was at its highest level of the five-year period.

The gross profit margin was stable, a positive sign in light of new store openings featuring many "sale" and discounted items to attract customers, and the firm managed to improve its operating profit margin in 2013. The increase in operating profit margin is especially noteworthy because it occurred during an expansionary period with sizable increases in operating expenses, especially lease payments required for new stores. The net profit margin also improved in spite of increased interest and tax expenses and a reduction in interest revenue from cash equivalents.

Sage Inc.	2013	2012	2011	2010	2009	Industry Average 2013
Return on assets	9.86%	7.79%	8.91%	14.35%	15.34%	9.09%
Return on equity	20.45%	15.61%	17.53%	24.25%	25.46%	17.72%
Cash return on assets	10.52%	(4.96)%	8.64%	15.01%	15.98%	*

*Not available

After declining steadily through 2012, return on assets, return on equity, and cash return on assets rebounded strongly in 2013. The return on assets and return on equity ratios measure the overall success of the firm in generating profits, whereas the cash return on assets measures the firm's ability to generate cash from its investment and management strategies. It would appear that Sage Inc. is well positioned for future growth. As discussed earlier, it will be important to monitor the firm's management of inventories, which account for half of total assets and have been problematic in the past. The expansion will necessitate a continuation of expenditures for advertising, at least at the current level, to attract customers to both new and old areas. Sage Inc. has financed much of its expansion with debt, and thus far its shareholders have benefited from the use of debt through financial leverage.

Sage Inc. experienced a negative cash flow from operations in 2012, another problem that bears watching in the future. The negative cash flow occurred in a year of only modest sales and earnings growth:

Sage Inc.	2013	2012	2011	2010	2009
Sales growth	40.9%	8.7%	25.5%	21.6%	27.5%
Earnings growth	59.0%	0.2%	5.2%	16.9%	19.2%

Sales expanded rapidly in 2013 as the economy recovered and the expansion of retail outlets began to pay off. The outlook is for continued economic recovery.

Relating the Ratios—The Du Pont System

Having looked at individual financial ratios as well as groups of financial ratios measuring short-term liquidity, operating efficiency, capital structure and long-term solvency, and profitability, it is helpful to complete the evaluation of a firm by considering the interrelationship among the individual ratios. That is, how do the various pieces of financial measurement work together to produce an overall return? The Du Pont System helps the analyst see how the firm's decisions and activities over the course of an accounting period—which is what financial ratios are measuring—interact to produce an overall return to the firm's shareholders, the return on equity. The summary ratios used are the following:

(1) **Net profit margin**	×	(2) **Total asset turnover**	=	(3) **Return on investment**
$\frac{\text{Net income}}{\text{Net sales}}$	×	$\frac{\text{Net sales}}{\text{Total assets}}$	=	$\frac{\text{Net income}}{\text{Total assets}}$
(3) **Return on investment**	×	(4) **Financial leverage**	=	(5) **Return on equity**
$\frac{\text{Net income}}{\text{Total assets}}$	×	$\frac{\text{Total assets}}{\text{Stockholders' equity}}$	=	$\frac{\text{Net income}}{\text{Stockholders' equity}}$

By reviewing this series of relationships, the analyst can identify strengths and weaknesses as well as trace potential causes of any problems in the overall financial condition and performance of the firm.

The first three ratios reveal that the (3) return on investment (profit generated from the overall investment in assets) is a product of the (1) net profit margin (profit generated from sales) and the (2) total asset turnover (the firm's ability to produce sales from its assets). Extending the analysis, the remaining three ratios show how the (5) return on equity (overall return to shareholders, the firm's owners) is derived from the product of (3) return on investment and (4) financial leverage (proportion of debt in the capital structure). Using this system, the analyst can evaluate changes in the firm's condition and performance, whether they are indicative of improvement or deterioration or some combination. The evaluation can then focus on specific areas contributing to the changes.

Evaluating Sage Inc. using the Du Pont System over the five-year period from 2009 to 2013 would show the following relationships:

Du Pont System Applied to Sage Inc.

	(1) NPM	×	(2) TAT	=	(3) ROI	×	(4) FL	=	(5) ROE
2009	5.20	×	2.95	=	15.34	×	1.66	=	25.46
2010	5.00	×	2.87	=	14.35	×	1.69	=	24.25
2011	4.19	×	2.13	=	8.92	×	1.97	=	17.57
2012	3.86	×	2.02	=	7.80	×	2.00	=	15.60
2013	4.36	×	2.26	=	9.85	×	2.07	=	20.39

As discussed earlier in the chapter, return on equity is below earlier year levels but has improved since its low point in 2012. The Du Pont System helps provide clues as to why these changes have occurred. Both the profit margin and the asset turnover are lower in 2013 than in 2009 and 2010. The combination of increased debt (financial leverage) and the improvement in profitability and asset utilization has produced an improved overall return in 2013 relative to the two previous years. Specifically, the firm has added debt to finance capital asset expansion and has used its debt effectively. Although debt carries risk and added cost in the form of interest expense, it also has the positive benefit of financial leverage when employed successfully, which is the case for Sage Inc. The 2013 improvement in inventory management has impacted the firm favorably, showing up in the improved total asset turnover ratio. The firm's ability to control operating costs while increasing sales during expansion has improved the net profit margin. The overall return on investment is now improving as a result of these combined factors.

Projections and Pro Forma Statements

Some additional analytical tools and financial ratios are relevant to financial statement analysis, particularly for investment decisions and long-range planning. Although an in-depth discussion of these tools is beyond the scope of this chapter, we provide an introductory treatment of projections, pro forma financial statements, and several investment-related financial ratios.

The investment analyst, in valuing securities for investment decisions, must project the future earnings stream of a business enterprise. References that provide earnings forecasts are found in the "Other Sources" section earlier in the chapter.

Pro forma financial statements are projections of financial statements based on a set of assumptions regarding future revenues, expenses, level of investment in assets, financing methods and costs, and working capital management. Pro forma financial statements are utilized primarily for long-range planning and long-term credit decisions. A bank considering the extension of $1.5 million in new credit to Sage Inc. would want to look at the firm's pro forma statements, assuming the loan is granted, and determine—using different scenarios regarding the firm's performance—whether cash flow from operations would be sufficient to service the debt. Sage Inc.'s CEO, who is making a decision about new store expansion, would develop pro forma statements based on varying estimates of performance outcomes and financing alternatives.

It is important that the above described pro forma financial statements not be confused with "pro forma" earnings or "pro forma" financial statements that many firms now report in their annual reports and financial press releases. Many companies in recent years have made up their own definition of *pro forma* in order to present more favorable financial information than the generally accepted accounting principles (GAAP)-based number required to be reported. By eliminating items such as depreciation, amortization, interest, and tax expense from earnings, for example, some firms have tried to convince users of their annual reports to focus on the "pro forma" amount that is usually a profit, instead of the GAAP-based amount that is usually a loss. (This topic was discussed in Appendix 3A.)

Summary of Analysis

The analysis of any firm's financial statements consists of a mixture of steps and pieces that interrelate and affect each other. No one part of the analysis should be interpreted in isolation. Short-term liquidity affects profitability; profitability begins with sales, which relate to the liquidity of assets. The efficiency of asset management influences the cost and availability of credit, which shapes the capital structure. Every aspect of a firm's financial condition, performance, and outlook affects the share price. The last step of financial statement analysis is to integrate the separate pieces into a whole, leading to conclusions about the business enterprise. The specific conclusions drawn will be affected by the original objectives established at the initiation of the analytical process.

The major findings from the analysis of Sage Inc.'s financial statements can be summarized by the following strengths and weaknesses.

Strengths

1. Favorable economic and industry outlook; firm well-positioned geographically to benefit from expected economic and industry growth
2. Aggressive marketing and expansion strategies
3. Recent improvement in management of accounts receivable and inventory
4. Successful use of financial leverage and solid coverage of debt service requirements
5. Effective control of operating costs
6. Substantial sales growth, partially resulting from market expansion and reflective of future performance potential
7. Increased profitability in 2013 and strong, positive generation of cash flow from operations

Weaknesses

1. Highly sensitive to economic fluctuations and weather conditions
2. Negative cash flow from operating activities in 2012
3. Historical problems with inventory management and some weakness in overall asset management efficiency
4. Increased risk associated with debt financing

The answers to specific questions regarding Sage Inc. are determined by the values placed on each of the strengths and weaknesses. In general, the outlook for the firm is promising. Sage Inc. appears to be a sound credit risk with attractive investment potential. The management of inventories, a continuation of effective cost controls, and careful timing of further expansion will be critically important to the firm's future success.

Financial Statements: A Map

This book began with the notion that financial statements should serve as a map to successful business decision making, even though the user of financial statement data would confront mazelike challenges in seeking to find and interpret the necessary information. The chapters have covered the enormous volume of material found in corporate financial reporting, the complexities and confusions created by accounting rules and choices, the potential for management manipulations of financial statement

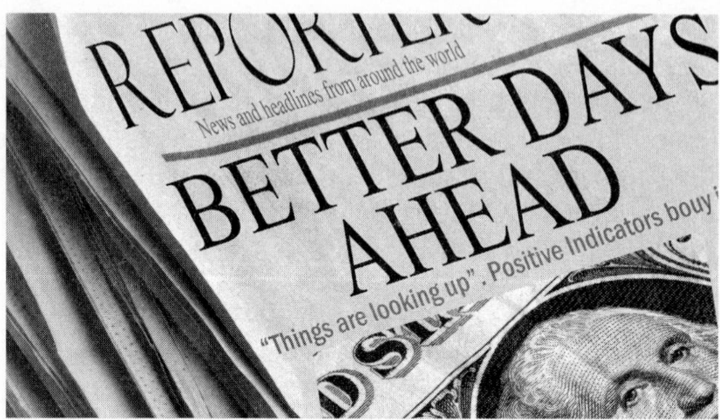

Shutterstock

results, and the difficulty in finding necessary information. The exploration of financial statements has required a close examination of the form and content of each financial statement presented in corporate annual reporting as well as the development of tools and techniques for analyzing the data. It is the hope of the authors that readers of this book will find that financial statements are a map, leading to sound and profitable business decisions.

Appendix 5A: The Analysis of Segmental Data

The FASB requires companies to disclose supplementary financial data for each reportable segment including foreign operations, sales to major customers, and information for enterprises that have only one reportable segment. Segmental disclosures are valuable to the financial analyst in identifying areas of strength and weakness within a company, proportionate contribution to revenue and profit by each division, the relationship between capital expenditures and rates of return for operating areas, and segments that should be de-emphasized or eliminated. The information on segments is presented as a supplementary section in the notes to the financial statements, as part of the basic financial statements, or in a separate schedule that is referenced to and incorporated into the financial statements. (Information is provided at the end of this appendix regarding the definition of a segment and the FASB's disclosure requirements.)

Analyzing Segmental Data: An Illustration

The following analysis of Sage Inc.'s segment disclosures provides an illustration of how to interpret segmental data. The analytical tools used to assess the segmental data of Sage Inc. are applicable to any company with segmental disclosures. Minor variations and/or additions to the tables prepared for Sage may be appropriate for a particular company, but the basic analysis should include, by segment and for at least a three-year period:

1. Percentage contribution to revenue
2. Percentage contribution to operating profit
3. Operating profit margin
4. Capital expenditures
5. Return on investment
6. An assessment of the relationship between the size of a division and its relative contribution

Exhibit 5A.1 contains the information from Note 6, Segment Information, for the Sage Inc. financial statements. Segmental reporting does not include complete financial statements, but it is feasible to perform an analysis of the key financial data presented.

EXHIBIT 5A.1 Sage Inc. Note 6—Segment Information

Sage Inc. has three reportable segments: sporting apparel, footwear, and sporting gear and equipment.

- Sporting apparel includes men's, women's and children's sports clothing.
- Footwear includes tennis, running, walking, aerobic, and golf shoes, as well as ski and hiking boots.
- Sporting gear and equipment includes hunting and fishing gear, sporting goods equipment and an extensive line of golf, ski, and cycling equipment.

Segment information is as follows (in thousands):

	Year Ended December 31		
	2013	**2012**	**2011**
Net sales:			
Sporting apparel	$ 62,524	$ 45,288	$ 39,959
Footwear	36,652	26,163	27,858
Sporting gear and equipment	116,424	81,549	72,883
Total	$215,600	$153,000	$140,700
Operating profit:			
Sporting apparel	$ 8,992	$ 6,443	$ 5,928
Footwear	518	(124)	98
Sporting gear and equipment	10,538	6,252	6,033
Corporate and other	(805)	(765)	(803)
Total	$ 19,243	$ 11,806	$ 11,256
Depreciation and amortization:			
Sporting apparel	$ 793	$ 681	$ 300
Footwear	1,202	1,190	1,200
Sporting gear and equipment	1,642	887	800
Corporate and other	361	226	201
Total	$ 3,998	$ 2,984	$ 2,501
Identifiable assets:			
Sporting apparel	$ 15,663	$ 13,463	$ 10,011
Footwear	23,760	29,444	30,893
Sporting gear and equipment	31,554	13,600	11,300
Corporate and other	24,321	19,402	18,116
Total	$ 95,298	$ 75,909	$ 70,320
Capital expenditures:			
Sporting apparel	$ 32	$ 24	$ 25
Footwear	35	75	78
Sporting gear and equipment	43	28	23
Corporate and other	28	16	18
Total	$ 138	$ 143	$ 144

In order to analyze the performance for each segment, six tables have been prepared from computations based on the figures provided in Exhibit 5A.1. Table 5A.1 shows the percentage contribution to total revenue by segment.

TABLE 5A.1 Contribution by Segment to Revenue (Percentages)

	2013	*2012*	*2011*
Sporting apparel	29.00	29.60	28.40
Footwear	17.00	17.10	19.80
Sporting gear and equipment	54.00	53.30	51.80
Total revenue	100.00	100.00	100.00

Note the change in trends over the three-year period. Sporting gear and equipment not only continues to be the largest revenue producer, but also is contributing more each year to total revenues. Sporting apparel has also increased its relative contribution to total revenue over the three-year period from 2011 to 2013. Footwear, on the other hand, has contributed less to revenue each of the past three years.

TABLE 5A.2 Contribution by Segment to Operating Profit (Percentages)

	2013	*2012*	*2011*
Sporting apparel	46.73	54.57	52.66
Footwear	2.69	(1.05)	0.87
Sporting gear and equipment	54.76	52.96	53.60
Corporate and other	(4.18)	(6.48)	(7.13)
Total operating profit	100.00	100.00	100.00

Table 5A.2 reveals the contribution by segment to operating profit and loss and provides a basis for assessing the ability of a segment to translate revenue into profit. Sporting gear and equipment was the leading contributor to operating profit in 2013 and 2011, with sporting apparel contributing the most to operating profits in 2012. It is not surprising that these two segments contribute the most to operating profit given the level of sales in each segment. Footwear contributed the least to operating profits all three years and in 2012 incurred an operating loss. The MD&A for Sage Inc. explains that the firm had decreases in unit sales and retail prices in the athletic footwear area in 2012. It appears the firm has made strategic changes to remedy this challenge in 2013.

Operating profit margin (operating profit divided by revenue) is presented for each segment in Table 5A.3. The operating profit margin shows the percent of every sales dollar that is converted to (before-tax) profit. Sporting apparel produced the highest profit margins in all three years. Operating profit margin increased in 2013 in the sporting gear and equipment segment after a decline in 2012. Operating profit margin for footwear has improved in 2013 after generating a negative operating profit margin in 2012.

TABLE 5A.3 Operating Profit Margin by Segment (Percentages)

	2013	*2012*	*2011*
Sporting apparel	14.38	14.23	14.84
Footwear	1.41	(0.47)	0.35
Sporting gear and equipment	9.05	7.67	8.28

Table 5A.4 is a percentage breakdown of capital expenditures by segment. Sage Inc. has chosen to invest more heavily in sporting gear and equipment, especially in 2013. This investment has resulted in increased revenues, operating profit, and operating profit margin. Heavier investment has also occurred in the sporting apparel area, leading to a slightly higher operating profit margin in 2013 compared to 2012. In 2011 and 2012, Sage Inc. invested significant amounts in the footwear segment, which did not result in better revenues or operating profits. The firm has reduced capital expenditures in this area in 2013 and shifted those dollars to more profitable areas.

TABLE 5A.4 Capital Expenditures by Segment (Percentages)

	2013	*2012*	*2011*
Sporting apparel	23.19	16.78	17.36
Footwear	25.36	52.45	54.17
Sporting gear and equipment	31.16	19.58	15.97
Corporate and other	20.29	11.19	12.50
Total capital expenditures	100.00	100.00	100.00

It is important to examine the relationship between investment and return, and this information is provided in Table 5A.5, which shows return on investment by segment (operating profit divided by identifiable assets). Sporting apparel consistently generates solid return on investment each year, despite the lower investment in capital expenditures compared to the other two segments. Sporting gear and equipment generates significant return on investment; however, the return is decreasing significantly from 2011 to 2013. Capital expenditures, in 2013, for this segment were higher than in all other segments. This segment should be monitored to see if the increase in expenditures will result in higher returns again in the next few years.

TABLE 5A.5 Return on Investment by Segment (Percentages)

	2013	*2012*	*2011*
Sporting apparel	57.41	47.86	59.21
Footwear	2.18	(0.42)	0.32
Sporting gear and equipment	33.40	45.97	53.39

Table 5A.6 compares a ranking of segments in 2013 by segment assets with percentage contribution to operating profit, operating profit margin, and return on investment.

Sporting apparel is the largest segment when considering total investment in assets. This segment generates the highest operating profit margin and return on investment with the least amount of capital expenditures required. Footwear does not produce impressive operating profit or return on investment for the significant capital expenditures that have been allocated to this segment. Sporting gear and equipment requires the least investment in assets; however, despite the positive operating profit margin and good return on investment, the return on investment for this segment is dropping significantly from 2011 to 2013.

TABLE 5A.6 Ranking of Segments in 2013

	Percentage of Total Segment Assets	*Percentage Contribution to Operating Profit*	*Operating Profit Margin*	*Return on Investment*
Sporting gear and equipment	44.45	54.76	9.05	33.40
Footwear	33.48	2.69	1.41	2.18
Sporting apparel	22.07	46.73	14.38	57.41

Summary

The analytical tools used to assess the segmental data of Sage Inc. are applicable to any company with segmental disclosures. Minor variations and/or additions to the tables prepared for Sage may be appropriate for a particular company, but the basic analysis should include, by segment and for at least a three-year period: (1) percentage contribution to revenue, (2) percentage contribution to operating profit, (3) operating profit margin, (4) capital expenditures, (5) return on investment, and (6) an examination of the relationship between the size of a division and its relative contribution.

Operating Segment—Definition

An operating segment is defined by FASB as a component of a business enterprise:

1. That engages in business activities from which it may earn revenues and incur expenses.
2. Whose operating results are regularly reviewed by the company's chief operating decision maker to make decisions about resources allocated to the segment and assesses its performance.
3. For which discrete financial information is available

A segment is considered to be reportable if any one of three criteria is met:

1. Revenue is 10% or more of combined revenue, including intersegment revenue.
2. Operating profit or loss is 10% or more of the greater of combined profit of all segments with profit or combined loss of all segments with loss.
3. Segment assets exceed 10% or more of combined assets of all segments.

Disclosure Requirements

The following information must be disclosed according to FASB:

1. General Information. The "management approach" is used to identify operating segments in the enterprise. The management approach is based on the way that management organizes the segments within the company for making operating decisions and assessing performance. A company must identify how it is organized and what factors were used to identify operating segments and describe the types of products and services from which each operating segment derives its revenues.
2. Information about Profit or Loss. A company must report a measure of profit or loss for each reportable segment. In addition, certain amounts must be disclosed if the specified amounts are included in information reviewed by the chief operating decision maker. For companies basing profit or loss on pretax income from continuing operations, the following amounts must be disclosed:[1]

   - Revenues (separated into sales to external customers and intersegment sales)
   - Interest revenue
   - Interest expense
   - Depreciation, depletion, and amortization expense

3. Information about Assets. A company must report a measure of the total operating segments' assets. Only assets included in reports to the chief operating decision maker should be included. The total capital expenditures that have been added to long-lived assets must also be reported for each operating segment.

The total of the operating segments' revenues, profit or loss, assets, and any other items reported shall be reconciled to the company's total consolidated amounts for each of these items.

SELF-TEST

Solutions are provided in Appendix B.

_______ **1.** What is the first step in an analysis of financial statements?
(a) Check the auditor's report.
(b) Check references containing financial information.
(c) Specify the objectives of the analysis.
(d) Do a common-size analysis.

_______ **2.** What is a creditor's objective in performing an analysis of financial statements?
(a) To decide whether the borrower has the ability to repay interest and principal on borrowed funds.
(b) To determine if the firm would be a good place to obtain employment.
(c) To determine the company's taxes for the current year.
(d) To determine whether an investment is warranted by estimating a company's future earnings stream.

[1]If more complex profit measures are used, the company must also disclose any unusual items, equity income, income tax expense, extraordinary items, and other significant noncash items.

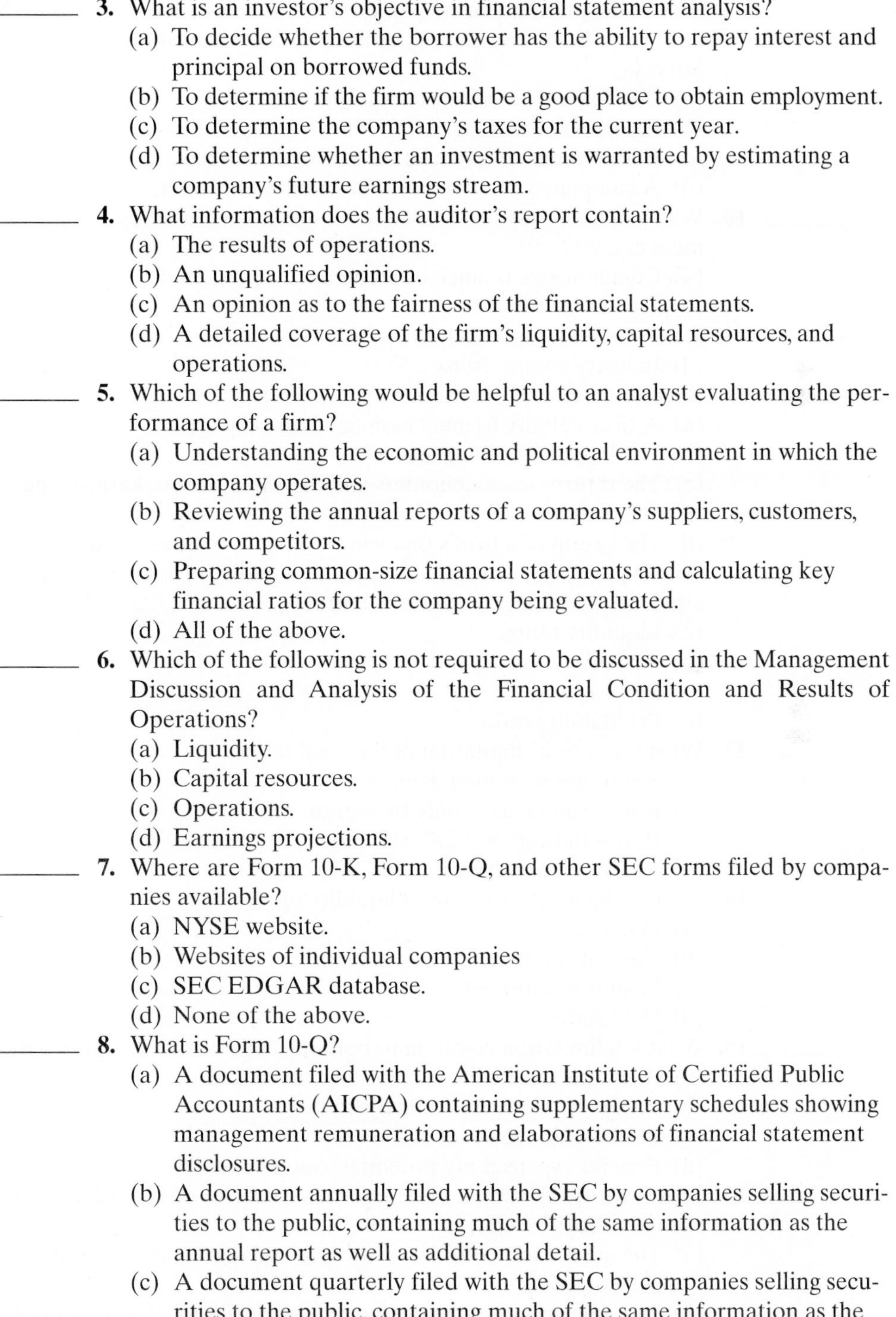

______ **3.** What is an investor's objective in financial statement analysis?
(a) To decide whether the borrower has the ability to repay interest and principal on borrowed funds.
(b) To determine if the firm would be a good place to obtain employment.
(c) To determine the company's taxes for the current year.
(d) To determine whether an investment is warranted by estimating a company's future earnings stream.

______ **4.** What information does the auditor's report contain?
(a) The results of operations.
(b) An unqualified opinion.
(c) An opinion as to the fairness of the financial statements.
(d) A detailed coverage of the firm's liquidity, capital resources, and operations.

______ **5.** Which of the following would be helpful to an analyst evaluating the performance of a firm?
(a) Understanding the economic and political environment in which the company operates.
(b) Reviewing the annual reports of a company's suppliers, customers, and competitors.
(c) Preparing common-size financial statements and calculating key financial ratios for the company being evaluated.
(d) All of the above.

______ **6.** Which of the following is not required to be discussed in the Management Discussion and Analysis of the Financial Condition and Results of Operations?
(a) Liquidity.
(b) Capital resources.
(c) Operations.
(d) Earnings projections.

______ **7.** Where are Form 10-K, Form 10-Q, and other SEC forms filed by companies available?
(a) NYSE website.
(b) Websites of individual companies
(c) SEC EDGAR database.
(d) None of the above.

______ **8.** What is Form 10-Q?
(a) A document filed with the American Institute of Certified Public Accountants (AICPA) containing supplementary schedules showing management remuneration and elaborations of financial statement disclosures.
(b) A document annually filed with the SEC by companies selling securities to the public, containing much of the same information as the annual report as well as additional detail.
(c) A document quarterly filed with the SEC by companies selling securities to the public, containing much of the same information as the annual report but less extensively.
(d) A document quarterly filed with the SEC containing nonpublic information.

______ **9.** What information can be gained from sources such as Industry Norms and Key Business Ratios, Annual Statement Studies, and Industry Surveys?
(a) The general economic condition.
(b) Forecasts of earnings.
(c) Elaborations of financial statement disclosures.
(d) A company's relative position within its industry.

______ **10.** Which of the following is not a tool or technique used by a financial statement analyst?
(a) Common-size financial statements.
(b) Trend analysis.
(c) Random sampling analysis.
(d) Industry comparisons.

______ **11.** What do market ratios measure?
(a) A firm's ability to meet cash needs as they arise.
(b) The liquidity of fixed assets.
(c) The returns to stockholders and the value the marketplace puts on a company's stock.
(d) The extent of a firm's financing with debt relative to equity.

______ **12.** Which category of ratio measures the liquidity of specific assets and the efficiency of managing assets by a firm?
(a) Liquidity ratios.
(b) Activity ratios.
(c) Leverage ratios.
(d) Profitability ratios.

______ **13.** What is a serious limitation of financial ratios?
(a) Ratios are screening devices.
(b) Ratios can be used only by themselves.
(c) Ratios indicate weaknesses only.
(d) Ratios are not predictive.

______ **14.** What is the most widely used liquidity ratio?
(a) Quick ratio.
(b) Current ratio.
(c) Inventory turnover.
(d) Debt ratio.

______ **15.** What is a limitation common to both the current and the quick ratio?
(a) Accounts receivable may not be truly liquid.
(b) Inventories may not be truly liquid.
(c) Marketable securities are not liquid.
(d) Prepaid expenses are potential sources of cash.

______ **16.** Why is the quick ratio a more rigorous test of short-run solvency than the current ratio?
(a) The quick ratio considers only cash and marketable securities as current assets.
(b) The quick ratio eliminates prepaid expenses for the numerator.
(c) The quick ratio eliminates prepaid expenses for the denominator.
(d) The quick ratio eliminates inventories from the numerator.

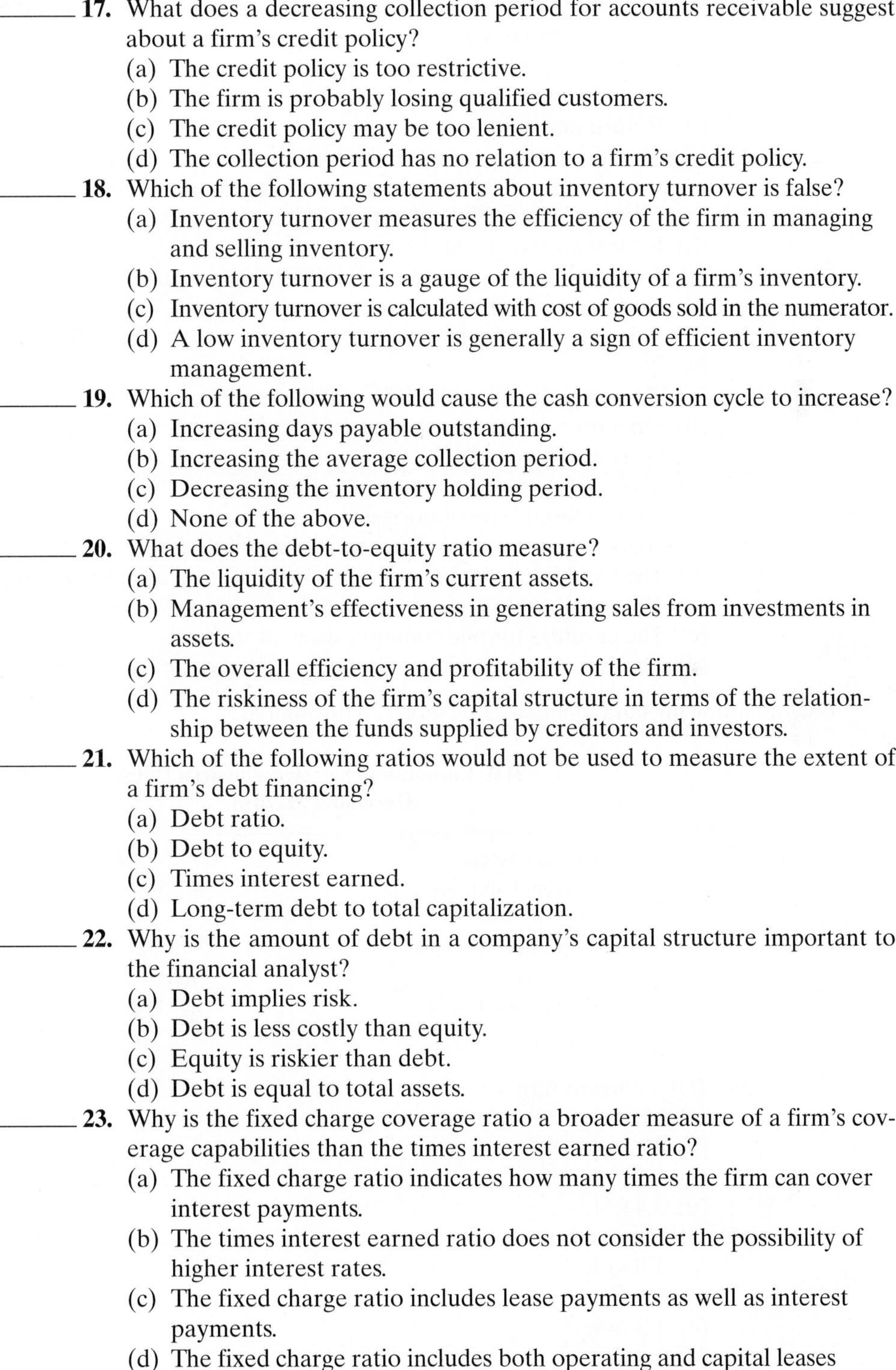

_______ **17.** What does a decreasing collection period for accounts receivable suggest about a firm's credit policy?
(a) The credit policy is too restrictive.
(b) The firm is probably losing qualified customers.
(c) The credit policy may be too lenient.
(d) The collection period has no relation to a firm's credit policy.

_______ **18.** Which of the following statements about inventory turnover is false?
(a) Inventory turnover measures the efficiency of the firm in managing and selling inventory.
(b) Inventory turnover is a gauge of the liquidity of a firm's inventory.
(c) Inventory turnover is calculated with cost of goods sold in the numerator.
(d) A low inventory turnover is generally a sign of efficient inventory management.

_______ **19.** Which of the following would cause the cash conversion cycle to increase?
(a) Increasing days payable outstanding.
(b) Increasing the average collection period.
(c) Decreasing the inventory holding period.
(d) None of the above.

_______ **20.** What does the debt-to-equity ratio measure?
(a) The liquidity of the firm's current assets.
(b) Management's effectiveness in generating sales from investments in assets.
(c) The overall efficiency and profitability of the firm.
(d) The riskiness of the firm's capital structure in terms of the relationship between the funds supplied by creditors and investors.

_______ **21.** Which of the following ratios would not be used to measure the extent of a firm's debt financing?
(a) Debt ratio.
(b) Debt to equity.
(c) Times interest earned.
(d) Long-term debt to total capitalization.

_______ **22.** Why is the amount of debt in a company's capital structure important to the financial analyst?
(a) Debt implies risk.
(b) Debt is less costly than equity.
(c) Equity is riskier than debt.
(d) Debt is equal to total assets.

_______ **23.** Why is the fixed charge coverage ratio a broader measure of a firm's coverage capabilities than the times interest earned ratio?
(a) The fixed charge ratio indicates how many times the firm can cover interest payments.
(b) The times interest earned ratio does not consider the possibility of higher interest rates.
(c) The fixed charge ratio includes lease payments as well as interest payments.
(d) The fixed charge ratio includes both operating and capital leases whereas the times interest earned ratio includes only operating leases.

_______ **24.** Which profit margin measures the overall operating efficiency of the firm?
(a) Gross profit margin.
(b) Operating profit margin.
(c) Net profit margin.
(d) Return on equity.

_______ **25.** Which ratio or ratios measure the overall efficiency of the firm in managing its investment in assets and in generating return to shareholders?
(a) Gross profit margin and net profit margin.
(b) Return on investment.
(c) Total asset turnover and operating profit margin.
(d) Return on investment and return on equity.

_______ **26.** What does a financial leverage index greater than one indicate about a firm?
(a) The unsuccessful use of financial leverage.
(b) Operating returns more than sufficient to cover interest payments on borrowed funds.
(c) More debt financing than equity financing.
(d) An increased level of borrowing.

_______ **27.** What does the price to earnings ratio measure?
(a) The "multiple" that the stock market places on a firm's earnings.
(b) The relationship between dividends and market prices.
(c) The earnings for one common share of stock.
(d) The percentage of dividends paid to net earnings of the firm.

Use the following data to answer questions 28 through 31:

JDL Corporation Selected Financial Data, December 31, 2013

Current assets	$125,000
Current liabilities	125,000
Inventories	37,500
Accounts receivable	75,000
Net sales	900,000
Cost of goods sold	675,000

_______ **28.** JDL's current ratio is:
(a) 1.0 to 1.
(b) 0.7 to 1.
(c) 1.5 to 1.
(d) 2.4 to 1.

_______ **29.** JDL's quick ratio is:
(a) 1.0 to 1.
(b) 0.7 to 1.
(c) 1.5 to 1.
(d) 2.4 to 1.

______ **30.** JDL's average collection period is:
(a) 6 days.
(b) 11 days.
(c) 16 days.
(d) 30 days.

______ **31.** JDL's inventory turnover is:
(a) 1.25 times.
(b) 13.5 times.
(c) 18.0 times.
(d) 37.5 times.

Use the following data to answer questions 32 through 35:

RQM Corporation Selected Financial Data, December 31, 2013

Net sales	$2,000,000
Cost of goods sold	1,200,000
Operating expenses	350,000
Net operating income	450,000
Net income	390,000
Total stockholders' equity	1,000,000
Total assets	1,500,000
Cash flow from operating activities	50,000

______ **32.** RQM's gross profit margin, operating profit margin, and net profit margin, respectively, are:
(a) 40.00%, 22.50%, 19.50%.
(b) 60.00%, 19.50%, 10.83%.
(c) 60.00%, 22.50%, 19.50%.
(d) 40.00%, 22.50%, 10.83%.

______ **33.** RQM's return on equity is:
(a) 26%.
(b) 54%.
(c) 42%.
(d) 39%.

______ **34.** RQM's return on investment is:
(a) 22.5%.
(b) 26.5%.
(c) 19.5%.
(d) 40.0%.

______ **35.** RQM's cash flow margin is:
(a) 1.4%.
(b) 2.5%.
(c) 10.8%.
(d) 12.8%.

Study Questions and Problems

5.1. Explain how the credit analyst's focus will differ from the investment analyst's focus.

5.2. What are the limitations of financial ratios?

5.3. What do liquidity ratios measure? Activity ratios? Leverage ratios? Profitability ratios? Market ratios?

5.4. How is the Du Pont System helpful to the analyst?

5.5. Eleanor's Computers is a retailer of computer products. Using the financial data provided, complete the financial ratio calculations for 2013. Advise management of any ratios that indicate potential problems and provide an explanation of possible causes of the problems.

Financial Ratios	2011	2012	2013	Industry Averages 2013
Current ratio	1.71X	1.65X		1.70X
Quick ratio	0.92X	0.89X		0.95X
Average collection period	60 days	60 days		65 days
Inventory turnover	4.20X	3.90X		4.50X
Fixed asset turnover	3.20X	3.33X		3.00X
Total asset turnover	1.40X	1.35X		1.37X
Debt ratio	59.20%	61.00%		60.00%
Times interest earned	4.20X	3.70X		4.75X
Gross profit margin	25.00%	23.00%		22.50%
Operating profit margin	12.50%	12.70%		12.50%
Net profit margin	6.10%	6.00%		6.50%
Return on total assets	8.54%	8.10%		8.91%
Return on equity	20.93%	20.74%		22.28%

Income Statement for Year Ended 12/31/13		Balance Sheet at 12/31/13	
Sales	$1,500,000	Cash	$ 125,000
Cost of goods sold	1,200,000	Accounts receivable	275,000
Gross profit	$ 300,000	Inventory	325,000
Operating expenses	100,000	Current assets	$ 725,000
Operating profit	$ 200,000	Fixed assets (net)	$ 420,000
Interest expense	72,000	Total Assets	$1,145,000
Earnings before tax	128,000	Accounts payable	$ 150,000
Income tax (40%)	51,200	Notes payable	225,000
Net Income	$ 76,800	Accrued liabilities	100,000
		Current liabilities	475,000
		Long-term debt	400,000
		Total liabilities	$ 875,000
		Equity	270,000
		Total liabilities and equity	$1,145,000

5.6. Luna Lighting, a retail firm, has experienced modest sales growth over the past three years but has had difficulty translating the expansion of sales into improved profitability. Using three years' financial statements, you have developed the following ratio calculations and industry comparisons. Based on this information, suggest possible reasons for Luna's profitability problems.

	2013	2012	2011	Industry Averages 2013
Current	2.3X	2.3X	2.2X	2.1X
Average collection period	45 days	46 days	47 days	50 days
Inventory turnover	8.3X	8.2X	8.1X	8.3X
Fixed asset turnover	2.7X	3.0X	3.3X	3.5X
Total asset turnover	1.1X	1.2X	1.3X	1.5X
Debt ratio	50%	50%	50%	54%
Times interest earned	8.1X	8.2X	8.1X	7.2X
Fixed charge coverage	4.0X	4.5X	5.5X	5.1X
Gross profit margin	43%	43%	43%	40%
Operating profit margin	6.3%	7.2%	8.0%	7.5%
Net profit margin	3.5%	4.0%	4.3%	4.2%
Return on assets	3.7%	5.0%	5.7%	6.4%
Return on equity	7.4%	9.9%	11.4%	11.8%

5.7. RareMetals Inc. sells a rare metal found only in underdeveloped countries overseas. As a result of unstable governments in these countries and the rarity of the metal, the price fluctuates significantly. Financial information is given assuming the use of the first-in, first-out (FIFO) method of inventory valuation and also the last-in, first-out (LIFO) method of inventory valuation. Current assets other than inventory total $1,230 and current liabilities total $1,600. The ending inventory balances are $1,350 for FIFO and $525 for LIFO.

RareMetals Inc. Income Statements (in Thousands)

	FIFO	LIFO
Net sales	$3,000	$3,000
Cost of goods sold	1,400	2,225
Gross profit	1,600	775
Selling, general, and administrative	600	600
Operating profit	1,000	175
Interest expense	80	80
Earnings before taxes	920	95
Provision for income taxes	322	33
Net earnings	$ 598	$ 62

Required

(a) Calculate the following ratios assuming RareMetals Inc. uses the FIFO method of inventory valuation: gross profit margin, operating profit margin, net profit margin, current ratio, and quick ratio.
(b) Calculate the ratios listed in (a) assuming RareMetals Inc. uses the LIFO method of inventory valuation.
(c) Evaluate and explain the differences in the ratios calculated in (a) and (b).
(d) Will cash flow from operating activities differ depending on the inventory valuation method used? If so, estimate the difference and explain your answer.

5.8. ABC Company and XYZ Company are competitors in the manufacturing industry. The following ratios and financial information have been compiled for these two companies for the most recent year:

Financial ratios	**ABC**	**XYZ**
Liquidity		
Current (times)	0.92	1.51
Quick (times)	0.61	1.20
Cash flow liquidity (times)	0.35	0.85
Cash flow from operations (in millions of $)	995	2,520
Activity		
Accounts receivable turnover (times)	5.48	6.20
Inventory turnover (times)	4.75	4.00
Payables turnover (times)	2.82	3.55
Fixed asset turnover (times)	2.49	3.62
Total asset turnover (times)	1.10	1.10
Leverage		
Debt ratio (%)	76.02	51.21
Times interest earned (times)	12.31	17.28
Cash interest coverage (times)	9.89	30.19
Cash flow adequacy (times)	0.43	1.35
Profitability		
Gross profit margin (%)	43.08	43.11
Operating profit margin (%)	16.23	8.84
Net profit margin (%)	11.26	4.80
Cash flow margin (%)	6.98	12.59
Return on assets (%)	9.77	4.63
Return on equity (%)	40.86	10.23
Cash return on assets (%)	6.87	12.54
Earnings per share	4.59	1.19
Closing stock price	$41 per share	$35 per share

Required

(a) Compare and evaluate the strengths and weaknesses of ABC and XYZ Companies.
(b) Calculate the price-to-earnings (P/E) ratios for both firms. Explain what a P/E ratio tells an analyst. What could be the cause of the difference between ABC's and XYZ's P/E ratios?

5.9. Determine the effect on the current ratio, the quick ratio, net working capital (current assets less current liabilities), and the debt ratio (total liabilities to total assets) of each of the following transactions. Consider each transaction separately and assume that prior to each transaction the current ratio is 2X, the quick ratio is 1X, and the debt ratio is 50%. The company uses an allowance for doubtful accounts.

Use I for increase, D for decrease, and N for no change.

	Current Ratio	Quick Ratio	Net Working Capital	Debt Ratio
(a) Borrows $10,000 from bank on short-term note				
(b) Writes off a $5,000 customer account				
(c) Issues $25,000 in new common stock for cash				
(d) Purchases for cash $7,000 of new equipment				
(e) Inventory of $5,000 is destroyed by fire				
(f) Invests $3,000 in short-term marketable securities				
(g) Issues $10,000 long-term bonds				
(h) Sells equipment with book value of $6,000 for $7,000				
(i) Issues $10,000 stock in exchange for land				
(j) Purchases $3,000 inventory for cash				
(k) Purchases $5,000 inventory on credit				
(l) Pays $2,000 to supplier to reduce account payable				

5.10. Laurel Street, president of Uvalde Manufacturing Inc., is preparing a proposal to present to her board of directors regarding a planned plant expansion that will cost $10 million. At issue is whether the expansion should be financed with debt (a long-term note at First National Bank of Uvalde with an interest rate of 15%) or through the issuance of common stock (200,000 shares at $50 per share).

Uvalde Manufacturing currently has a capital structure of:

Debt (12% interest)	40,000,000
Equity	50,000,000

The firm's most recent income statement is presented next:

Sales	$100,000,000
Cost of goods sold	65,000,000
Gross profit	35,000,000
Operating expenses	20,000,000
Operating profit	15,000,000
Interest expense	4,800,000
Earnings before tax	10,200,000
Income tax expense (40%)	4,080,000
Net income	$ 6,120,000
Earnings per share (800,000 shares)	$ 7.65

Laurel Street is aware that financing the expansion with debt will increase risk but could also benefit shareholders through financial leverage. Estimates are that the plant expansion will increase operating profit by 20%. The tax rate is expected to stay at 40%. Assume a 100% dividend payout ratio.

Required

(a) Calculate the debt ratio, times interest earned, earnings per share, and the financial leverage index under each alternative, assuming the expected increase in operating profit is realized.
(b) Discuss the factors the board should consider in making a decision.

5.11. Using the ratios and information given for Walmart, a retailer, analyze the short-term liquidity and operating efficiency of the firm as of January 31, 2011.

Financial ratios for the years ended January 31,	2011	2010
Liquidity		
Current (times)	0.89	0.86
Quick (times)	0.27	0.28
Cash flow liquidity (times)	0.53	0.61
Average collection period	5 days	4 days
Days inventory held	42 days	40 days
Days payable outstanding	39 days	37 days
Cash conversion cycle	8 days	7 days
Activity		
Fixed asset turnover (times)	3.99	4.07
Total asset turnover (times)	2.32	2.38
Other information		
Cash flow from operations (in millions of $)	23,643	26,249
Revenues (in millions of $)	418,952	405,132

5.12. Using the ratios and information given for AMC Entertainment Inc., owner and operator of movie theaters, analyze the capital structure, long-term solvency, and profitability of AMC as of 2010.

Financial ratios	2010	2009
Leverage		
Debt ratio (%)	79.2	72.1
Long-term debt to total capital (%)	70.6	61.8
Times interest earned (times)	0.8	(3.3)
Cash interest coverage (times)	3.2	2.7
Fixed charge coverage (times)	1.0	0.8
Cash flow adequacy (times)	0.3	1.2
Profitability		
Gross profit margin (%)	58.6	59.8
Operating profit margin (%)	4.4	(0.2)
Net profit margin (%)	2.9	(3.6)
Cash flow margin (%)	10.7	8.9
Return on assets (%)	1.9	(2.2)
Return on equity (%)	9.2	(7.8)
Cash return on assets (%)	7.1	5.4
Other Information		
Cash flow from operations (in thousands of $)	258,015	200,701
Revenues (in thousands of $)	2,417,739	2,265,487

5.13. Writing Skills Problem

Sage Inc.'s staff of accountants finished preparing the financial statements for 2013 and will meet next week with the company's CEO as well as the Director of Investor Relations and representatives from the marketing and art departments to design the current year's annual report.

Required:

Write a paragraph in which you present the main idea(s) you think the company should present to shareholders in the annual report.

5.14. Research Problem

Using the articles referenced in footnote 3 in this chapter regarding cash flow ratios, create a list of cash flow ratios that you believe would be a good set of ratios to assess the cash flows of a firm. Choose an industry and locate four companies in that industry. Calculate the cash flow ratios for each company and then create an industry average of all four companies. Comment on how well you think your industry average would work as a guide when analyzing other firms in this industry.

5.15. Internet Problem

Choose an industry and find four companies in that industry. Using a financial Internet database such as www.marketwatch.com, calculate or locate the four market ratios discussed in the chapter for each of the four companies. Write an analysis comparing the market ratios of the four companies.

CASES

Case 5.1 Intel Case

The 2010 Intel Annual Report can be found at the following Web site: www.pearsoninternationaleditions.com/fraser. Using the annual report, answer the following questions:

(a) Using the Intel Annual Report, calculate key financial ratios for all years presented.
(b) Using the library, find industry averages to compare to the calculations in (a).
(c) Write a report to the management of Intel. Your report should include an evaluation of short-term liquidity, operating efficiency, capital structure and long-term solvency, profitability, market measures, and a discussion of any quality of financial reporting issues. In addition, strengths and weaknesses should be identified, and your opinion of the investment potential and the creditworthiness of the firm should be conveyed to management.

Hint: Use the information from the Intel Problems at the end of Chapters 1 through 4 to complete this problem.

Case 5.2 Avnet Comprehensive Analysis Case Using the Financial Statement Analysis Template

Each chapter in the textbook contains a continuation of this problem. The objective is to learn how to do a comprehensive financial statement analysis in steps as the content of each chapter is learned. Using the 2010 Avnet Form 10-K, which can be found at wwww.pearsoninternationaleditions.com/fraser, complete the following requirements:

(a) Open the financial statement analysis template that you have been using in the prior chapters. Link to the "Ratios" and the "Growth Rate Analysis" by clicking on the tabs at the bottom of the template. All of the ratios should be automatically calculated for you, assuming you have input all required data from prior chapters. Print these pages.

(b) Using all of your data and calculations for Avnet from prior chapters, write a comprehensive analysis of the company. Use Figure 5.2 as a guide.

Case 5.3 Spartech Corporation

The following excerpts are from the 2010 Form 10-K of Spartech Corporation.

Item 1. Business

General

Spartech Corporation (the "Company" or "Spartech") was incorporated in the state of Delaware in 1968, succeeding a business that had commenced operations in 1960. The Company, together with its subsidiaries, is an intermediary processor of engineered thermoplastics, polymeric compounds and concentrates. The Company converts base polymers or resins purchased from commodity suppliers into extruded plastic sheet and rollstock, thermoformed packaging, specialty film laminates, acrylic products, specialty plastic alloys, color concentrates and blended resin compounds. Its products are sold to original equipment manufacturers and other customers in a wide range of end markets.

In 2009, the Company sold its wheels and profiles businesses and closed and liquidated three businesses including a manufacturer of boat components sold to the marine market and one compounding and one sheet business that previously serviced single customers. These businesses are classified as discontinued operations in accordance with Financial Accounting Standards Board ("FASB") Accounting Standards Codification ("ASC") 205, Discontinued Operations. All amounts presented within this Form 10-K are presented on a continuing basis, unless otherwise noted. See the notes to the consolidated financial statements for further details of these divestitures and closures. The wheels, profiles and marine businesses were previously reported in the Engineered Products segment, and due to these dispositions, the Company no longer has this reporting segment.

SPARTECH CORPORATION AND SUBSIDIARIES
CONSOLIDATED STATEMENTS OF OPERATIONS
(Dollars in thousands, except per share data)

	2010	2009	2008
Net sales	$ 1,022,896	$ 926,777	$ 1,321,169
Costs and expenses			
Cost of sales	914,293	810,469	1,204,932
Selling, general and administrative expenses	88,852	77,868	88,073
Amortization of intangibles	3,774	4,479	5,163
Goodwill impairments	56,149	—	217,974
Other intangible and fixed asset impairments	13,674	2,592	9,031
Restructuring and exit costs	7,290	5,234	2,230
Total costs and expenses	1,084,032	900,642	1,527,403
Operating (loss) earnings	(61,136)	26,135	(206,234)
Interest, net of interest income*	12,025	15,379	19,403
Debt extinguishment costs	729	—	—
(Loss) earnings from continuing operations before income taxes	(73,890)	10,756	(225,637)
Income tax (benefit) expense	(24,247)	7,451	(53,988)
Net (loss) earnings from continuing operations	(49,643)	3,305	(171,649)
Net (loss) earnings from discontinued operations, net of tax	(732)	5,046	(20,463)
Net (loss) earnings	$ (50,375)	$ 8,351	$ (192,112)
Basic (loss) earnings per share:			
(Loss) earnings from continuing operations	$ (1.60)	$ 0.11	$ (5.61)
(Loss) earnings from discontinued operations, net of tax	(0.03)	0.16	(0.68)
Net (loss) earnings per share	$ (1.63)	$ 0.27	$ (6.29)
Diluted (loss) earnings per share:			
(Loss) earnings from continuing operations	$ (1.60)	$ 0.11	$ (5.61)
(Loss) earnings from discontinued operations, net of tax	(0.03)	0.16	(0.68)
Net (loss) earnings per share	$ (1.63)	$ 0.27	$ (6.29)
Dividends declared per share	$ —	$ 0.05	$ 0.37

The accompanying notes are an integral part of these consolidated financial statements.

*(Note: Interest, net of interest income, is comprised only of interest expense.)

SPARTECH CORPORATION AND SUBSIDIARIES
CONSOLIDATED BALANCE SHEETS
(Dollars in thousands, except share data)

	October 30, 2010	October 31, 2009
Assets		
Current assets:		
Cash and cash equivalents	$ 4,900	$ 26,925
Trade receivables, net of allowances of $3,404 and $2,470, respectively	134,902	130,355
Inventories, net of inventory reserves of $6,539 and $5,430, respectively	79,691	62,941
Prepaid expenses and other current assets, net	35,789	33,299
Assets held for sale	3,256	2,907
Total current assets	258,538	256,427
Property, plant, and equipment, net	211,844	229,003
Goodwill	87,921	144,345
Other intangible assets, net	14,559	28,404
Other long-term assets	4,279	3,892
Total assets	$ 577,141	$ 662,071
Liabilities and shareholders' equity		
Current liabilities:		
Current maturities of long-term debt	$ 880	$ 36,079
Accounts payable	129,037	103,484
Accrued liabilities	34,112	39,505
Total current liabilities	164,029	179,068
Long-term debt, less current maturities	171,592	180,355
Other long-term liabilities:		
Deferred taxes	42,648	58,736
Other long-term liabilities	5,866	7,033
Total liabilities	384,135	425,192
Shareholders' equity		
Preferred stock (authorized: 4,000,000 shares, par value $1.00)		
Issued: None	—	—
Common stock (authorized: 55,000,000 shares, par value $0.75)		
Issued: 33,131,846 shares; outstanding: 30,884,503 and 30,719,277 shares, respectively	24,849	24,849
Contributed capital	204,966	204,183
Retained earnings	10,036	60,411
Treasury stock, at cost, 2,247,343 and 2,412,569 shares, respectively	(52,730)	(54,860)
Accumulated other comprehensive income	5,885	2,296
Total shareholders' equity	193,006	236,879
Total liabilities and shareholders' equity	$ 577,141	$ 662,071

The accompanying notes are an integral part of these consolidated financial statements.

SPARTECH CORPORATION AND SUBSIDIARIES
CONSOLIDATED STATEMENTS OF CASH FLOWS
(Dollars in thousands)

	2010	2009	2008
Cash flows from operating activities			
Net (loss) earnings	$ (50,375)	$ 8,351	$ (192,112)
Adjustments to reconcile net (loss) earnings to net cash provided by operating activities:			
Depreciation and amortization	36,632	44,030	47,201
Stock-based compensation expense	3,107	3,071	3,634
Goodwill impairment	56,424	–	238,641
Other intangible and fixed asset impairments	13,674	2,592	15,846
Restructuring and exit costs	2,849	2,114	659
Gain on disposition of assets, net	(1,116)	(6,242)	–
Provision for bad debt expense	8,111	4,321	4,763
Deferred taxes	(22,067)	2,523	(59,100)
Change in current assets and liabilities:			
Trade receivables	(12,175)	36,254	31,326
Inventories	(16,467)	29,343	19,026
Prepaid expenses and other current assets	2,868	(9,635)	1,727
Accounts payable	24,283	(47,519)	(11,691)
Accrued liabilities	(5,837)	(4,736)	(2,766)
Other, net	(581)	797	(542)
Net cash provided by operating activities	39,330	65,264	96,612
Cash flows from investing activities			
Capital expenditures	(21,432)	(8,098)	(17,276)
Proceeds from the disposition of assets	3,560	32,677	584
Business acquisitions	–	–	(792)
Net cash (used) provided by investing activities	(17,872)	24,579	(17,484)
Cash flows from financing activities			
Bank credit facility borrowings (payments), net	45,900	(41,600)	(49,903)
Payments on notes and bank term loan	(87,582)	(18,936)	(7,876)
Payments on bonds and leases	(515)	(1,183)	573
Debt issuance costs	(1,174)	(215)	(2,424)
Cash dividends on common stock	–	(3,057)	(13,926)
Issuance of common stock	–	–	2,812
Stock-based compensation exercised	(194)	(15)	16
Treasury stock acquired	–	–	(9,667)
Net cash used by financing activities	(43,565)	(65,006)	(80,395)
Effect of exchange rate changes on cash and cash equivalents	82	(30)	(24)
(Decrease) increase in cash and cash equivalents	(22,025)	24,807	(1,291)
Cash and cash equivalents at beginning of year	26,925	2,118	3,409
Cash and cash equivalents at end of year	$ 4,900	$ 26,925	$ 2,118

	2010	2009	2008
Supplemental Disclosures:			
Cash paid during the year for:			
Interest	$ 12,780	$ 16,222	$ 18,829
Income taxes	5,711	6,598	257
Schedule of business acquisitions:			
Fair value of assets acquired	—	—	187
Liabilities assumed	—	—	605
Purchase price adjustments	—	—	—
Total cash paid	$ —	$ —	$ 792

The accompanying notes are an integral part of these consolidated financial statement.

Item 3. Legal Proceedings

The Company is part of an environmental investigation initiated by the New Jersey Department of Environmental Protection ("NJDEP") and the United States Environmental Protection Agency ("USEPA") as well as associated litigation initiated by the NJDEP, and if the Company's liability is materially different from the amount accrued, it could impact the Company's results of operations, financial position and cash flows.

In September 2003, NJDEP issued a directive to approximately 30 companies, including Franklin-Burlington Plastics, Inc., a subsidiary of the Company ("Franklin-Burlington"), to undertake an assessment of natural resource damage and perform interim restoration of the Lower Passaic River, a 17-mile stretch of the Passaic River in northern New Jersey. The directive, insofar as it relates to the Company and its subsidiary, pertains to the Company's plastic resin manufacturing facility in Kearny, New Jersey, located adjacent to the Lower Passaic River. The Company acquired the facility in 1986, when it purchased the stock of the facility's former owner, Franklin Plastics Corp. The Company acquired all of Franklin Plastics Corp.'s environmental liabilities as part of the acquisition.

Also in 2003, the USEPA requested that companies located in the area of the Lower Passaic River, including Franklin-Burlington, cooperate in an investigation of contamination of the Lower Passaic River. In response, the Company and approximately 70 other companies (collectively, the "Cooperating Parties") agreed, pursuant to an Administrative Order of Consent with the USEPA, to assume responsibility for completing a Remedial Investigation/Feasibility Study ("RIFS") of the Lower Passaic River. The RIFS is currently estimated to cost approximately $85 million to complete (in addition to USEPA oversight costs) and is currently expected to be completed by late 2012 or early 2013. However, the RIFS costs are exclusive of any costs that may ultimately be required to remediate the Lower Passaic River area being studied or costs associated with natural resource damages that may be assessed. By agreeing to bear a portion of the cost of the RIFS, the Company did not admit to or agree to bear any such remediation or natural resource damage costs. In 2007, the USEPA issued a draft study that evaluated nine (9) alternatives for early remedial action of a portion of the Lower Passaic River. The estimated cost of the alternatives ranged from $900 million to $2.3 billion. The Cooperating Parties provided comments to the USEPA regarding this draft study and to date the USEPA has not taken further action. Given that the USEPA has not finalized its study and that the RIFS is still ongoing, the Company does not believe that remedial costs can be reliably estimated at this time.

In 2009, the Company's subsidiary and over 300 other companies were named as third-party defendants in a suit brought by the NJDEP in Superior Court of New Jersey, Essex County against Occidental Chemical Corporation and certain related entities (collectively, the "Occidental Parties") with respect to alleged contamination of the Newark Bay Complex, including the Lower Passaic River. The third-party complaint seeks contribution from the third-party defendants with respect to any award to NJDEP of damages against the Occidental Parties in the matter.

As of October 30, 2010, the Company had approximately $0.8 million accrued related to these Lower Passaic River matters representing funding of the RIFS costs and related legal expenses of the RIFS and this litigation. Given the uncertainties pertaining to this matter, including that the RIFS is ongoing, the ultimate remediation has not yet been determined and the extent to which the Company may be responsible for such remediation or natural resource damages is not yet known, it is not possible at this time to estimate the Company's ultimate liability related to this matter. Based on currently known facts and circumstances, the Company does not believe that this matter is reasonably likely to have a material impact on the Company's results of operations, consolidated financial position, or cash flows because the Company's Kearny, New Jersey, facility could not have contributed contamination along most of the river's length and did not store or use the contaminants that are of the greatest concern in the river sediments, and because there are numerous other parties who will likely share in the cost of remediation and damages. However, it is possible that the ultimate liability resulting from this matter could materially differ from the October 30, 2010, accrual balance and in the event of one or more adverse determinations related to this matter, the impact on the Company's results of operations, consolidated financial position or cash flows could be material to any specific period.

Item 5. Market for Registrant's Common Equity, Related Stockholder Matters and Issuer Purchases of Equity Securities

Spartech's common stock is listed for trading on the New York Stock Exchange ("NYSE") under the symbol "SEH."

The Company's Board of Directors periodically reviews the dividend policy based upon the Company's financial results and cash flow projections. On January 12, 2011, the Company entered into concurrent amendments to its Amended and

Restated Credit and 2004 Senior Note agreements. Under the amendments, the Company is not permitted to pay dividends or complete purchases of its common stock during fiscal 2011. The Company did not complete any purchases of its common stock during 2010 or 2009.

Item 6. Selected Financial Data

	2010	2009	2008
Dividends Declared per Share	–	0.05	0.37

Item 7. Management's Discussion and Analysis of Financial Condition and Results of Operations

Executive Summary

Net sales of $1.0 billion in 2010 increased 10% from 2009 reflecting a 5% increase in volume and the pass-through of higher raw material costs as selling price increases. The sales volume increase occurred across several end markets reflecting a modest recovery in demand from 2009 levels. Despite the increase in sales volume, operating earnings excluding special items decreased from $34.0 million in 2009 to $17.3 million in 2010. This decrease was primarily caused by the impact of inefficiencies due to disruptions from plant consolidation efforts, equipment line moves and organizational changes, the impact of increases in material costs in the first half of 2010 that were not passed through timely as selling price increases, margin compression from increased competition and reinstatement of temporary compensation reductions that were in effect in 2009. Over the past few years, the Company has reduced its fixed cost structure through asset consolidations, realigned production lines across the Company, changed its organizational structure, enhanced the management team and implemented a new company-wide ERP reporting system. Although these internally focused changes helped the Company manage through the recession, the Company's 2010 results were adversely impacted by the breadth and speed of the changes. The Company's priorities in 2011 are to strengthen operations with a focus on product quality and cost management, and to re-establish itself as having the highest quality and broadest material capabilities. The Company believes that this transition in priorities, a continued U.S. based economic recovery and a more efficient cost structure will lead to improved shareholder returns.

Outlook

Although the Company experienced modest increases in sales volumes in most of our end markets in 2010, we expect the overall market recovery to continue at a slow pace. The Company's results were adversely impacted by disruptions caused by its significant internal changes in 2010 and it is focused on strengthening operations in 2011. In addition, the Company expects to continue to manage through a volatile raw material pricing environment. The Company believes it has emerged from 2010 as a stronger company with a lower fixed cost structure that is better positioned to generate profitable growth and improved shareholder returns in the future.

Results of Operations

Comparison of 2010 and 2009:
Selling, general and administrative expenses were $88.9 million in 2010 compared to $77.9 million in 2009. The 2010 increase was caused by $4.4 million of higher bad debts expense because of a provision for one customer, $1.4 million associated with the separation of the Company's former President and Chief Executive Officer (CEO) in the fourth quarter of 2010, higher professional fees and other expenses associated with accelerating progress on resolving contingencies and the reinstatement of temporary compensation reductions that were in effect in 2009.

Notes to Consolidated Financial Statements

5) Property, Plant and Equipment

Property, plant and equipment at October 30, 2010, and October 31, 2009, consisted of the following:

	2010	2009
Land	$ 9,820	$ 11,211
Buildings and leasehold improvements	96,946	102,155
Machinery and equipment	373,898	376,360
Computer equipment and software	39,428	38,456
Furniture and fixtures	4,663	5,245
	524,755	533,427
Accumulated depreciation	(312,911)	(304,424)
	$ 211,844	$ 229,003

9) Long-Term Debt

Long-term debt at October 30, 2010, and October 31, 2009, consisted of the following:

	2010	2009
2006 Senior Notes	$ —	$ 45,684
2004 Senior Notes	113,972	137,054
Credit facility	45,900	—
Euro Bank term loan	—	20,292
Other	12,600	13,404
Total debt	172,472	216,434
Less current maturities	880	36,079
Total long-term debt	$ 171,592	$ 180,355

The Company's other debt consists primarily of industrial revenue bonds and capital lease obligations used to finance capital expenditures. These financings mature between 2012 and 2019 and have interest rates ranging from 2.00% to 12.47%. Scheduled maturities of long-term debt for the next five years and thereafter are:

Year Ended	Maturities
2011	$ 880
2012	23,333
2013	23,186
2014	69,007
2015	23,133
Thereafter	32,933
	$ 172,472

The Company was in compliance with all debt covenants as of October 30, 2010. On January 12, 2011, the Company entered into concurrent amendments (collectively, the "Amendments") to its Amended and Restated Credit and 2004 Senior Note agreements (collectively, the "Agreements"). The Amendments are effective starting in the Company's first quarter of 2011. Under the Amendments, the Company's maximum Leverage Ratio is amended from 3.5 to 1 during the term of the Agreements to 4.25 to 1 in the first quarter of 2011, 4.5 to 1 in the second quarter of 2011, 3.75 to 1 in the third quarter of 2011, 3.5 to 1 in the fourth quarter of 2011, 3.25 to 1 in the first quarter of 2012 through the third quarter of 2012, 3.0 to 1 in the fourth quarter of 2012 through the third quarter of 2013, and 2.75 to 1 in the fourth quarter of 2013 through the end of the Agreements. Under the Amendments, annual capital expenditures are limited to $30,000 when the Company's Leverage Ratio exceeds 3.0 to 1, and during 2011 the Company is not permitted to pay dividends, complete purchases of its common stock, or prepay its Senior Notes. In addition, the Company is subject to certain restrictions on its ability to complete acquisitions. Capitalized fees incurred in the first quarter of 2011 for the Amendments were approximately $1,500. During the term of the Agreements, the Company is subject to an additional fee in the event the Company's credit profile rating decreases to a defined level. The additional fee would be based on the Company's debt level at that time and would have been approximately $1,100 as of October 30, 2010.

While the Company was in compliance with its covenants and currently expects to be in compliance with its covenants during the next twelve months, the Company's failure to comply with its covenants or other requirements of its financing arrangements is an event of default and could, among other things, accelerate the payment of indebtedness, which could have a material adverse impact on the Company's results of operations, financial condition and cash flows.

14) Commitments and Contingencies

The Company conducts certain of its operations in facilities under operating leases. Rental expense in 2010, 2009 and 2008 was $7,220, $7,525 and $8,530, respectively. Future minimum lease payments under non-cancelable operating leases, by year, are as follows:

Year Ended	Operating Leases
2011	$ 4,841
2012	2,663
2013	1,891
2014	1,421
2015	1,042
Thereafter	3,382
	$ 15,240

The Company has various short-term take-or-pay arrangements associated with the purchase of raw materials. As of October 30, 2010, these commitments totaled $2,358.

18) Former President and Chief Executive Officer's Arrangement

Effective September 8, 2010, Mr. Odaniell resigned as President, Chief Executive Officer and a Director of the Company. Pursuant to the terms of his employment, non-compete and severance agreements with the Company, Mr. Odaniell received the following payments and benefits:

- Severance compensation of $1,998 representing an amount equal to two times his former salary and the average of the bonus payments he earned during the prior two fiscal years. Of this amount, $490 was paid in 2010, and the remaining $1,508 will be paid over the two year period following the Separation Date.
- As a result of stock-based compensation and bonus forfeitures, $494 of stock-based compensation expense and $218 of accrued bonus expense was recaptured during 2010. The Company also recorded $100 of expense for estimated health care coverage costs and other supplementary benefits. The net charge to operating earnings was $1,369 during the fourth quarter and is included in selling, general and administrative expenses in the consolidated statements of operations.

SPARTECH CORPORATION AND SUBSIDIARIES
SCHEDULE II—VALUATION AND QUALIFYING ACCOUNTS
FOR THE YEARS ENDED 2010, 2009, AND 2008
(Dollars in thousands)

Description	Balance at Beginning of Period	Additions and Charges to Costs and Expenses (1)	Write-Offs (2)	Balance End of Period
October 30, 2010				
Trade receivable allowance for doubtful accounts	$ 2,470	$ 1,566	$ (632)	$ 3,404
Note receivable allowance for doubtful accounts	–	6,500	–	6,500
October 31, 2009				
Trade receivable allowance for doubtful accounts	4,550	4,321	(6,401)	2,470
November 1, 2008				
Trade receivable allowance for doubtful accounts	1,572	4,763	(1,785)	4,550

1. Includes provision for bad debt expense related to discontinued operations of $0, $644 and $67 in 2010, 2009, and 2008, respectively.
2. Includes accounts receivable write-offs related to discontinued operations of $0, $129 and $124 in 2010, 2009, and 2008, respectively.

Required:

1. Analyze Spartech's financial statements and excerpts from the company's 2010 Form 10-K. Your analysis should include the preparation of common-size financial statements, key financial ratios, and an evaluation of short-term solvency, operating efficiency, capital structure and long-term solvency, profitability, and market measures. (The financial statement analysis template can be accessed and used at www.pearsoninternationaleditions.com/fraser.)*
2. Using your analysis, list reasons for and against investment in Spartech's common stock.
3. Using your analysis, list reasons for and against lending Spartech additional funds.

*Note: If using the financial statement analysis template, the stock ticker symbol may be autocorrected to an incorrect symbol. Should this happen, follow the links in Microsoft Excel to prevent this from happening: File; Options; Proofing; Autocorrect Options; then make sure the box next to "Replace text as you type" is not checked.

Case 5.4 Applied Materials Inc

The following excerpts are from the 2010 Form 10-K of Applied Materials Inc.

APPLIED MATERIALS INC.
CONSOLIDATED STATEMENTS OF OPERATIONS

Fiscal Year	2010	2009	2008
	(In thousands, except per share amounts)		
Net sales	$ 9,548,667	$ 5,013,607	$ 8,129,240
Cost of products sold	5,833,665	3,582,802	4,686,412
Gross margin	3,715,002	1,430,805	3,442,828
Operating expenses:			
Research, development, and engineering	1,143,521	934,115	1,104,122
General and administrative	535,820	406,946	505,762
Marketing and selling	406,028	327,572	459,402
Restructuring charges and asset impairments (Note 12)	245,925	155,788	39,948
Gain on sale of facility	—	—	21,837
Total operating expenses	2,331,294	1,824,421	2,087,397
Income (loss) from operations	1,383,708	(393,616)	1,355,431
Pre-tax loss of equity-method investment	—	34,983	35,527
Impairments of investments and strategic investments (Note 3)	12,665	84,480	—
Interest expense	21,507	21,304	20,506
Interest income	37,430	48,580	109,320
Income (loss) before income taxes	1,386,966	(485,803)	1,408,718
Provision (benefit) for income taxes	449,100	(180,476)	447,972
Net income (loss)	$ 937,866	$ (305,327)	$ 960,746
Earnings (loss) per share:			
Basic	$ 0.70	$ (0.23)	$ 0.71
Diluted	$ 0.70	$ (0.23)	$ 0.70
Weighted average number of shares:			
Basic	1,339,949	1,333,091	1,354,176
Diluted	1,348,804	1,333,091	1,374,507

See accompanying notes to consolidated financial statements.

APPLIED MATERIALS INC.
CONSOLIDATED BALANCE SHEETS

	October 31, 2010	October 25, 2009
	(In thousands, except per share amounts)	
Assets		
Current assets:		
Cash and cash equivalents (Note 3)	$ 1,857,664	$ 1,576,381
Short-term investments (Note 3)	726,918	638,349
Accounts receivable, net (Note 6)	1,831,006	1,041,495
Inventories (Note 7)	1,547,378	1,627,457
Deferred income taxes, net (Note 15)	512,944	356,336
Income taxes receivable (Note 15)	857	184,760
Other current assets	288,548	264,169
Total current assets	6,765,315	5,688,947
Long-term investments (Note 3)	1,307,283	1,052,165
Property, plant, and equipment, net (Note 7)	963,004	1,090,433
Goodwill, net (Note 8)	1,336,426	1,170,932
Purchased technology and other intangible assets, net (Note 8)	286,821	306,416
Deferred income taxes and other assets (Note 15)	284,496	265,350
Total assets	$ 10,943,345	$ 9,574,243
Liabilities and Stockholders' Equity		
Current liabilities:		
Current portion of long-term debt	$ 1,258	$ 1,240
Accounts payable and accrued expenses (Note 7)	1,765,966	1,061,502
Customer deposits and deferred revenue (Note 7)	847,231	864,280
Income taxes payable (Note 15)	273,421	12,435
Total current liabilities	2,887,876	1,939,457
Long-term debt (Note 11)	204,271	200,654
Employee benefits and other liabilities (Note 14)	315,085	339,524
Total liabilities	3,407,232	2,479,635
Commitments and contingencies (Note 16)		
Stockholders' equity (Note 13):		
Preferred stock: $.01 par value per share; 1,000 shares authorized; no shares issued	—	—
Common stock: $.01 par value per share; 2,500,000 shares authorized; 1,327,998 and 1,340,917 shares outstanding at 2010 and 2009, respectively	13,280	13,409
Additional paid-in capital	5,406,598	5,195,437
Retained earnings	11,510,843	10,934,004
Treasury stock: 537,056 and 508,254 shares at 2010 and 2009, respectively, net	(9,396,274)	(9,046,562)
Accumulated other comprehensive income (loss)	1,666	(1,680)
Total stockholders' equity	7,536,113	7,094,608
Total liabilities and stockholders' equity	$ 10,943,345	$ 9,574,243

See accompanying notes to consolidated financial statements.

APPLIED MATERIALS INC.
CONSOLIDATED STATEMENTS OF CASH FLOWS

Fiscal Year	2010	2009	2008
		(In thousands)	
Cash flows from operating activities:			
Net income (loss)	$ 937,866	$ (305,327)	$ 960,746
Adjustments required to reconcile net income (loss) to cash provided by operating activities:			
Depreciation and amortization	304,515	291,203	320,051
Loss on fixed asset retirements	20,034	24,017	6,826
Provision for bad debts	17,000	62,539	2,456
Restructuring charges and asset impairments	245,925	155,788	39,948
Deferred income taxes	(186,057)	18,863	(58,259)
Net recognized loss on investments	20,473	10,231	4,392
Pre-tax loss of equity method investment	—	34,983	35,527
Impairments of investments	12,665	84,480	—
Excess tax benefits from share-based compensation plans	—	—	(7,491)
Share-based compensation	126,070	147,160	178,943
Changes in operating assets and liabilities, net of amounts acquired:			
Accounts receivable	(766,937)	586,993	421,834
Inventories	144,626	359,560	(638,256)
Income taxes receivable	183,903	(59,155)	(125,605)
Other current assets	(4,590)	94,740	94,247
Other assets	(6,690)	(6,530)	(394)
Accounts payable and accrued expenses	469,049	(660,006)	(260,041)
Customer deposits and deferred revenue	(22,908)	(361,455)	622,645
Income taxes payable	261,909	(229,128)	133,731
Employee benefits and other liabilities	(34,000)	83,709	(20,832)
Cash provided by operating activities	1,722,853	332,665	1,710,468
Cash flows from investing activities:			
Capital expenditures	(169,081)	(248,427)	(287,906)
Cash paid for acquisitions, net of cash acquired	(322,599)	—	(235,324)
Proceeds from sale of facility	—	—	42,210
Proceeds from sales and maturities of investments	1,407,804	1,317,365	5,939,509
Purchases of investments	(1,777,736)	(956,249)	(5,534,475)
Cash provided by (used in) investing activities	(861,612)	112,689	(75,986)

(*continued*)

Fiscal Year	2010	2009	2008
		(In thousands)	
Cash flows used for financing activities:			
Debt repayments, net	(6,441)	(750)	(2,117)
Proceeds from common stock issuances	128,832	61,824	393,978
Common stock repurchases	(350,000)	(22,906)	(1,499,984)
Excess tax benefits from share-based compensation plans	—	—	7,491
Payments of dividends to stockholders	(348,522)	(319,507)	(325,405)
Cash used in financing activities	(576,131)	(281,339)	(1,426,037)
Effect of exchange rate changes on cash and cash equivalents	(3,827)	742	457
Increase in cash and cash equivalents	281,283	164,757	208,902
Cash and cash equivalents—beginning of year	1,576,381	1,411,624	1,202,722
Cash and cash equivalents—end of year	$ 1,857,664	$ 1,576,381	$ 1,411,624
Supplemental cash flow information:			
Cash payments for income taxes	$ 388,144	$ 206,537	$ 490,826
Cash refunds for income taxes	$ 200,660	$ 72,297	$ 122,367
Cash payments for interest	$ 14,485	$ 14,372	$ 14,580

See accompanying notes to consolidated financial statements.

Item 1: Business

Incorporated in 1967, Applied, a Delaware corporation, provides manufacturing equipment, services, and software to the global semiconductor, flat panel display, solar photovoltaic (PV), and related industries. Applied's customers include manufacturers of semiconductor wafers and chips, flat panel liquid crystal displays (LCDs), solar PV cells and modules, and other electronic devices. These customers may use what they manufacture in their own end products or sell the items to other companies for use in advanced electronic components. The Company's fiscal year ends on the last Sunday in October.

Applied is the world's largest semiconductor fabrication equipment supplier based on revenue, with the capability to provide global deployment and support services. Applied also is a leading supplier of LCD fabrication equipment to the flat panel display industry and is the leading supplier of solar PV manufacturing systems to the solar industry, based on revenue.

Item 5: Market for Registrant's Common Equity, Related Stockholder Matters, and Issuer Purchases of Equity Securities

Applied's common stock is traded on the NASDAQ Global Select Market under the symbol AMAT.

Dividends

During fiscal 2010, Applied's Board of Directors declared three quarterly cash dividends in the amount of $0.07 per share and one quarterly cash dividend in the amount of $0.06 per share. The fourth quarterly cash dividend of $0.07 per share declared in fiscal 2010 will be paid on December 15, 2010, to stockholders of record as of November 24, 2010. During fiscal 2009, Applied's Board of Directors declared four quarterly cash dividends in the amount of $0.06 per share each.*

Item 7: Management's Discussion and Analysis of Financial Condition and Results of Operations

Applied's business was subject to cyclical industry conditions in fiscal 2010, 2009, and 2008. As a result of these conditions and the changing global economic environment, there were significant fluctuations in Applied's quarterly new orders and net sales, both within and across the three fiscal years. Demand for manufacturing equipment has historically been volatile as a result of sudden changes in chip, LCD, and solar PV supply and demand and other factors, including global economic and market conditions and rapid technological advances in fabrication processes.

New orders more than doubled to $10.2 billion in fiscal 2010 compared to fiscal 2009. The increase was principally due to greater demand for semiconductor equipment and services, primarily from memory and foundry customers, as well as increased demand for c-Si solar manufacturing products and display equipment. The increase in new orders reflected the general recovery in the semiconductor equipment industry and the LCD market from the steep downturn experienced in fiscal 2009.

New orders decreased 55 percent to $4.1 billion in fiscal 2009 compared to fiscal 2008. The decrease in new orders was across all segments, and particularly in the semiconductor and display businesses, reflecting the challenging economic and industry conditions prevalent during fiscal 2009. Customer demand for semiconductor and LCD equipment began to recover in the second half of fiscal 2009.

Net sales of $9.5 billion for fiscal 2010 increased 90 percent from fiscal 2009, primarily due to higher sales of semiconductor equipment. Net sales decreased 38 percent to $5.0 billion in fiscal 2009 compared to fiscal 2008, as a result of significantly lower sales of equipment and services to semiconductor and display customers, partially offset by increased sales of solar manufacturing equipment. Net sales decreased 16 percent to

*Note: Applied also declared four quarterly cash dividends in the amount of $0.06 per share in fiscal year 2008.

$8.1 billion in fiscal 2008 compared to fiscal 2007, due to decreased investment from memory and logic chip manufacturers, partially offset by increased demand from solar and LCD customers.

SCHEDULE II
VALUATION AND QUALIFYING ACCOUNTS
ALLOWANCE FOR DOUBTFUL ACCOUNTS

Fiscal Year	Balance at Beginning of Fiscal Year	Additions — Charged to Income	Additions — Business Combinations	Deductions — Recoveries	Deductions — Not Charged to Income	Balance at End of Fiscal Year
			(In thousands)			
2010	$ 67,313	$ 17,000	$ —	$ (7,500)	$ (2,873)	$ 73,940
2009	$ 5,275	$ 62,539	$ —	$ (501)	$ —	$ 67,313
2008	$ 4,136	$ 2,456	$ 501	$ (1,818)	$ —	$ 5,275

NOTES TO CONSOLIDATED FINANCIAL STATEMENTS

Note 7 Balance Sheet Detail

	Useful Life	October 31, 2010	October 25, 2009
	(In Years)	(In thousands)	
Property, Plant, and Equipment, Net			
Land and improvements		$ 227,202	$ 228,057
Buildings and improvements	3–30	1,233,850	1,164,384
Demonstration and manufacturing equipment	3–5	669,473	654,779
Furniture, fixtures, and other equipment	3–15	719,119	713,505
Construction in progress		19,144	146,232
Gross property, plant, and equipment		2,868,788	2,906,957
Accumulated depreciation		(1,905,784)	(1,816,524)
		$ 963,004	$ 1,090,433
Accounts Payable and Accrued Expenses			
Accounts payable		$ 657,971	$ 477,148
Compensation and employee benefits		435,021	134,949
Warranty		155,242	117,537
Restructuring reserve		104,229	31,581
Other accrued taxes		98,634	36,954
Dividends payable		92,960	80,455
Other		221,909	182,878
		$ 1,765,966	$ 1,061,502

Note 16 Warranty, Guarantees, and Contingencies

Leases

Applied leases some of its facilities and equipment under non-cancelable operating leases and has options to renew most leases, with rentals to be negotiated. Total rent expense was $52 million for fiscal 2010, $64 million for fiscal 2009, and $68 million for fiscal 2008.

As of October 31, 2010, future minimum lease payments is expected to be as follows:

	Lease Payments
	(In thousands)
2011	$ 41,765
2012	28,924
2013	16,100
2014	14,211
2015	12,114
Thereafter	30,376
	$ 143,490

Note 17 Industry Segment Operations

Applied's four reportable segments are: Silicon Systems Group, Applied Global Services, Display, and Energy and Environmental Solutions. Applied's chief operating decision-maker has been identified as the President and Chief Executive Officer, who reviews operating results to make decisions about allocating resources and assessing performance for the entire Company. Segment information is presented based upon Applied's management organization structure as of October 31, 2010, and the distinctive nature of each segment. Future changes to this internal financial structure may result in changes to the Company's reportable segments.

The Silicon Systems Group segment includes semiconductor capital equipment for etch, rapid thermal processing, deposition, chemical mechanical planarization, metrology and inspection, and wafer packaging.

The Applied Global Services segment includes technically differentiated products and services to improve operating efficiency, reduce operating costs, and lessen the environmental impact of semiconductor, display, and solar customers' factories. Applied Global Services' products consist of spares, services, certain earlier generation products, and remanufactured equipment. Customer demand for these products and services is fulfilled through a global distribution system with trained service engineers located in close proximity to customer sites.

The Display segment includes products for manufacturing LCDs for TVs, personal computers, and other video-enabled devices.

The Energy and Environmental Solutions segment includes products for fabricating solar photovoltaic cells and modules, high throughput roll-to-roll coating systems for flexible electronics and web products, and systems used in the manufacture of energy-efficient glass.

Information for each reportable segment as of October 31, 2010, October 25, 2009, and October 26, 2008, and for the fiscal years then ended, is as follows:

	Net Sales	Operating Income (Loss)	Depreciation/ Amortization	Capital Expenditures	Segment Assets
			(In thousands)		
2010:					
Silicon Systems Group	$ 5,304,028	$ 1,892,307	$ 66,465	$ 38,514	$ 2,317,023
Applied Global Services	1,864,938	337,386	25,306	5,453	1,285,405
Display	898,998	267,495	7,820	4,534	418,874
Energy and Environmental Solutions	1,480,703	(466,124)	56,717	41,412	1,401,634
Total Segment	$ 9,548,667	$ 2,031,064	$ 156,308	$ 89,913	$ 5,422,936
2009:					
Silicon Systems Group	$ 1,960,225	$ 200,829	$ 53,504	$ 23,167	$ 1,194,929
Applied Global Services	1,396,643	115,170	33,641	14,952	1,043,022
Display	501,692	51,226	11,924	14,428	444,619
Energy and Environmental Solutions	1,155,047	(234,259)	80,095	51,320	1,853,283
Total Segment	$ 5,013,607	$ 132,966	$ 179,164	$ 103,867	$ 4,535,853
2008:					
Silicon Systems Group	$ 4,005,141	$ 1,229,432	$ 104,130	$ 61,518	$ 1,773,348
Applied Global Services	2,328,930	545,065	34,831	19,694	1,306,158
Display	975,582	300,607	8,397	11,478	658,744
Energy and Environmental Solutions	819,587	(206,211)	106,663	7,544	2,075,516
Total Segment	$ 8,129,240	$ 1,868,893	$ 254,021	$ 100,234	$ 5,813,766

The following companies accounted for at least 10 percent of Applied's net sales in fiscal 2010, 2009, and/or 2008, which were for products in multiple reportable segments.

	2010	2009	2008
Samsung Electronics Co., Ltd.	14 %	10 %	16 %
Taiwan Semiconductor Manufacturing Company Limited	11 %	*	*
Intel Corporation	*	12 %	*

* Less than 10%.

As of October 31, 2010, accounts receivable for those customers that accounted for at least 10% of Applied's net sales in fiscal 2010 were as follows:

	October 31, 2010
Taiwan Semiconductor Manufacturing Company Limited	14 %
Samsung Electronics Co., Ltd.	7 %

Required:

1. Analyze Applied Materials' financial statements and excerpts from the company's 2010 Form 10-K. Your analysis should include the preparation of common-size financial statements, key financial ratios, and an evaluation of short-term solvency, operating efficiency, capital structure and long-term solvency, profitability, and market measures. (The financial statement analysis template can be accessed and used at www.pearsoninternationaleditions.com/fraser.)*
2. Complete a segmental analysis for Applied Materials using the illustration in Appendix 5A.
3. Identify the strengths and weaknesses of the company.
4. What is your opinion of the investment potential and the creditworthiness of Applied Materials Inc.?

Appendix A: Summary of Financial Ratios

Ratio	Method of Computation	Significance
Liquidity:		
Current	$\frac{\text{Current assets}}{\text{Current liabilities}}$	Measures short-term liquidity, the ability of a firm to meet needs for cash as they arise.
Quick or acid-test	$\frac{\text{Current assets} - \text{inventory}}{\text{Current liabilities}}$	Measures short-term liquidity more rigorously than the current ratio by eliminating inventory, usually the least liquid current asset.
Cash flow liquidity	$\frac{\text{Cash and cash equivalents} + \text{marketable securities} + \text{cash flow from operating activities}}{\text{Current liabilities}}$	Measures short-term liquidity by considering as cash resources (numerator) cash plus cash equivalents plus cash flow from operating activities.
Average collection period	$\frac{\text{Net accounts receivable}}{\text{Average daily sales}}$	Indicates days required to convert receivables into cash.
Days inventory held	$\frac{\text{Inventory}}{\text{Average daily cost of sales}}$	Indicates days required to sell inventory.
Days payable outstanding	$\frac{\text{Accounts payable}}{\text{Average daily cost of sales}}$	Indicates days required to pay suppliers.
Cash conversion or net trade cycle	Average collection period + days inventory held − days payable outstanding	Indicates the days in the normal operating cycle or cash conversion cycle of a firm.

Activity:		
Accounts receivable turnover	$\frac{\text{Net sales}}{\text{Net accounts receivable}}$	Indicates how many times receivables are collected during a year, on average.
Inventory turnover	$\frac{\text{Cost of goods sold}}{\text{Inventories}}$	Measures efficiency of the firm in managing and selling inventory.
Payables turnover	$\frac{\text{Cost of goods sold}}{\text{Accounts payable}}$	Measures efficiency of the firm in paying suppliers.
Fixed asset turnover	$\frac{\text{Net sales}}{\text{Net property, plant, and equipment}}$	Measures efficiency of the firm in managing fixed assets.
Total asset turnover	$\frac{\text{Net sales}}{\text{Total assets}}$	Measures efficiency of the firm in managing all assets.
Leverage:		
Debt ratio	$\frac{\text{Total liabilities}}{\text{Total assets}}$	Shows proportion of all assets that are financed with debt.
Long-term debt to total capitalization	$\frac{\text{Long-term debt}}{\text{Long-term debt} + \text{stockholders' equity}}$	Measures the extent to which long-term debt is used for permanent financing.
Debt to equity	$\frac{\text{Total liabilities}}{\text{Stockholders' equity}}$	Measures debt relative to equity base.
Financial leverage index	$\frac{\text{Return on equity}}{\text{Adjusted return on assets}}$	Indicates whether a firm is employing debt successfully.
Times interest earned	$\frac{\text{Operating profit}}{\text{Interest expense}}$	Measures how many times interest expense is covered by operating earnings.
Cash interest coverage	$\frac{\text{Cash flow from operating activities} + \text{interest paid} + \text{taxes paid}}{\text{Interest paid}}$	Measures how many times interest payments are covered by cash flow from operating activities.
Fixed charge coverage	$\frac{\text{Operating profit} + \text{lease payments}}{\text{Interest expense} + \text{lease payments}}$	Measures coverage capability more broadly than times interest earned by including operating lease payments as a fixed expense.
Cash flow adequacy	$\frac{\text{Cash flow from operating activities}}{\text{Capital expenditures} + \text{debt repayments} + \text{dividends paid}}$	Measures how many times capital expenditures, debt repayments, and cash dividends are covered by operating cash flow.

Profitability:		
Gross profit margin	Gross profit / Net sales	Measures profit generated after consideration of cost of products sold.
Operating profit margin	Operating profit / Net sales	Measures profit generated after consideration of operating expenses.
Effective tax rate	Income taxes / Earnings before income taxes	Measures the percentage the company recognizes as tax expense relative to income before taxes.
Net profit margin	Net profit / Net sales	Measures profit generated after consideration of all expenses and revenues.
Cash flow margin	Cash flow from operating activities / Net sales	Measures the ability of the firm to generate cash from sales.
Return on total assets	Net earnings / Total assets	Measures overall efficiency of firm in managing assets and generating profits.
Return on equity	Net earnings / Stockholders' equity	Measures rate of return on stockholders' (owners') investment.
Cash return on assets	Cash flow from operating activities / Total assets	Measures the return on assets on a cash basis.
Market:		
Earnings per common share	Net earnings / Average common shares outstanding	Shows return to common stock shareholders for each share owned.
Price to earnings	Market price of common stock / Earnings per share	Expresses a multiple that the stock market places on a firm's earnings.
Dividend payout	Dividends per share / Earnings per share	Shows percentage of earnings paid to shareholders.
Dividend yield	Dividends per share / Market price of common stock	Shows the rate earned by shareholders from dividends relative to current price of stock.

Appendix B: Solutions to Self-Tests

Chapter 1

1. (d)
2. (d)
3. (c)
4. (c)
5. (a)
6. (a), (c)
7. (b), (c), (d)
8. (c)
9. (b), (c)
10. (b)
11. (b)
12. (a)
13. (c)
14. (c)
15. (1) c
    (2) b
    (3) a
    (4) c
    (5) b
    (6) a
    (7) d
    (8) b
    (9) d
    (10) a or b

Chapter 2

1. (b), (d)
2. (a)
3. (d)
4. (d)
5. (a), (c)
6. (a)
7. (d)
8. (c)
9. (a)
10. (c)
11. (d)
12. (c)
13. (c)
14. (b)
15. (d)
16. (c)
17. (b)
18. (b)
19. (d)
20. (d)
21. (c)
22. (a) NC
    (b) C
    (c) C
    (d) C or NC
    (e) NC
    (f) C
    (g) C
    (h) C
    (i) NC
    (j) NC
23. (a) 4
    (b) 5
    (c) 8
    (d) 7
    (e) 1
    (f) 2
    (g) 2
    (h) 5
    (i) 8
    (j) 5
    (k) 3
    (l) 2
    (m) 1
    (n) 6
    (o) 8
24. (a) 7
    (b) 1
    (c) 5
    (d) 9
    (e) 4
    (f) 6
    (g) 10
    (h) 2
    (i) 3
    (j) 8

Chapter 3

1. (c)
2. (b)
3. (a)
4. (a)
5. (b)
6. (c)
7. (d)
8. (d)
9. (d)
10. (b)
11. (b)
12. (a)
13. (a)
14. (c)
15. (d)
16. (c)
17. (c)
18. (d)
19. (a) 4
    (b) 9
    (c) 13
    (d) 8
    (e) 5
    (f) 14
    (g) 1
    (h) 6
    (i) 11
    (j) 2
    (k) 10
    (l) 12
    (m) 3
    (n) 7

20. (1) c
(2) d
(3) a
(4) c
(5) d
(6) a
(7) e
(8) c
(9) c
(10) b
(11) d
(12) c

Chapter 4

1. (c)
2. (c)
3. (d)
4. (d)
5. (b)
6. (c)
7. (b)
8. (d)
9. (c)
10. (b)
11. (b)
12. (c)
13. (a)
14. (d)
15. (d)
16. (c)
17. (d)
18. (d)
19. (b)
20. (d)
21. (c)
22. (b)
23. (c)
24. (c)
25. (b)
26. (b)

Chapter 5

1. (c)
2. (a)
3. (d)
4. (c)
5. (d)
6. (d)
7. (c)
8. (c)
9. (d)
10. (c)
11. (c)
12. (b)
13. (d)
14. (b)
15. (a)
16. (d)
17. (a)
18. (d)
19. (b)
20. (d)
21. (c)
22. (a)
23. (c)
24. (b)
25. (d)
26. (b)
27. (a)
28. (a)
29. (b)
30. (d)
31. (c)
32. (a)
33. (d)
34. (b)
35. (b)

Appendix C: Glossary

Accelerated Cost Recovery System The system established by the Economic Recovery Tax Act of 1981 to simplify depreciation methods for tax purposes and to encourage investment in capital by allowing rapid write-off of asset costs over predetermined periods, generally shorter than the estimated useful lives of the assets. The system remains in effect for assets placed in service between 1981 and 1986 but was modified by the Tax Reform Act of 1986 for assets placed in service after 1986. *See* Modified Accelerated Cost Recovery System.

Accelerated depreciation An accounting procedure under which larger amounts of expense are apportioned to the earlier years of an asset's depreciable life and lesser amounts to the later years.

Accounting period The length of time covered for reporting accounting information.

Accounting principles The methods and procedures used in preparing financial statements.

Accounts payable Amounts owed to creditors for items or services purchased from them.

Accounts receivable Amounts owed to an entity, primarily by its trade customers.

Accounts receivable turnover *See* Summary of financial ratios, Appendix A.

Accrual basis of accounting A method of earnings determination under which revenues are recognized in the accounting period when earned, regardless of when cash is received, and expenses are recognized in the period incurred, regardless of when cash is paid.

Accrued liabilities Obligations resulting from the recognition of an expense prior to the payment of cash.

Accumulated depreciation A balance sheet account indicating the amount of depreciation expense taken on plant and equipment up to the balance sheet date.

Accumulated other comprehensive income or loss An account that includes unrealized gains or losses in the market value of investments of marketable securities classified as available for sale, specific types of pension liability adjustments, certain gains and losses on derivative financial instruments, and foreign currency translation adjustments resulting when financial statements from a foreign currency are converted into U.S. dollars.

Acid-test ratio *See* Summary of financial ratios, Appendix A.

Activity ratio A ratio that measures the liquidity of specific assets and the efficiency of the firm in managing assets.

Additional paid-in-capital The amount by which the original sales price of stock shares sold exceeds the par value of the stock.

Adverse opinion Opinion rendered by an independent auditor stating that the financial statements have not been presented fairly in accordance with generally accepted accounting principles.

Allowance for doubtful accounts The balance sheet account that measures the amount of outstanding accounts receivable expected to be uncollectable.

Amortization The process of expense allocation applied to the cost expiration of intangible assets.

Annual report The report to shareholders published by a firm; contains information required by generally accepted accounting principles and/or by specific Securities and Exchange Commission requirements.

Asset impairment The decline in value of assets.

Assets Items possessing service or use potential to owner.

Auditor's report Report by independent auditor attesting to the fairness of the financial statements of a company.

Average collection period *See* Summary of financial ratios, Appendix A.

Average cost method Amethod of valuing inventory and cost of products sold; all costs, including those in beginning inventory, are added together and divided by the total number of units to arrive at a cost per unit.

Balance sheet The financial statement that shows the financial condition of a company on a particular date.

Balancing equation Assets = Liabilities + Stockholders' equity.

Basic earnings per share The earnings per share figure calculated by dividing net earnings available to common shareholders by the average number of common shares outstanding.

Book value *See* Net book value.

Calendar year The year starting January 1 and ending December 31.

Capital assets *See* Fixed assets.

Capital in excess of par value *See* Additional paid-in-capital.

Capital lease A leasing arrangement that is, in substance, a purchase by the lessee, who accounts for the lease as an acquisition of an asset and the incurrence of a liability.

Capital structure The permanent long-term financing of a firm represented by long-term debt, preferred stock, common stock, and retained earnings.

Capitalize The process whereby initial expenditures are included in the cost of assets and allocated over the period of service.

Cash basis of accounting A method of accounting under which revenues are recorded when cash is received and expenses are recognized when cash is paid.

Cash conversion cycle The amount of time (expressed in number of days) required to sell inventory and collect accounts receivable, less the number of days to pay suppliers.

Cash equivalents Security investments that are readily converted to cash.

Cash flow adequacy *See* Summary of financial ratios, Appendix A.

Cash flow from financing activities On the statement of cash flows, cash generated from/used by financing activities.

Cash flow from investing activities On the statement of cash flows, cash generated from/used by investing activities.

Cash flow from operating activities On the statement of cash flows, cash generated from/used by operating activities.

Cash flow from operations The amount of cash generated from/used by a business enterprise's normal, ongoing operations during an accounting period.

Cash flow liquidity ratio *See* Summary of financial ratios, Appendix A.

Cash flow margin *See* Summary of financial ratios, Appendix A.

Cash flow return on assets *See* Summary of financial ratios, Appendix A.

Cash interest coverage *See* Summary of financial ratios, Appendix A.

Commercial paper Unsecured promissory notes of large companies.

Commitments Contractual agreements that will have a significant impact on the company in the future.

Common-size financial statements A form of financial ratio analysis that allows the comparison of firms with different levels of sales or total assets by introducing a common denominator. A common-size balance sheet expresses each item on the balance sheet as a percentage of total assets, and a common-size income statement expresses each item as a percentage of net sales.

Common stock Shares of stock representing ownership in a company.

Complex capital structure Capital structures including convertible securities, stock options, and warrants.

Comprehensive income The concept that income should include all revenues, expenses, gains, and losses recognized during an accounting period, regardless of whether they are the results of operations.

Conservatism The accounting concept holding that in selecting among accounting methods the choice should be the one with the least favorable effect on the firm.

Consolidation The combination of financial statements for two or more separate legal entities when one company, the parent, owns more than 50% of the voting stock of the other company or companies.

Contingencies Potential liabilities of a company.

Contra-asset account An account shown as a deduction from the asset to which it relates in the balance sheet.

Convertible securities Securities that can be converted or exchanged for another type of security, typically common stock.

Core earnings *See* Pro forma earnings.

Cost flow assumption An assumption regarding the order in which inventory is sold; used to value cost of goods sold and ending inventory.

Cost method A procedure to account for investments in the voting stock of other companies under which the investor recognizes investment income only to the extent of any cash dividends received.

Cost of goods sold The cost to the seller of products sold to customers.

Cost of goods sold percentage The percentage of cost of goods sold to net sales.

Cost of sales *See* Cost of goods sold.

Cumulative effect of change in accounting principle The difference in the actual amount of retained earnings at the beginning of the period in which a change in accounting principle is instituted and the amount of retained earnings that would have been reported at that date if the new accounting principle had been applied retroactively for all prior periods.

Current (assets/liabilities) Items expected to be converted into cash or paid out in cash in one year or one operating cycle, whichever is longer.

Current maturities of long-term debt The portion of long-term debt that will be repaid during the upcoming year.

Current ratio *See* Summary of financial ratios, Appendix A.

Days inventory held *See* Summary of financial ratios, Appendix A.

Days payable outstanding *See* Summary of financial ratios, Appendix A.

Debt ratio *See* Summary of financial ratios, Appendix A.

Debt to equity ratio *See* Summary of financial ratios, Appendix A.

Deferred credits *See* Unearned revenue.

Deferred taxes The balance sheet account that results from temporary differences in the recognition of revenue and expense for taxable income and reported income.

Depletion The accounting procedure used to allocate the cost of acquiring and developing natural resources.

Depreciation The accounting procedure used to allocate the cost of an asset, which will benefit a business enterprise for more than a year, over the asset's service life.

Derivatives Financial instruments that derive their value from an underlying asset or index.

Diluted earnings per share The earnings per share figure calculated using all potentially dilutive securities in the number of shares outstanding.

Direct method On the statement of cash flows, a method of calculating cash flow from operating activities that shows cash collections from customers; interest and dividends collected; other operating cash receipts; cash paid to suppliers and employees; interest paid; taxes paid; and other operating cash payments.

Disclaimer of opinion Independent auditor could not evaluate the fairness of the financial statements and, as a result, expresses no opinion on them.

Discontinued operations The financial results of selling a major business segment.

Discretionary items Revenues and expenses under the control of management with respect to budget levels and timing.

Dividend payout ratio *See* Summary of financial ratios, Appendix A.

Dividend yield *See* Summary of financial ratios, Appendix A.

Double-declining balance method An accounting procedure for depreciation under which the straight-line rate of depreciation is doubled and applied to the net book value of the asset.

Du Pont System An analytical technique used to evaluate the profitability and return on equity for a firm.

EBITDA Earnings before interest, taxes, depreciation, and amortization. *See* Pro forma earnings.

Earnings before income taxes The profit recognized before the deduction of income taxes.

Earnings before interest and taxes The operating profit of a firm.

Earnings per common share *See* Summary of financial ratios, Appendix A.

Earnings statement *See* Income statement.

Effective tax rate *See* Summary of financial ratios, Appendix A.

Equity *See* Stockholders' equity.

Equity method The procedure used for an investment in common stock when the investor company can exercise significant influence over the investee company; the investor recognizes investment income of the investee's net income in proportion to the percentage of stock owned.

Expenses Cost incurred to produce revenue.

Extraordinary transactions Items that are unusual in nature and not expected to recur in the foreseeable future.

Financial Accounting Standards Board (FASB) The private-sector organization primarily responsible for establishing generally accepted accounting principles.

Financial leverage The extent to which a firm finances with debt, measured by the relationship between total debt and total assets.

Financial leverage index *See* Summary of financial ratios, Appendix A.

Financial ratios Calculations made to standardize, analyze, and compare financial data; expressed in terms of mathematical relationships in the form of percentages or times.

Financial statements Accounting information regarding the financial position of a firm, the results of operations, and the cash flows. Four statements comprise the basic set of financial statements: the balance sheet, the income statement, the statement of stockholder's equity, and the statement of cash flows.

Financing activities On the statement of cash flows, transactions that include borrowing from creditors and repaying the principal; obtaining resources from owners and providing them with a return on the investment.

Finished goods Products for which the manufacturing process is complete.

First-in, first-out (FIFO) A method of valuing inventory and cost of goods sold under which the items purchased first are assumed to be sold first.

Fiscal year A 12-month period starting on a date other than January 1 and ending 12 months later.

Fixed assets Tangible, long-lived assets that are expected to provide service benefit for more than one year.

Fixed asset turnover *See* Summary of financial ratios, Appendix A.

Fixed charge coverage *See* Summary of financial ratios, Appendix A.

Foreign currency translation effects Adjustment to the equity section of the balance sheet resulting from the translation of foreign financial statements.

Form 10-K An annual document filed with the Securities and Exchange Commission by companies that sell securities to the public.

Form 10-Q A quarterly report filed with the Securities and Exchange Commission by companies that sell securities to the public.

Generally accepted accounting principles The accounting methods and procedures used to prepare financial statements.

Goodwill An intangible asset representing the unrecorded assets of a firm; appears in the accounting records only if the firm is acquired for a price in excess of the fair market value of its net assets.

Gross margin *See* Gross profit.

Gross profit The difference between net sales and cost of goods sold.

Gross profit margin *See* Summary of financial ratios, Appendix A.

Historical cost The amount of cash or value of other resources used to acquire an asset; for some assets, historical cost is subject to depreciation, amortization, or depletion.

Impairment charges *See* Asset impairment.

Income statement The financial statement presenting the revenues and expenses of a business enterprise for an accounting period.

Indirect method On the statement of cash flows, a method of calculating cash flow from operating activities that adjusts net income for deferrals, accruals, and noncash and nonoperating items.

Industry comparisons Average financial ratios compiled for industry groups.

In-process research and development Onetime charges taken at the time of an acquisition to write-off amounts of research and development that are not considered viable.

Intangible assets Assets such as goodwill that possess no physical characteristics but have value for the company.

Integrated disclosure system A common body of information required by the Securities and Exchange Commission for both the 10-K Report filed with the Securities and Exchange Commission and the annual report provided to shareholders.

Interim statements Financial statements issued for periods shorter than one year.

International Accounting Standards Board (IASB) The international organization responsible for establishing accounting standards and promoting worldwide acceptance of those standards.

International Financial Reporting Standards (IFRS) The accounting standards established by the International Accounting Standards Board.

Inventories Items held for sale or used in the manufacture of products that will be sold.

Inventory turnover *See* Summary of financial ratios, Appendix A.

Investing activities On the statement of cash flows, transactions that include acquiring and selling or otherwise disposing of (1) securities that are not cash equivalents and (2) productive assets that are expected to benefit the firm for long periods of time; lending money and collecting on loans.

Last-in, first-out (LIFO) A method of valuing inventory and cost of goods sold under which the items purchased last are assumed to be sold first.

Leasehold improvement An addition or improvement made to a leased structure.

Leverage ratio A ratio that measures the extent of a firm's financing with debt relative to equity and its ability to cover interest and other fixed charges.

Liabilities Claims against assets.

Line of credit A prearranged loan allowing borrowing up to a certain maximum amount.

Liquidity The ability of a firm to generate sufficient cash to meet cash needs.

Liquidity ratio A ratio that measures a firm's ability to meet needs for cash as they arise.

Long-term debt Obligations with maturities longer than one year.

Long-term debt to total capitalization *See* Summary of financial ratios, Appendix A.

Lower of cost or market method A method of valuing inventory under which cost or market, whichever is lower, is selected for each item, each group, or for the entire inventory.

Management Discussion and Analysis (MD&A) of the Financial Condition and Results of Operation A section of the annual and 10-K report that is required and monitored by the Securities and Exchange Commission in which management presents detailed coverage of the firm's liquidity, capital resources, and operations.

Market ratio A ratio that measures returns to stockholders and the value the marketplace puts on a company's stock.

Marketable securities Cash not needed immediately in the business and temporarily invested to earn a return; also referred to as short-term investments.

Matching principle The accounting principle holding that expenses are to be matched with the generation of revenues to determine net income for an accounting period.

Merchandise inventories Goods purchased for resale to the public.

Minority interest Claims of shareholders other than the parent company against the net assets and net income of a subsidiary company.

Modified accelerated cost recovery system (MACRS) A modification of the accelerated tax recovery system (ACRS) in the Tax Reform Act of 1986 for assets placed in service after 1986.

Multiple-step format A format for presenting the income statement under which several intermediate profit measures are shown.

Net assets Total assets less total liabilities.

Net book value of capital assets The difference between original cost of property, plant, and equipment and any accumulated depreciation to date.

Net earnings The firm's profit or loss after consideration of all revenue and expense reported during the accounting period.

Net income *See* Net earnings.

Net profit margin *See* Summary of financial ratios, Appendix A.

Net sales Total sales revenue less sales returns and sales allowances.

Net trade cycle *See* Cash conversion cycle and Summary of financial ratios, Appendix A.

Noncurrent assets/liabilities Items expected to benefit the firm for/with maturities of more than one year.

Notes payable A short-term obligation in the form of a promissory note to suppliers or financial institutions.

Notes to the financial statements Supplementary information to financial statements that explain the firm's accounting policies and provide detail about particular accounts and other information such as pension plans.

Off-balance-sheet financing Financial techniques for raising funds that do not have to be recorded as liabilities on the balance sheet.

Operating activities On the statement of cash flows, transactions that include delivering or producing goods for sale and providing services; the cash effects of transactions and other events that enter into the determination of income.

Operating cycle The time required to purchase or manufacture inventory, sell the product, and collect the cash.

Operating efficiency The efficiency of a firm in managing its assets.

Operating expenses Costs related to the normal functions of a business.

Operating lease A rental agreement wherein no ownership rights are transferred to the lessee at the termination of the rental contract.

Operating profit Sales revenue less the expenses associated with generating sales. Operating profit measures the overall performance of a company on its normal, ongoing operations.

Operating profit margin *See* Summary of financial ratios, Appendix A.

Options *See* Stock options.

Par value The floor price below which stock cannot be sold initially.

Payables turnover *See* Summary of financial ratios, Appendix A.

Plant and equipment *See* Fixed assets.

Preferred stock Capital stock of a company that carries certain privileges or rights not carried by all outstanding shares of stock.

Premature revenue recognition Recording revenue before it should be recorded in order to increase earnings.

Prepaid expenses Expenditures made in the current or prior period that will benefit the firm at some future time.

Price-earnings ratio *See* Summary of financial ratios, Appendix A.

Principal The original amount of a liability.

Prior period adjustment A change in the retained earnings balance primarily resulting from the correction of errors made in previous accounting periods.

Pro forma earnings Alternative earnings numbers that adjust net income in some way for items not expected to be part of ongoing business operations.

Pro forma financial statements Projections of future financial statements based on a set of assumptions regarding future revenues, expenses, level of investment in assets, financing methods and costs, and working capital management.

Profitability ratio A ratio that measures the overall performance of a firm and its efficiency in managing assets, liabilities, and equity.

Property, plant, and equipment *See* Fixed assets.

Proxy statement A document required by the SEC that companies use to solicit shareholders' votes and that contains information about directors, director and executive compensation plans, and the audit committee report.

Public Company Accounting Oversight Board (PCAOB) A private, nonprofit organization with the authority to register, inspect, and discipline auditors of all publicly owned companies.

Publicly held companies Companies that operate to earn a profit and issue shares of stock to the public.

Qualified opinion An opinion rendered by an independent auditor when the overall financial statements are fairly presented "except for" certain items (which the auditor discloses).

Quality of financial reporting A subjective evaluation of the extent to which financial reporting is free of manipulation and accurately reflects the financial condition and operating success of a business enterprise.

Quick ratio *See* Summary of financial ratios, Appendix A.

Raw materials Basic commodities or natural resources that will be used in the production of goods.

Replacement cost The estimated cost of acquiring new and substantially equivalent property at current prices.

Reported income The net income published in financial statements.

Reserve accounts Accounts used to estimate obligations, recorded as accrued liabilities; also to record declines in asset values, recorded as contra-asset accounts.

Restructuring charges Costs to reorganize a company.

Retained earnings The sum of every dollar a company has earned since its inception, less any payments made to shareholders in the form of cash or stock dividends.

Return on equity *See* Summary of financial ratios, Appendix A.

Return on investment *See* Return on total assets, Appendix A.

Return on total assets *See* Summary of financial ratios, Appendix A.

Revenue The inflow of assets resulting from the sale of goods or services.

Reverse stock split Decreasing the number of shares of outstanding stock to existing stockholders in proportion to current ownership, usually to increase the market price of a firm's stock.

Sales allowance A deduction from the original sales invoice price.

Sales return A cancellation of a sale.

Salvage value The amount of an asset estimated to be recoverable at the conclusion of the asset's service life.

Sarbanes-Oxley Act of 2002 Legislation passed by the U.S. Congress in hopes of ending future accounting scandals and renewing investor confidence in the marketplace.

Securities and Exchange Commission (SEC) The public-sector organization primarily responsible for establishing generally accepted accounting principles.

Segment A component of a business enterprise that sells primarily to outside markets and for which information about revenue and profit is accumulated.

Segment operating expenses Expenses relating to unaffiliated customers and segment revenue; expenses not directly traceable to segments are allocated to segments on a reasonable basis.

Segment operating profit/loss Segment revenue less all operating expenses.

Segment revenue Sales of products and services to unaffiliated customers and intersegment sales, with company transfer prices used to determine sales between segments.

Selling and administrative expenses Costs relating to the sale of products or services and to the management function of the firm.

Short-term Generally indicates maturity of less than a year.

Single-step format A format for presenting the income statement under which all items of revenue are grouped together and then all items of expense are deducted to arrive at net income.

Stated value The floor price below which stock cannot be sold initially; *see also* par value.

Statement of cash flows The financial statement that provides information about the cash inflows and outflows from operating, financing, and investing activities during an accounting period.

Statement of financial position *See* Balance sheet.

Statement of retained earnings The financial statement that presents the details of the transactions affecting the retained earnings account during an accounting period.

Statement of stockholders' equity A financial statement that summarizes changes in the shareholders' equity section of the balance sheet during an accounting period.

Stock dividends The issuance of additional shares of stock to existing shareholders in proportion to current ownership.

Stock options A contract that conveys the right to purchase shares of stock at a specified price within a specified time period.

Stock splits The issuance of additional shares of stock to existing shareholders in proportion to current ownership, usually to lower the market price of a firm's stock.

Stockholders' equity Claims against assets by the owners of the business; represents the amount owners have invested including income retained in the business since inception.

Straight-line depreciation An accounting procedure under which equal amounts of expense are apportioned to each year of an asset's life.

Structural analysis Analysis looking at the internal structure of a business enterprise.

Summary of financial ratios *See* Summary of financial ratios, Appendix A.

Tangible Having physical substance.

Taxable income The net income figure used to determine taxes payable to governments.

Temporary differences Differences between pretax accounting income and taxable income caused by reporting items of revenue or expense in one period for accounting purposes and in an earlier or later period for income tax purposes.

Times interest earned *See* Summary of financial ratios, Appendix A.

Total asset turnover *See* Summary of financial ratios, Appendix A.

Treasury stock Shares of a company's stock that are repurchased by the company and not retired.

Trend analysis Evaluation of financial data over several accounting periods.

Unearned revenue A liability caused by receipt of cash in advance of earning revenue.

Units-of-production method An accounting method under which depreciation expense is based on actual usage.

Unqualified opinion An opinion rendered by an independent auditor of financial statements stating that the financial statements have been presented fairly in accordance with generally accepted accounting principles.

Unqualified opinion with explanatory language An opinion rendered by an independent auditor of financial statements stating that the financial statements have been presented fairly in accordance with generally accepted accounting principles, but there are items which the auditor wishes to explain to the user.

Unrealized gains (losses) on marketable equity securities The gains (losses) disclosed in the equity section resulting from the accounting rule that requires investments in marketable equity securities to be carried at the lower of cost or market value.

Warrant A certificate issued by a corporation that conveys the right to buy a stated number of shares of stock at a specified price on or before a predetermined date.

Work-in-process Products for which the manufacturing process is only partially completed.

Working capital The amount by which current assets exceed current liabilities.

Index

T

U

V

W

Z